# ◆ THE FLAVORS OF ◆
# BON APPÉTIT

# ◆ THE FLAVORS OF ◆

# BON APPÉTIT

## ◆1997◆

*from the Editors of Bon Appétit*

Condé Nast Books ◆ Pantheon
*New York*

For *Bon Appétit* Magazine

William J. Garry, *Editor-in-Chief*
Laurie Glenn Buckle, *Editor, Bon Appétit Books*
Marcy MacDonald, *Editorial Business Manager*
John Hartung and Carri Marks, *Editorial Production Director*
Sybil Shimazu Neubauer, *Editorial Coordinator*
Marcia Lewis, *Editorial Support*
Angeline Vogl, *Supplemental Text*
Norman Kolpas, *Supplemental Text*
Mara Papatheodorou, *Research*

For Condé Nast Books

Jill Cohen, *President*
Ellen Maria Bruzelius, *Division Vice President*
Lucille Friedman, *Fulfillment Manager*
Tom Downing, *Direct Marketing Manager*
Jill Neal, *Direct Marketing Manager*
Jennifer Metz, *Direct Marketing Associate*
Paul DiNardo, *Direct Marketing Assistant*

*Produced in association with Patrick Filley Associates, Inc.*
*Designed by Laura Hammond Hough*

*Front Jacket:* Grilled Vegetables with Lemon, Thyme and Mustard Basting Sauce (page 140).

*Back Jacket:* Phyllo-wrapped Brie with Apricot and Rosemary Chutney (page 14);
Asian Risotto with Pancetta and Mussels (page 102);
Summer Pudding (page 198).

*Contents Page:* Top: Phyllo-wrapped Brie with Apricot and Rosemary Chutney (page 14);
Lower Left: Steak with Horseradish and Dijon Mustard Crust (page 49);
Lower Right: Warm Lentil Salad with Jicama (page 161).

ISBN 0-679-44277-4

Random House Web Address: http://www.randomhouse.com/

*Printed in the United States of America*

FIRST EDITION

2 4 6 8 9 7 5 3 1

# •Contents•

# ◆Introduction◆

Putting together this fourth annual collection of *The Flavors of Bon Appétit*, we faced, as always, the daunting task of selecting some 200 recipes from the 1,200 or so that appeared in the magazine last year. What qualities, we had to wonder, made a recipe so good that, having already passed the magazine's high selection standards, it deserved to join the ranks of the year's very best in this compilation of our favorites?

It wasn't easy, this winnowing process. In the end, we chose different recipes for different reasons. Some are here because they offer combinations of tastes and textures so unusual and delicious we can honestly say we've never experienced anything like them before. Others are included because they provide new takes on classic dishes by employing unexpected ingredients, seasonings or styles of presentation.

Still others made the cut because they share techniques for cooking favorite foods in lighter, healthier new ways. And some won their places because they make it possible to entertain lavishly while spending a minimum of time in the kitchen.

Every recipe here reveals a secret, a special something—be it a technique, a combination of flavors, an ingredient—that will make your good cooking great. Read on to discover them.

# ·Starters·

A great first course is at once interesting and appealing on its own, as it builds anticipation for the main course that follows. But as the appetizer, soup and beverage recipes in this chapter demonstrate, no two successful starters accomplish this same goal in exactly the same way.

A special ingredient or technique might be what elevates a first-course recipe from the everyday to the extraordinary. Cornmeal, for example, adds rich taste and crunchy texture to Cornmeal Blini with Tomato-Corn Salsa (page 18). Roasting the vegetables for the Black Bean and Roasted Tomato Soup (page 30) contributes a wonderful depth of flavor.

Sometimes the secret to success has to do with how easily an impressive starter is made. Both the Roasted Pepper and Artichoke Tapenade (page 16) and the Grilled Pesto Breadsticks with Goat Cheese-Pesto Spread (page 16) use purchased ingredients.

With so much interest today in healthful eating, still other first courses exceed expectations as they find ingenious ways to impress us with flavor and texture while reducing fat. Cherry Tomatoes and Cucumber Rounds with Herbed Tuna Filling (page 21) and Shrimp and Lime Tostadas (page 19) both offer great taste and good looks without a lot of fat. Sherried Winter Squash Bisque (page 31), though rich and creamy, is made with nonfat milk— a cooking secret everyone can benefit from.

*Mussels on the Half Shell with Pesto (page 20); Shrimp and Lime Tostadas (page 19); Cherry Tomatoes and Cucumber Rounds with Herbed Tuna Filling (page 21); Cornmeal Blini with Tomato-Corn Salsa (page 18)*

# Crab Cakes with Spicy Thai Sauce

◆ ◆ ◆

CRAB CAKES

| | |
|---|---|
| 12 | ounces cooked crabmeat |
| ¼ | cup minced red onion |
| 2 | tablespoons minced red bell pepper |
| 1 | large egg white, beaten to blend |
| 1½ | teaspoons black sesame seeds or regular sesame seeds |
| ¼ | teaspoon ground allspice |
| ¼ | teaspoon white pepper |
| ⅛ | teaspoon hot pepper sauce (such as Tabasco) |
| ¾ | cup (about) fresh sourdough breadcrumbs |

SAUCE

| | |
|---|---|
| ½ | cup rice vinegar |
| 5 | tablespoons sugar |
| 2 | tablespoons fresh lime juice |
| 2 | tablespoons water |
| 2 | teaspoons minced seeded red jalapeño chili |
| 1 | teaspoon minced garlic |
| 1 | teaspoon black sesame seeds or regular sesame seeds |
| ¼ | cup finely grated seeded peeled cucumber |

| | |
|---|---|
| 4 | tablespoons (about) butter |

FOR CAKES: Mix first 8 ingredients in large bowl. Mix in enough breadcrumbs to form stiff mixture. Shape mixture into sixteen ¼-inch-thick patties. *(Can be made 8 hours ahead. Cover; chill.)*

FOR SAUCE: Combine rice vinegar, sugar, lime juice, water, red chili, garlic and sesame seeds in small bowl; stir until sugar dissolves. Mix in cucumber. Let sauce stand for 30 minutes at room temperature to allow flavors to blend.

Preheat oven to 250°F. Melt 1 tablespoon butter in heavy large skillet over medium heat. Working in batches, add crab cakes and cook until golden, about 4 minutes per side, adding more butter to skillet as necessary. Transfer to paper towels; drain. Transfer to baking sheet; keep warm in oven. Divide crab cakes among 8 plates. Spoon sauce around cakes and serve.

8 SERVINGS

# Croutons with Shrimp, Andouille Sausage and Red Bell Pepper

◆ ◆ ◆

2      tablespoons olive oil
½      cup chopped andouille sausage or hot links
¼      cup diced shallots or red onion
6      ounces uncooked shrimp, peeled, deveined, coarsely chopped
¼      cup diced roasted red bell peppers from jar
2      tablespoons chopped fresh Italian parsley
1      tablespoon chopped fresh thyme
1      tablespoon Dijon mustard

24    ½-inch-thick diagonal slices French bread baguette, toasted

Heat oil in heavy large skillet over medium-high heat. Add sausage; sauté until golden, about 2 minutes. Using slotted spoon, transfer sausage to bowl. Add shallots to same skillet and sauté 3 minutes. Add shrimp and sauté until cooked through, about 3 minutes. Mix in peppers, parsley, fresh thyme, mustard and sausage. Season with salt and pepper.

Spoon shrimp mixture onto croutons. Arrange on platter.

MAKES 24

## SAUSAGE SHOPPING

There are hundreds of varieties of sausages available now, from the ordinary to the ethnic, from traditional to new wave. New varieties turn up every day, some exotically seasoned, others lightened versions of the classics. Here are some to look for.

◆ Andouille: This spicy smoked pork sausage has French origins; it's a key ingredient in Cajun cooking.

◆ Bockwurst: A German sausage in origin, made of veal and pork and flavored with chives, coriander, nutmeg or garlic. Bockwurst can be served with sauerkraut or for breakfast with eggs.

◆ Boudin blanc: The classic French boudin is a bland white sausage made from eggs, cream and any white meat. The Cajun version tends to be spicy.

◆ Bratwurst: This mild veal and pork sausage is popular in German and Swiss cooking.

◆ Chorizo: Red in color from the addition of paprika, this piquant pork sausage is used in Spanish and Mexican cooking.

◆ Kielbasa: Widely available both fresh and dried, kielbasa is a big, highly seasoned Polish sausage.

◆ ◆ ◆

## OLIVE OPTIONS

If you're still limiting your olive purchases to the tried-and-true black variety from California, consider branching out and sampling some of the many other kinds now available. Look for the following at supermarkets and specialty foods stores.

◆ Gaeta olives from Italy are small, black, wrinkled and chewy. They are dry-cured and salty.

◆ Kalamata olives from Greece are a shiny purple-black color, with a distinctive wine or vinegar flavor from their brine cure.

◆ Manzanillo olives from Spain are brine-cured, bitter, salty and firm.

◆ Niçoise olives from France are tiny and brownish in color with a sharp, nutty flavor. Brine-cured, they are often packed with herbs.

◆ Picholine olives from France are medium green-colored. Crisp and tart, they are brine-cured.

◆ Sicilian green olives from California are big, sour-tasting and salty.

◆ ◆ ◆

# Provençal Stuffed Tomatoes and Pattypan Squash

◆ ◆ ◆

2 tablespoons olive oil
1 medium zucchini, cut into ¼-inch pieces
½ small onion, finely chopped
1 large garlic clove, minced
2 ounces thinly sliced prosciutto, chopped
6 brine-cured black olives (such as Kalamata), pitted, chopped
¼ cup freshly grated Parmesan cheese
2 tablespoons chopped seeded tomato
2 tablespoons chopped fresh basil or 2 teaspoons dried
1 tablespoon chopped fresh parsley
1½ teaspoons chopped fresh tarragon or ½ teaspoon dried
1 egg yolk

12 2-inch-diameter yellow or green pattypan squash, stems trimmed
12 large plum tomatoes, halved crosswise, seeded

Heat 2 tablespoons oil in heavy medium skillet over medium heat. Add zucchini, onion and garlic and sauté until tender but not brown, about 5 minutes. Add prosciutto and next 6 ingredients. Sauté 1 minute. Remove from heat. Cool. Season filling to taste with salt and pepper. Mix in egg yolk.

Using melon baller, scoop out centers of squash, leaving generous ¼-inch-thick shell. Blanch squash shells in pot of boiling salted water 3 minutes. Drain; cool. Cut thin slice from rounded end of tomato halves if necessary to stand flat.

Lightly brush heavy baking sheet with olive oil. Fill vegetables using about 1 heaping tablespoon filling for each tomato half and 1 heaping teaspoon for each squash. Arrange vegetables on prepared baking sheet. *(Can be prepared 1 day ahead. Cover and refrigerate.)*

Preheat oven to 400°F. Bake vegetables uncovered until tender, about 30 minutes. Serve warm or at room temperature.

MAKES 36

# Deviled Eggs with Radishes, Chives and Thyme

◆ ◆ ◆

10   large eggs, hard-boiled, peeled
¼   cup plain nonfat yogurt or low-fat mayonnaise
4   teaspoons Dijon mustard
⅓   cup finely chopped radishes
4   teaspoons chopped fresh chives
4   teaspoons chopped fresh thyme

    Additional chopped fresh chives, thyme and radishes
    Whole radishes

Halve eggs lengthwise and transfer yolks to medium bowl. Mash yolks with fork. Mix in yogurt (or mayonnaise) and mustard. Mix in ⅓ cup radishes, 4 teaspoons chives and thyme. Season filling to taste with salt and generous amount of pepper.

Spoon filling into egg whites, mounding in center. Top with additional chopped chives, thyme and radishes. Arrange on platter. Garnish platter with whole radishes.

6 SERVINGS

◆ ◆ ◆

These old-fashioned (and high-fat) favorites take a lighter turn when prepared with nonfat yogurt or low-fat mayonnaise; radishes and herbs give the eggs a modern twist.

# Sun-dried Tomato Aioli Dip with Crudités

◆ ◆ ◆

6   garlic cloves, peeled, halved
½   teaspoon salt
12   oil-packed sun-dried tomatoes, drained, patted dry, chopped
2   cups nonfat cottage cheese
⅔   cup plain nonfat yogurt
½   cup low-fat mayonnaise
    Assorted fresh vegetables

Place garlic on cutting board. Sprinkle with ½ teaspoon salt. Using flat side of knife, crush garlic. Add sun-dried tomatoes; mince to coarse paste. Puree cottage cheese in processor. Add yogurt and mayonnaise and blend well. Add garlic paste; process to blend. Season with salt. *(Can be made 1 day ahead. Cover and refrigerate.)* Serve aioli with assorted vegetables.

20 SERVINGS

To begin a phyllo rose, fold one inch of phyllo over, starting at one long side. Continue to roll up loosely.

Stand phyllo strip on one long edge and gently wind up into coil.

Gather bottom edge of coiled phyllo strip together and pinch, forcing coil to open into rose shape.

# Phyllo-wrapped Brie with Apricot and Rosemary Chutney

◆ ◆ ◆

CHUTNEY

| 12 | ounces dried apricots, chopped |
| 1 | large red onion, chopped |
| 1 | cup water |
| ⅔ | cup cider vinegar |
| ⅔ | cup (packed) golden brown sugar |
| 3 | ounces dried tart cherries (¾ cup) |
| 1½ | tablespoons chopped fresh rosemary |
| 3 | large garlic cloves, finely chopped |
| 2 | teaspoons grated lemon peel |
| ½ | teaspoon salt |
| ⅛ | teaspoon cayenne pepper |
| ½ | cup blanched slivered almonds, toasted |

| 1 | cup (2 sticks) unsalted butter, melted |
| 1 | pound fresh phyllo pastry sheets or frozen, thawed |
| 4½ | tablespoons chopped fresh rosemary |

| 1 | 32- to 36-ounce wheel of Brie |

Fresh herb sprigs (such as rosemary, sage and chives)
Additional dried apricots and dried cherries
Fresh baguettes, thinly sliced
Thinly sliced apples

FOR CHUTNEY: Combine first 11 ingredients in heavy large saucepan. Bring to boil over medium-high heat, stirring until sugar dissolves. Reduce heat to medium-low; simmer until most liquid has evaporated and chutney is thick, stirring occasionally, about 25 minutes. Mix in almonds. Transfer chutney to bowl. Chill until cold, about 3 hours. *(Can be made 1 week ahead. Cover; keep chilled.)*

Brush heavy large baking sheet with butter; set aside. Unroll pastry. Cover with plastic wrap and damp kitchen towel. Transfer 2 stacked phyllo sheets to work surface, arranging 1 short side parallel to edge of work surface. Arrange 2 more stacked phyllo sheets on work surface, overlapping long side of first sheets by about 5 to 7 inches and forming rectangle about 18 x 17 inches. Brush pastry with butter; sprinkle 1½ tablespoons rosemary over. Place 2 more stacked sheets atop first set of 2 sheets, then 2 more stacked sheets atop second set of 2 sheets. Brush with butter and sprinkle with 1½ tablespoons rosemary. Repeat layering 1 more time with phyllo, butter and 1½ tablespoons rosemary. (You will use 12 sheets.)

Using sharp knife or scissors, trim phyllo corners, forming approximately 17-inch oval. Place Brie in center of phyllo. Spread 1½ cups chutney evenly over cheese. Slide hand under 1 rounded corner of phyllo. Lift phyllo and fold onto top of cheese. Brush folded pastry with butter. Continue to lift phyllo in sections and to fold snugly over top of cheese, brushing with butter and pressing each section to adhere until cheese is wrapped (the top center 2 to 3 inches of cheese will not be covered). Use hand and metal spatula to transfer wrapped cheese to prepared baking sheet.

Place 1 phyllo sheet on work surface. Brush with butter. Starting at 1 long side, fold 1 inch of pastry over. Continue folding pastry loosely over itself, forming 1-inch-wide strip of pastry. Roll up strip into coil. Gather bottom edge of coil together, pinching to force top slightly open and forming rose. Place rose atop uncovered center of cheese. Brush with butter. Repeat with 2 more sheets of phyllo, forming 2 more roses. Place atop cheese, covering opening completely. Refrigerate for 3 hours. *(Can be made 1 day ahead. Cover with plastic; keep refrigerated.)*

Position rack in center of oven and preheat to 400°F. Bake cheese until pastry is deep golden brown, covering roses loosely with foil if browning too quickly, about 25 minutes. (If cheese leaks from pastry during baking, press piece of foil over tear in pastry; continue baking.) Cool cheese on sheet 45 minutes.

Using metal spatula, transfer cheese to platter. Arrange herbs, fruit, baguette and apple around cheese and serve.

16 SERVINGS

# PHYLLO KNOW-HOW

For many years, what we knew about phyllo (or filo) was limited to our experience with baklava, that sweet, flaky Middle Eastern dessert. More recently, though, these paper-thin sheets of stretched pastry dough are turning up in a variety of dishes, from appetizers to casseroles to pastries both sweet and savory.

Sheets of phyllo (the name means "leaf" in Greek) are generally sold in one-pound packages in the refrigerator or freezer sections of most supermarkets; Middle Eastern markets and specialty foods stores also carry it. If your are using frozen phyllo be sure to allow it to thaw in the refrigerator to prevent condensation from forming inside the package.

Though fragile in appearance, phyllo is actually very pliable and easy to handle. Keep the sheets from drying out by covering them with plastic wrap and a damp kitchen towel as you work. When layering the phyllo, brush butter in between the layers for that crispy result everyone loves. You can also use butter to repair tears and cracks, and to patch with small pieces of dough.

◆ ◆ ◆

## INSTANT APPETIZERS

One of the quickest ways there is to make up an appetizer platter is to head for the nearest Mediterranean deli and look for these delicious relishes, condiments and spreads. All you need to add is an assortment of raw vegetables and some crusty bread.

◆ Caponata: This sweet and sour vegetable stew from Sicily is similar to ratatouille (see below), but with the addition of celery, Kalamata olives and capers. Serve it at room temperature with toast.

◆ Olivada: A savory spread of pureed black olives and olive oil, olivada is great spread on toast or a pizza crust. Try topping with anchovies, garlic and/or basil.

◆ Ratatouille: This Provençal classic makes the most of fresh vegetables, including onions, peppers, eggplant and zucchini, all cooked until tender and juicy. Serve it at room temperature as a dip.

◆ Tapenade: Another Provençal dish, this pungent blend of finely chopped oil-cured olives, anchovies, capers, garlic, olive oil and basil is good as a dip with crudités or spread on toast.

◆ ◆ ◆

# Roasted Pepper and Artichoke Tapenade

◆ ◆ ◆

1   7-ounce jar roasted red bell peppers, drained, coarsely chopped
1   6-ounce jar marinated artichoke hearts, drained, coarsely chopped
½   cup minced fresh parsley
½   cup freshly grated Parmesan cheese
⅓   cup olive oil
¼   cup drained capers
4   garlic cloves, chopped
1   tablespoon fresh lemon juice

Combine all ingredients in processor. Process using on/off turns until mixture is well blended and finely chopped. Transfer mixture to medium bowl. Season to taste with salt and pepper. *(Tapenade can be prepared 1 day ahead. Cover with plastic and refrigerate.)*

MAKES ABOUT 1¾ CUPS

# Grilled Pesto Breadsticks with Goat Cheese-Pesto Spread

◆ ◆ ◆

11   ounces soft fresh goat cheese (such as Montrachet), room temperature
2   7-ounce containers prepared pesto*

1   1-pound French bread baguette, cut into 6-inch lengths
¼   cup olive oil

Puree goat cheese in processor. Mix in 7 ounces pesto. Transfer to medium bowl. *(Can be made 1 day ahead. Cover; chill. Bring to room temperature before serving.)*

Prepare barbecue (medium-high heat). Halve each bread piece lengthwise, then cut each half lengthwise into 1¼-inch-wide strips. Combine 7 ounces pesto and oil in small bowl. Brush bread with pesto mixture. Grill until brown, about 45 seconds per side. Serve with pesto cheese spread.

*Available at specialty foods stores and many supermarkets.*

10 TO 12 SERVINGS

## Clams with Red Bell Pepper and Garlic

❖ ❖ ❖

4    dozen littleneck clams, scrubbed
¼    cup yellow cornmeal
1    tablespoon salt

1½    cups dry white wine
2    red bell peppers, cut into thin strips
¼    cup (½ stick) butter
¼    cup olive oil
3    garlic cloves, minced
2    teaspoons grated lemon peel
½    cup chopped fresh cilantro

Place clams in large bowl. Add enough cold water to cover. Sprinkle with cornmeal and salt. Let stand 1 hour. Drain; rinse well.

Combine wine, bell peppers, butter, oil, garlic and lemon peel in large pot. Bring to simmer over medium heat. Cover and cook 2 minutes. Increase heat to high and add all clams and chopped cilantro. Cover pot and cook until clams open, about 8 minutes. Discard any clams that do not open. Ladle clams and broth into shallow bowls and serve immediately.

8 SERVINGS

❖ ❖ ❖

Once the clams have soaked for a bit, it's only about 10 minutes to this attractive first-course shellfish dish.

❖ ❖ ❖

◆ ◆ ◆

# Cornmeal Blini with Tomato-Corn Salsa

◆ ◆ ◆

BLINI

| | |
|---|---|
| 1 | cup plus 2 tablespoons low-fat milk |
| 2 | tablespoons water |
| ¼ | cup sugar |
| 1 | teaspoon dry yeast |
| | |
| ¾ | cup unbleached all purpose flour |
| ⅔ | cup yellow cornmeal |
| 1 | teaspoon salt |
| ½ | cup buttermilk |
| 2 | large eggs, separated |
| | |
| 5 | teaspoons (about) vegetable oil |

SALSA

| | |
|---|---|
| 2 | cups frozen corn, thawed, drained |
| 1½ | pounds tomatoes, seeded, chopped |
| ½ | small red onion, finely chopped |
| 6 | tablespoons chopped fresh cilantro |
| 2 | jalapeño chilies, seeded, minced |
| 1 | tablespoon balsamic vinegar |
| | |
| ½ | cup nonfat plain yogurt |

FOR BLINI: Heat milk and water to lukewarm (105°F to 115°F) in small saucepan. Pour into large bowl. Mix in sugar and yeast. Let mixture stand for 10 minutes.

Stir flour, cornmeal and salt in medium bowl to blend. Stir into yeast mixture. Mix in buttermilk and egg yolks. Cover with plastic and let stand in warm area until very spongy, about 2 hours.

Using electric mixer, beat egg whites in another medium bowl until stiff but not dry. Gently fold into cornmeal mixture in 2 additions.

Preheat oven to 250°F. Brush large nonstick skillet with 1 teaspoon oil. Heat over medium-high heat. Working in batches and brushing with additional oil as necessary, drop batter by tablespoonfuls into skillet, spreading gently to 2-inch rounds. Cook until golden on bottoms and bubbles begin to break on surface, about 2 minutes. Using spatula, turn over; cook until golden, 1 minute. Arrange in single layer on baking sheets. Keep warm in oven.

FOR SALSA: Mix all ingredients except yogurt in medium bowl

to blend. Season with salt and pepper. *(Blini and salsa can be made 8 hours ahead. Cool blini. Cover blini and salsa separately and chill. Reheat blini uncovered in 350°F oven about 10 minutes.)*

Spread small amount of yogurt over blini. Divide salsa over blini. Arrange on platters and serve warm.

MAKES 64

# Shrimp and Lime Tostadas

◆ ◆ ◆

9    5- to 6-inch corn tortillas, each cut into 6 wedges

     Nonstick vegetable oil spray

3    garlic cloves, unpeeled

1    tablespoon cumin seeds

1½   pounds uncooked medium shrimp, peeled, deveined

3½   teaspoons finely grated lime peel

6    tablespoons fresh lime juice

6    tablespoons plain nonfat yogurt

6    tablespoons chopped fresh cilantro

2½   teaspoons minced seeded serrano or jalapeño chili

Preheat oven to 325°F. Place tortilla wedges in single layer on 2 large baking sheets. Bake until crisp, turning once, about 30 minutes. Cool tortilla chips on baking sheet.

Spray baking dish with oil spray. Add garlic; cover with foil. Bake until tender, 30 minutes. Cool slightly. Peel; mash in bowl.

Heat small skillet over medium heat. Add cumin seeds; stir until fragrant, about 1 minute. Grind in spice grinder or in mortar with pestle. Add to garlic in bowl.

Bring large pot of water to boil. Add shrimp and lime peel and cook until shrimp are opaque, about 3 minutes. Drain shrimp and lime peel in fine strainer. Cool. Coarsely chop shrimp. Transfer shrimp and lime peel to bowl.

*(Tortillas, garlic mixture and shrimp can be made 1 day ahead. Store tortillas in airtight containers at room temperature. Chill garlic mixture and shrimp separately.)*

Add lime juice, yogurt, chopped cilantro, chili and garlic mixture to shrimp. Season with salt and pepper. Spoon atop tortilla chips.

MAKES 54

◆ ◆ ◆

These mini tostadas make terrific low-fat appetizers. The chopped shrimp topping is seasoned with cumin, serrano chili and cilantro.

## ITALIAN FOR TOAST

Popular in Italy since Roman times, bruschetta is a relative new-comer to this country—but already ubiquitious in Italian restaurants from coast to coast. And it's easy to see why. This wonderful appetizer is, at its simplest, a thick slice of coarse-textured peasant bread (often *ciabatta*) toasted over an open fire, rubbed with garlic and dipped into fruity olive oil. Popular refinements include toppings of sliced ripe tomato, basil and, perhaps, some red onion or roasted red pepper. Its name reflects the original cooking method: The word *bruschetta* derives from the Italian *bruscare*, which means to "roast over coals."

Along with bruschetta, we have recently discovered *crostini*, "little toasted crusts." Thinner and smaller than bruschetta, crostini are grilled over an open fire, broiled, baked or fried, brushed with good olive oil and then topped with everything from chopped olives and anchovy paste to liver pâté and *tapenade*.

◆ ◆ ◆

# Smoked Salmon Bruschetta with Tomato-Avocado Salsa

◆ ◆ ◆

SALSA

3   large plum tomatoes (about 8 ounces), seeded, chopped
½   yellow bell pepper, seeded, chopped
3   tablespoons chopped red onion
1   jalapeño chili, seeded, chopped
1   tablespoon fresh lime juice
1   teaspoon olive oil
½   avocado, peeled, cut into small cubes
3   tablespoons chopped fresh basil

TOASTS

4   ½-inch-thick bread slices from crusty round loaf
    Olive oil
¼   pound thinly sliced smoked salmon

FOR SALSA: Combine all ingredients in small mixing bowl. Season salsa with salt and pepper.

FOR TOASTS: Preheat broiler. Brush 1 side of bread with olive oil. Sprinkle with pepper. Broil both sides until golden, about 2 minutes per side. Arrange bread, oil side up, on work surface. Top with salmon. Cut each toast in half. Arrange on platter. Top each with some salsa. Serve, passing remaining salsa separately.

4 SERVINGS

# Mussels on the Half Shell with Pesto

◆ ◆ ◆

1   cup dry white wine
1   cup water
¼   cup chopped shallots
2   tablespoons white wine vinegar
4   garlic cloves, crushed with side of knife
40  fresh mussels, scrubbed, debearded

4   cups fresh basil leaves
4   garlic cloves, chopped
3   tablespoons olive oil
6   tablespoons freshly grated Parmesan cheese
2   tablespoons low-fat mayonnaise

Bring first 5 ingredients to boil in large pot. Working in batches, add mussels to pot. Cover; cook until mussels open, about 4 minutes. Using slotted spoon, transfer mussels to large bowl. Discard any mussels that do not open. Cool mussels. Strain cooking liquid; reserve 1 cup mussel cooking liquid.

Remove mussels from shells, reserving half of each shell. Transfer mussels to medium bowl and refrigerate.

Finely chop basil and garlic in processor. With processor running, gradually add reserved 1 cup cooking liquid and oil and process until well blended. Blend in cheese and mayonnaise. Transfer pesto to large bowl. Season with salt and pepper. Add mussels and toss to coat. Chill at least 1 hour. *(Can be made 1 day ahead. Refrigerate shells.)*

Spoon mussels and pesto into shells. Arrange on platter.

MAKES 40

# Cherry Tomatoes and Cucumber Rounds with Herbed Tuna Filling

◆ ◆ ◆

| | |
|---|---|
| 2 | 6-ounce cans tuna in water, well drained |
| ½ | cup plain nonfat yogurt |
| ½ | cup minced shallots |
| 6 | tablespoons chopped fresh mint |
| 6 | tablespoons chopped fresh parsley |
| 4 | garlic cloves, minced |
| 3 | tablespoons fresh lemon juice |
| 1 | teaspoon ground cumin |
| | |
| 20 | cherry tomatoes |
| 1 | English hothouse cucumber |

Place tuna in medium bowl. Flake with fork. Mix in yogurt and next 6 ingredients. Season with salt and pepper.

Cut off ¼-inch from tops of tomatoes. Gently squeeze out seeds. Cut thin slice from bottoms of tomatoes so that they will stand upright. Turn tomatoes top side up. Using small knife or melon baller, scoop out insides of tomatoes. Using tines of fork, score sides of cucumber lengthwise. Cut into ½-inch-thick rounds. Using melon baller, scoop out some seeds in center of each round, being careful not to scoop through bottom. *(Tuna mixture, tomatoes and cucumbers can be prepared 8 hours ahead. Cover separately; chill.)* Spoon tuna into tomatoes and onto cucumber rounds.

MAKES ABOUT 40

# Twice-baked Goat Cheese Soufflés

❖ ❖ ❖

These first-course soufflés, which get baked once in soufflé dishes and again—briefly—after unmolding, are just right for entertaining because most of the preparation is done ahead of time.

❖ ❖ ❖

1¾ cups whole milk
¾ cup coarsely chopped onion
2 whole cloves
⅛ teaspoon ground nutmeg

6 tablespoons (¾ stick) butter
9 tablespoons all purpose flour
¼ teaspoon dry mustard
2 cups crumbled soft fresh goat cheese
(such as Montrachet; about 9 ounces)
6 large egg yolks
1¼ teaspoons salt
¾ teaspoon ground black pepper

8 large egg whites

1 cup whipping cream

Combine milk, onion, cloves and nutmeg in heavy medium saucepan over medium heat. Bring to boil. Remove from heat. Cover and let stand 30 minutes. Strain.

Preheat oven to 350°F. Butter eight 1¼-cup soufflé dishes. Melt 6 tablespoons butter in heavy large saucepan over medium heat. Add flour and dry mustard and whisk 2 minutes. Gradually whisk in strained milk. Boil until mixture is very thick and smooth, whisking constantly, about 2 minutes. Transfer soufflé base to large bowl. Gradually add 1½ cups goat cheese, whisking until melted and smooth. Add yolks, 1 teaspoon salt and pepper; whisk until smooth. Cool goat cheese mixture to lukewarm.

Beat egg whites and remaining ¼ teaspoon salt in another large bowl until stiff but not dry. Gently fold beaten egg whites into cheese mixture in 3 separate additions.

Divide batter equally among prepared soufflé dishes. Arrange dishes in heavy 17 x 12-inch roasting pan. Pour enough hot water into pan to come halfway up sides of dishes. Bake until soufflés are puffed and just firm to touch on top, about 20 minutes. Transfer pan to rack and completely cool soufflés in water. *(Can be prepared 2 hours ahead. Let stand at room temperature.)*

Preheat oven to 425°F. Butter heavy large baking sheet. Using small knife, cut around sides of soufflés to loosen. Invert each soufflé onto spatula and slide soufflés onto prepared sheet, spacing evenly. Sprinkle with remaining ½ cup goat cheese. Bake until soufflés are puffed, about 10 minutes.

Meanwhile, bring cream to boil in heavy small saucepan. Remove from heat and season with salt and pepper.

Using spatula, transfer soufflés to plates. Spoon seasoned cream around soufflés and serve hot.

MAKES 8

# Buttermilk-Herb Pancakes Topped with Caviar

◆ ◆ ◆

½   cup crème fraîche or sour cream
4   teaspoons minced lemon peel (yellow part only)
¾   cup all purpose flour
¾   cup buttermilk
⅓   cup beaten eggs (about 1½ large eggs)
¼   cup chopped mixed fresh herbs (such as parsley, chives and mint)
2   tablespoons chopped shallots
1½  tablespoons butter, melted
¾   teaspoon baking powder
¼   teaspoon baking soda

8   teaspoons (about) butter
3   tablespoons caviar

Stir crème fraîche and lemon peel in small bowl to blend. Season with salt and pepper. Set aside. Mix flour, buttermilk, beaten eggs, herbs, chopped shallots, melted butter, baking powder and baking soda in medium bowl until well blended.

Melt 2 teaspoons butter in large nonstick skillet over medium heat. Working in batches, drop batter by heaping tablespoonfuls into skillet, spreading each pancake to 3-inch round with back of spoon and adding 2 teaspoons butter to skillet for each batch. Cook until bottom is golden, about 3 minutes. Turn over and cook until bottom is golden, about 2 minutes. Transfer to plates. Top each pancake with dollop of lemon crème fraîche and caviar.

MAKES ABOUT 12

◆ ◆ ◆

Be sure to serve these pancakes immediately, since they do not keep well in a warm oven. You can top them with any type of caviar, but buy the best you can (this sage advice applies to Champagne, too).

# Minestrone with Basil

◆ ◆ ◆

½   cup dried red beans
5   cups water
2   cups shredded green cabbage
1½  cups chopped tomatoes
1   small onion, chopped
1   celery stalk, diced
1   carrot, diced
1   zucchini, diced
1   medium russet potato, peeled, left whole
1   small russet potato, peeled, diced
3   tablespoons extra-virgin olive oil
1½  tablespoons finely chopped garlic
1   teaspoon salt

½   cup small shell pasta
½   cup chopped fresh basil
    Freshly grated Parmesan cheese

Place beans in medium bowl. Add enough cold water to cover by 2 inches; soak overnight. Drain. Place beans in large Dutch oven. Add 5 cups water and next 11 ingredients and bring to boil. Reduce heat, cover and simmer until beans are tender, stirring occasionally, about 1 hour.

◆ ◆ ◆

Thickened by a red bean-and-potato puree, this satisfying soup makes an ideal lunch when served with a chunk of crusty bread.

◆ ◆ ◆

Transfer 2 cups soup and whole potato to blender and puree. Return puree to soup in pot. Add pasta and ¼ cup basil; simmer uncovered until pasta is cooked through and flavors blend, stirring occasionally, about 25 minutes. Season with salt and pepper. Mix in ¼ cup basil. Serve with Parmesan cheese.

6 SERVINGS

# Thai Shrimp Soup with Lemon

◆ ◆ ◆

| | |
|---|---|
| 1 | pound uncooked large shrimp |
| 3 | cups water |
| 2 | cups bottled clam juice |
| 1 | onion, sliced |
| 8 | quarter-size slices fresh ginger |
| 6 | tablespoons fresh lemon juice |
| 2 | jalapeño chilies, split lengthwise |
| 2 | bay leaves |
| 1 | tablespoon grated lemon peel |
| ½ | teaspoon whole black peppercorns |
| | |
| 1 | cup canned unsweetened coconut milk* |
| ½ | pound wafer-thin boneless pork loin chops, cut into thin strips |
| 1 | skinless boneless chicken breast half, cut crosswise into thin strips |
| 1 | tablespoon nam pla (fish sauce)* |
| 2 | teaspoons garlic chili sauce* |
| | |
| 3 | cups hot cooked white rice |
| ¼ | cup chopped green onions |
| ¼ | cup chopped fresh cilantro |

Peel and devein shrimp, reserving shells. Cut shrimp in half lengthwise. Cover and chill shrimp. Combine shrimp shells, water and next 8 ingredients in heavy large saucepan. Cover; simmer 30 minutes. Strain broth; return to saucepan.

Add coconut milk to broth. Bring to simmer. Add pork; cook 3 minutes. Add chicken and shrimp. Simmer until pork, chicken and shrimp are cooked through, about 3 minutes. Stir in fish sauce and garlic chili sauce. Season to taste with salt and pepper.

Divide rice and soup among 4 bowls. Sprinkle with chopped green onions and cilantro. Serve immediately.

*Available at Asian markets and some supermarkets.*

4 SERVINGS

◆ ◆ ◆

This exotically seasoned soup, made hearty by the addition of shrimp, pork and chicken, plus white rice, could work as a main course, too. Serve it with a spinach salad and frosty mugs of Asian beer.

◆ ◆ ◆

# A LOOK BACK AT CHOWDER

Although we think of chowder as a Yankee soup, it actually traces it origins to the coastal villages of France where, hundreds of years ago, the safe return of a fishing fleet would be celebrated with a communal feast. Each fisherman would toss a share of his catch into a huge copper pot called *la chaudière*.

Traveling from France to New Foundland and down the coast to New England, chowder became known as any thick broth made of fish or shellfish or both. Over time, the abundance of clams in the region led to a local preference for clam chowder.

While New Englanders debated among themselves what was essential to a true clam chowder, they united in protest when Manhattan clam chowder came on the scene, which uses tomatoes and water instead of cream. So heated was the "tomato question" that the 1939 Maine legislature actually considered a bill that would make it illegal to add tomatoes to the chowder pot—or so the story goes.

The chowder at right (shown opposite with the Green Onion and Sesame Corn Muffins from page 162) keeps to the original take on the theme, with lots of clams and potatoes and absolutely no tomatoes, though corn and chopped red pepper do add interest.

◆ ◆ ◆

# Classic Clam Chowder

◆ ◆ ◆

6   bacon slices, chopped
1½  large onions, chopped
1½  pounds russet potatoes (about 2 large), peeled, cut into ½-inch pieces
1   large red bell pepper, chopped
3   10-ounce cans baby clams, drained, liquid reserved
2   cups milk (do not use low-fat or nonfat)
½   cup bottled clam juice
2   15-ounce cans cream-style corn
3   tablespoons chopped fresh thyme or 1 tablespoon dried

Cook bacon in heavy large saucepan over medium heat until beginning to brown. Add onions and sauté until tender, 10 minutes. Add potatoes and bell pepper and sauté 1 minute. Add reserved liquid from clams, milk and clam juice. Simmer until vegetables are tender, 15 minutes. Add corn and clams to chowder; simmer until slightly thickened, 5 minutes. Mix in thyme. Season with salt and pepper. Ladle into bowls and serve.

6 SERVINGS

# Leek and Potato Soup

◆ ◆ ◆

3   tablespoons butter
3   large leeks (white and pale green parts only), halved lengthwise, thinly sliced (about 4½ cups)
2   large russet potatoes (about 18 ounces total), peeled, diced
4½  cups (or more) chicken stock or canned low-salt broth
2   tablespoons chopped fresh tchives

Melt butter in heavy large saucepan over medium heat. Add leeks; stir to coat with butter. Cover saucepan; cook until leeks are tender, stirring often, 10 minutes. Add potatoes. Cover and cook until potatoes begin to soften, stirring often, 10 minutes. Add 4½ cups stock. Bring to boil. Reduce heat, cover and simmer until vegetables are very tender, about 30 minutes.

Puree soup in batches in processor. Return to saucepan. Thin with additional stock if too thick. Season with salt and pepper. Bring soup to simmer. Ladle into bowls. Top with chives.

4 SERVINGS

# Acorn Squash Velouté with Ginger and Mustard Seeds

◆ ◆ ◆

3   tablespoons plus 1 teaspoon vegetable oil
2½  cups chopped onions
8   cups 1-inch pieces peeled acorn squash (about 3¾ pounds)
2   tablespoons chopped fresh ginger
4½  cups (or more) canned low-salt chicken broth

2   tablespoons tomato puree
    Pinch of cayenne pepper

1   tablespoon cumin seeds
1   tablespoon mustard seeds

Heat 3 tablespoons oil in heavy large pot over medium-high heat. Add onions; sauté until light golden, about 8 minutes. Add squash and ginger; sauté 5 minutes. Add 4½ cups broth. Simmer until squash is very tender, about 35 minutes.

Working in batches, puree soup in blender. Return to same pot. Add tomato puree and cayenne. Season to taste with salt and pepper. Simmer 10 minutes to blend flavors; add more broth if soup is too thick. *(Can be prepared 1 day ahead. Cover and refrigerate. Rewarm soup over medium heat before serving.)*

Heat 1 teaspoon oil in small skillet over medium heat. Add cumin and mustard seeds and stir until fragrant, about 2 minutes. Ladle soup into bowls. Top with seed mixture and serve.

6 SERVINGS

◆ ◆ ◆

Based on a classic French sauce called a *velouté*, this creamy soup is sparked with Indian seasonings. The result is rich and exotic, while still being easy to prepare.

◆ ◆ ◆

# Tortilla Soup with Chicken and Lime

◆ ◆ ◆

4   5- to 6-inch-diameter corn tortillas
2   teaspoons olive oil

2   14½-ounce cans low-salt chicken broth
2   cups water

| ¾ | cup canned Mexican-style stewed tomatoes with juices |
| 1 | bay leaf |
| 1 | garlic clove, pressed |
| ¼ | teaspoon ground cumin |
| ⅛ | teaspoon dried crushed red pepper |
| 12 | ounces skinless boneless chicken breast halves, cut into ½-inch-wide strips |
| 2 | green onions, sliced |
| ¼ | cup chopped fresh cilantro |
| 2 | tablespoons fresh lime juice |

Preheat oven to 350°F. Brush 1 side of tortillas with oil; cut in half. Stack halves and cut crosswise into ¼-inch-wide strips. Spread strips on nonstick baking sheet. Bake until golden, about 15 minutes. Cool tortilla strips on baking sheet.

Combine broth, water, tomatoes, bay leaf, garlic, cumin and red pepper in saucepan; bring to boil. Reduce heat; simmer 5 minutes. Add chicken; simmer until just cooked through, about 5 minutes. Stir in onions, cilantro and lime juice. Season with salt and pepper.

Ladle soup into bowls. Sprinkle with tortilla strips and serve.

4 SERVINGS

## ROASTING VEGETABLES

Roasting brings out the natural sugars in vegetables and seals in juices while creating a crisp outer layer. Smoky-flavored roasted vegetables make an excellent addition to salads and pastas, as well as giving rich taste to soups and stews.

◆ Garlic: Roast whole heads of garlic to bring out its sweet, fragrant taste. Bake in a thin layer of oil (or brush with oil and wrap in foil) until tender, 40 minutes.

◆ Onions: Roast onions in their skins. Cut a slice off the end so they will stand upright in the pan, rub with oil and prick with a fork, then bake for an hour or more, depending on size. Peel off the skin before serving.

◆ Peppers: Roast both bell peppers and chilies by charring them in a single layer in a pan a few inches under the broiler for 15 minutes. When the skin blackens, remove them from the broiler and place in a paper bag for 10 minutes. After that, the skin will easily peel off.

◆ Tomatoes: Cut tomatoes in half horizontally. Place cut-side up in an oiled baking dish, then sprinkle with herbs and dot with butter or brush with olive oil. Roast until warm and slightly browned, 8 to 10 minutes.

◆ ◆ ◆

# Black Bean and Roasted Tomato Soup

◆ ◆ ◆

1    pound plum tomatoes, halved lengthwise
1    large onion, halved lengthwise, cut into thin wedges
1    medium carrot, peeled, quartered
3    large garlic cloves, chopped
1    tablespoon olive oil
½    teaspoon dried oregano
2    cups (or more) canned vegetable broth
3¼    cups cooked black beans or two 15-ounce cans black beans, rinsed, drained

½    cup plain nonfat yogurt

Preheat oven to 350°F. Combine tomatoes, onion and carrot in large roasting pan. Add garlic, oil and oregano and stir to coat vegetables. Roast until vegetables are brown and tender, stirring occasionally, about 55 minutes. Cut carrot into small cubes and set aside. Transfer remaining vegetables to processor. Add 2 cups broth to roasting pan and scrape up any browned bits. Add broth and 2¼ cups beans to processor. Puree until almost smooth.

Transfer soup to heavy large saucepan. Add remaining 1 cup beans. Bring to boil. Reduce heat and simmer until flavors blend, adding more broth if soup is too thick, about 10 minutes. Stir in carrot. Season with salt and pepper. *(Can be made 1 day ahead. Cover; chill. Rewarm before continuing.)* Ladle soup into bowls. Top each with dollop of yogurt and serve.

4 SERVINGS

# Sherried Winter Squash Bisque

2    tablespoons olive oil

1    medium onion, chopped

1    2-pound butternut squash, peeled, cubed (about 6 cups)

1    14½-ounce can diced tomatoes, drained

2    tablespoons dry Sherry

2½   cups (or more) canned vegetable broth

⅔    cup nonfat milk

2    tablespoons chopped fresh thyme or 2 teaspoons dried

     Nonfat plain yogurt
     Fresh thyme sprigs

Heat olive oil in heavy large saucepan over medium-high heat. Add chopped onion and sauté until translucent, about 5 minutes. Add butternut squash and sauté until beginning to brown, about 10 minutes. Add tomatoes and Sherry. Boil until almost all liquid evaporates, about 30 seconds. Stir in 2½ cups vegetable broth. Bring to boil. Reduce heat, cover and simmer until squash is very tender, stirring occasionally, about 30 minutes.

Puree soup in blender in batches until smooth. Return soup to same saucepan. Stir in milk and chopped thyme. Bring to simmer. Season soup to taste with salt and pepper. *(Can be prepared 1 day ahead. Cover tightly and refrigerate. Bring soup to simmer before serving, thinning with more broth, if desired.)*

Ladle soup into bowls. Top with dollop of yogurt. Garnish with thyme sprigs. Serve immediately.

6 SERVINGS

Other varieties of sweet yellow-fleshed winter squash—such as acorn squash—would also work in this soup. Nonfat milk and vegetable broth keep it low in fat, but also give the soup a surprisingly velvety texture.

# Chilled Beet Soup with Chives

❖ ❖ ❖

The lovely color and tangy taste of this first-course soup make it a real crowd pleaser. And everyone will be even further pleased once they learn it's low in fat and calories (two grams of fat and 116 calories per serving).

❖ ❖ ❖

1½    teaspoons olive oil
3      medium carrots, peeled, chopped
1      onion, finely chopped
1½    tablespoons balsamic vinegar

2      15-ounce cans sliced beets with liquid
1      tablespoon sugar
2      cups buttermilk
       Chopped fresh chives

Heat oil in large nonstick skillet over low heat. Add carrots and onion. Cover; cook until vegetables are just tender, stirring occasionally, about 20 minutes. Add vinegar, cover and cook until vegetables are very tender, about 10 minutes longer.

Working in batches, add beets with their liquid, sugar and carrot mixture to blender. Puree. Transfer to large bowl. Mix in buttermilk. Season with salt and pepper. Chill until cold, about 3 hours. Ladle into bowls or mugs. Top with chives.

6 SERVINGS

# Cold Avocado Soup

❖ ❖ ❖

2      ripe medium avocados, halved, pitted
¾      cup buttermilk
½      cup plain yogurt
2      tablespoons fresh lime juice
1½    tablespoons chopped seeded jalapeño chili
½      teaspoon chili powder
½      cup (about) canned low-salt chicken broth

       Chopped red onion

Scrape avocados from skin into processor. Add buttermilk and yogurt; puree until smooth. Mix in lime juice, jalapeño and chili powder. With machine running, blend in ½ cup broth. Season with salt and pepper. Chill soup until cold.

Thin soup with more broth, if desired. Spoon into bowls. Sprinkle with chopped red onion.

4 SERVINGS

# Tomato-Orange Soup

◆ ◆ ◆

4    cups chicken stock or canned low-salt broth
1    28-ounce can whole peeled tomatoes with juices
1    large onion, thinly sliced
1    large carrot, thinly sliced
1    teaspoon grated lemon peel
2    bay leaves
½    teaspoon sugar

3    tablespoons butter
2    tablespoons all purpose flour
¼    cup orange juice

Purchased croutons

Combine stock, tomatoes with juices, onion, carrot, lemon peel, bay leaves and sugar in heavy large saucepan. Bring to boil over high heat, breaking up tomatoes with spoon. Reduce heat to medium and simmer until vegetables are very tender, about 40 minutes.

Melt butter in small saucepan over medium heat. Add flour; stir 2 minutes. Add 1 cup soup and stir until smooth. Return mixture to remaining soup in saucepan. Simmer until soup thickens, stirring occasionally, about 4 minutes. Discard bay leaves. Working in batches, puree soup in blender. Return soup to saucepan. Stir in orange juice. Season with salt and pepper. *(Can be prepared 1 day ahead. Cover with plastic and refrigerate.)*

Serve soup cold or bring to simmer and serve hot, if desired. Sprinkle soup  with purchased croutons.

4 TO 6 SERVINGS

◆ ◆ ◆

You can prepare this colorful soup a day ahead. Then, serve it chilled or rewarm it, depending on the rest of your menu—or the weather.

◆ ◆ ◆

# White Wine and Peach Sangria

◆ ◆ ◆

1    750-ml bottle dry white wine
¾    cup peach brandy
6    tablespoons frozen lemonade concentrate, thawed
¼    cup sugar
½    16-ounce package frozen unsweetened sliced peaches
¾    cup seedless green grapes, halved
¾    cup seedless red grapes, halved

Stir first 4 ingredients in large pitcher until sugar dissolves. Add frozen peaches and all grapes. Refrigerate sangria until well chilled, about 2 hours. Serve sangria over ice.

MAKES 6 CUPS

# Champagne and Passion Fruit Cocktails

◆ ◆ ◆

1    cup chilled passion fruit blend nectar
½    teaspoon Angostura bitters
1    cup chilled Champagne or other sparkling white wine
4    fresh raspberries or small strawberries
1    orange slice, cut in half

Divide nectar and bitters between 2 chilled Champagne flutes. Add Champagne. Drop 2 berries into each. Garnish with orange.

2 SERVINGS

◆ ◆ ◆

A bowl of macadamia nuts and these quick-to-prepare cocktails make an elegant start to dinner. You could use guava, peach or apricot nectar in place of the passion fruit blend with equally tasty results.

◆ ◆ ◆

# Jack Rose Cocktail

◆ ◆ ◆

1     cup ice cubes
½     cup applejack or apple brandy
¼     cup sweet and sour mix
2     tablespoons fresh lime juice
1     teaspoon sugar
1     teaspoon grenadine syrup
1     thin round lime slice, cut crosswise in half

Combine all ingredients except lime slice in shaker or pitcher. Shake or stir until blended and cold. Strain into 2 chilled Martini glasses. Cut slit in each lime half. Attach to rim of glasses.

2 SERVINGS

# Wasabi Bloody Mary

◆ ◆ ◆

6     tablespoons hot pepper vodka
4     teaspoons fresh lemon juice
1½    teaspoons wasabi powder*
½     teaspoon ground black pepper
1½    cups chilled tomato juice
1     teaspoon Worcestershire sauce

      Ice cubes
      Celery stalks with leaves

Stir vodka, lemon juice, wasabi and pepper in pitcher until wasabi dissolves. Stir in tomato juice and Worcestershire sauce. *(Can be prepared 1 day ahead. Cover and refrigerate. Stir before using.)*

Fill 2 tall glasses with ice cubes. Pour tomato juice mixture over. Garnish with celery stalks and serve.

*\*Available at Japanese markets and some supermarkets.*

MAKES 2

◆ ◆ ◆

Not your average Bloody Mary, this one gets its fire from hot pepper vodka and a Japanese horseradish powder called *wasabi.*

◆ ◆ ◆

# In the Pink

◆ ◆ ◆

1½   cups water
1    cup frozen pink lemonade concentrate
     (about 1⅓ six-ounce cans), thawed
¾    cup vodka
     Ice cubes
4    lemon slices

Mix first 3 ingredients in pitcher. Fill 4 tall glasses with ice. Pour lemonade mixture over. Attach lemon slice to rim of each glass.

4 SERVINGS

# Tennis Elbow

◆ ◆ ◆

4    cups chilled pineapple juice
3    cups chilled apricot nectar
2    cups chilled grapefruit juice

1⅓   cups gin
1    cup chilled tonic water
     Ice cubes
     Pineapple spears

Stir first 3 ingredients in large pitcher to blend. *(Can be prepared 1 day ahead. Cover and refrigerate.)*

Add gin and tonic water to fruit juices and stir to blend. Fill 8 tall glasses with ice. Pour drink over. Garnish with pineapple spears.

8 SERVINGS

◆ ◆ ◆

Its namesake ailment is no fun, but this tall and chilly gin-based drink is. Make it the start of a brunch to follow a game of mixed doubles.

◆ ◆ ◆

# Whiskey Punch

◆ ◆ ◆

1¾   cups Irish whiskey
¼    cup (packed) golden brown sugar
6    thick lemon slices
24   whole cloves
3    cups hot water

Mix whiskey and sugar in pitcher to dissolve sugar. Divide among 6 heatproof glasses. Stud each lemon slice with 4 cloves. Place 1 slice in each glass. Pour ½ cup hot water into each; stir to blend.

6 SERVINGS

# Waikaloa Breeze

◆ ◆ ◆

1¼ cups passion-orange-guava or other tropical fruit juice
1 cup thinly sliced hulled strawberries
½ cup gold rum
½ cup canned cream of coconut (such as Coco López)*
¼ cup half and half
8 ice cubes
 Whole strawberries

Puree first 6 ingredients in blender. Pour into glasses. Garnish with whole strawberries. Serve immediately

*Available in the liquor department of most supermarkets.*

4 SERVINGS

# Banana Colada

◆ ◆ ◆

20 ice cubes
3 ripe medium bananas, cut into chunks
1 cup canned cream of coconut (such as Coco López)*
1 cup pineapple juice
½ cup dark rum
½ cup light rum
4 tablespoons fresh lemon juice
4 fresh pineapple wedges
4 fresh mint sprigs

Place 4 tall glasses in freezer. Combine 10 ice cubes, 1½ bananas, ½ cup cream of coconut, ½ cup pineapple juice, ¼ cup dark rum, ¼ cup light rum and 2 tablespoons lemon juice in blender and blend until smooth. Divide between 2 frozen glasses. Attach pineapple wedge and mint sprig to side of each glass and serve. Repeat as described above to make second batch of drinks.

*Available in the liquor department of most supermarkets.*

4 SERVINGS

# Orange Sherbet Punch

◆ ◆ ◆

4 cups chilled orange juice
1 cup milk
3 tablespoons sugar
2 teaspoons grated orange peel
½ teaspoon ground nutmeg

1 cup chilled sparkling water
1 quart orange sherbet

Combine 4 cups orange juice, 1 cup milk, 3 tablespoons sugar, orange peel and nutmeg in large pitcher. Mix until sugar dissolves. *(Can be prepared 3 days ahead. Cover and refrigerate.)*

Pour sparkling water into orange juice mixture and stir to blend. Scoop sherbet into large glass punch bowl. Pour punch over and serve.

12 SERVINGS

# Old-fashioned Chocolate Milk Shakes

◆ ◆ ◆

1½ cups sugar
1 cup water
½ cup unsweetened cocoa (preferably Dutch process)
1 teaspoon vanilla extract

4 tablespoons milk
6 cups vanilla ice cream

Stir sugar and water in heavy medium saucepan over medium-low heat until sugar dissolves. Increase heat and bring to boil. Place cocoa in small bowl. Gradually whisk in sugar syrup. Return mixture to same saucepan. Boil 1 minute, whisking constantly. Pour into bowl. Whisk in vanilla extract and cool completely. Cover and refrigerate until cold, at least 1 hour. *(Syrup can be made 1 week ahead. Keep refrigerated.)*

Pour 3 tablespoons chocolate syrup and 1 tablespoon milk into blender. Add 1½ cups ice cream and blend until smooth. Pour into glass. Repeat in 3 more batches, using 3 tablespoons syrup, 1 tablespoon milk and 1½ cups ice cream for each milk shake.

4 SERVINGS

◆ ◆ ◆

This great-tasting drink is reminiscent of the classic Dreamsicles that used to be sold from neighborhood ice cream trucks. Kids will love it.

◆ ◆ ◆

# Hot Cider with Buttered Rum

◆ ◆ ◆

5   cups apple cider or apple juice
2   tablespoons sugar
10  whole allspice
8   whole cloves
2   cinnamon sticks
1   cup dark rum
½   cup (1 stick) unsalted butter

Combine first 5 ingredients in heavy large saucepan over medium heat. Bring to boil, stirring until sugar dissolves. Reduce heat to low. Simmer 5 minutes. Remove from heat. Add rum and butter. Stir until butter melts. Serve immediately.

6 SERVINGS

# Classic Irish Coffee

◆ ◆ ◆

¼   cup chilled whipping cream
3   teaspoons sugar

1⅓ cups hot strong coffee
6   tablespoons (3 ounces) Irish whiskey

Place cream and 2 teaspoons sugar in medium bowl. Whisk until cream holds firm peaks. Refrigerate up to 30 minutes.

Warm 2 Irish coffee glasses (small glass mugs with handles) or heatproof stemmed glasses by running very hot water into them. Dry quickly. Place ½ teaspoon sugar in each warm glass. Pour in hot coffee and stir to dissolve sugar. Add 3 tablespoons Irish whiskey to each. Spoon chilled cream over coffee in each glass and serve.

2 SERVINGS

## THE DRINK OF PIRATES

Rum and pirates are inextricably linked in history, chronicled in catchy songs and adventure rides in theme parks. Made from fermented sugarcane, this distilled spirit seems to have originated in Barbados in the 1600s, when sugarcane was the island's main crop. The rum trade spread throughout the Caribbean and as far as New England, becoming the drink of pirates—well, sailors—as well as Britain's Royal Navy.

These seamen took advantage of their access to the spirit, often overindulging, and soon enough a rum ration was declared. To stretch their limited supply, the sailors diluted it with warm water—and in so doing, set off a trend that's with us today: rum drinks.

Hot buttered rum (of which the recipe at left is a version) supposedly dates to those lean times, when sailors were drinking what was already lesser-quality rum made barely palatable by the addition of water. Somebody discovered that butter from the ship's galley, floated on top and melting into the harsh spirit, made things go down a little easier.

◆ ◆ ◆

# · Main Courses ·

An entrée doesn't need to be lavish or complex to be impressive. Sometimes it is the simplest dishes that we remember, the roast chicken with the crisp skin or the rich taste of a perfectly cooked steak, for example. Chefs know this, and they know simple secrets for making food more flavorful, secrets that don't usually leave their kitchens—that is, until *Bon Appétit* magazine comes calling. You'll find many of these divulged in the pages and recipes that follow.

Did you ever wonder, for example, about that roast chicken, how the meat stayed so succulent under the crisp and golden skin? You'll find surprisingly easy keys to success in the recipe for Lemon-Herb Roast Chicken (page 72). Have you ever had delicately crusted seafood and assumed you could never duplicate the dish at home? There's insider's knowledge in the recipe for Pecan-crusted Trout with Orange-Rosemary Butter Sauce (page 90).

In several instances, we've included step-by-step photos to help explain just how some of these tricks of the trade are done. In the Roast Stuffed Pork Loin with Applesauce (page 62), you'll discover how to butterfly, stuff and tie a pork loin roast. Turn to the recipe for Vegetable Frittata with Herbs and Goat Cheese (page106) to learn the ins and outs of cooking this tasty egg dish. Armed with these and the other pointers offered throughout this chapter, you will be cooking like a pro in no time.

*Smoked Salmon Bruschetta with Tomato-Avocado Salsa (page 20); Asian Risotto with Pancetta and Mussels (page 102); Hot Chocolate Cakes with Mango and Ginger (page 190)*

# Beef Tenderloin with Spring Vegetables and Champ

◆ ◆ ◆

2   cups beef stock or canned broth
1   cup chicken stock or canned low-salt broth

4   small carrots, peeled, halved lengthwise
16  green beans, trimmed
1   red bell pepper, cut into 8 strips
4   fresh shiitake mushrooms, stemmed
8   asparagus spears, trimmed
1   zucchini, trimmed, cut into ½-inch-thick rounds

4   8-ounce beef tenderloin steaks (about 1¼ inches thick)
2   tablespoons olive oil
½   cup dry red wine
6   tablespoons (¾ stick) chilled unsalted butter, cut into pieces

Olive oil

Champ (see recipe opposite)

Combine beef stock and chicken stock in medium saucepan. Boil until reduced to ¾ cup, about 20 minutes. Set aside.

Cook carrots in large saucepan of boiling salted water 3 minutes. Using slotted spoon, transfer carrots to strainer and rinse under cold water. Add beans to boiling water; cook 1 minute. Transfer to strainer with carrots and rinse under cold water. Drain well. Arrange carrots, beans, bell pepper, mushrooms, asparagus and zucchini in single layer on large baking sheet. *(Stock and vegetables can be prepared 4 hours ahead. Cover separately and refrigerate.)*

Preheat broiler. Sprinkle steaks with salt and pepper. Heat 2 tablespoons olive oil in heavy large skillet over medium-high heat. Add steaks; cook to desired doneness, about 4 minutes per side for medium-rare. Transfer steaks to plate; tent with aluminum foil to keep warm. Add dry red wine to same skillet. Boil until red wine is reduced to 1 tablespoon, scraping up browned bits, about 3 minutes. Add reduced stock and bring to boil. Remove from heat. Add chilled butter a few pieces at a time and whisk just until melted. Season sauce to taste with salt and pepper.

◆ ◆ ◆

This recipe is something of a new take on an Irish classic. Traditionally, champ is served with a well in the middle that has a dab of butter melting in it. The potatoes are usually eaten from "outside" to "inside," dipping each bite into the butter.

◆ ◆ ◆

Meanwhile, brush vegetables lightly with olive oil. Broil vegetables until crisp-tender, about 3 minutes per side for carrots, green beans, bell peppers and mushrooms and about 2 minutes per side for asparagus and zucchini.

Spoon Champ onto 4 plates. Place steaks atop Champ. Arrange vegetables decoratively around Champ. Spoon sauce over vegetables.

4 SERVINGS

# Champ
## (Green Onion Mashed Potatoes)

2    pounds russet potatoes, peeled, cut into 1-inch pieces

½    cup whipping cream
¼    cup (½ stick) butter
1    bunch green onions, sliced (about 1⅓ cups)

Cook potatoes in large pot of boiling salted water until very tender, about 15 minutes.

Meanwhile, bring cream and butter to simmer in heavy small saucepan over medium heat, stirring often. Mix in green onions. Remove from heat. Cover and let steep while potatoes cook.

Drain potatoes thoroughly. Return potatoes to same pot and mash. Add cream mixture and stir until blended. Season to taste with salt and pepper. *(Can be prepared 2 hours ahead. Cover; let stand at room temperature. Rewarm over low heat, stirring often.)*

4 SERVINGS

# Beef Stew with Shiitake Mushrooms and Baby Vegetables

All purpose flour
6 tablespoons (¾ stick) butter
3 pounds trimmed boneless beef chuck, cut into 1½-inch cubes

2 large onions, chopped
¼ cup tomato paste
3 cups dry red wine
2 14½-ounce cans beef broth
1 tablespoon dark brown sugar

1½ pounds baby red-skinned potatoes, quartered
30 baby carrots, trimmed
12 to 14 ounces baby pattypan squash, halved
1 pound fresh shiitake mushrooms, stemmed, caps thickly sliced
3 tablespoons chopped fresh marjoram or 1 tablespoon dried

Place flour in baking pan. Season with salt and pepper. Melt 4 tablespoons butter in heavy large Dutch oven over medium-high heat. Working in batches, coat meat with flour; add to pot and brown on all sides. Using slotted spoon, transfer to plate.

Melt 2 tablespoons butter in same pot over medium-high heat. Add onions; sauté until tender, about 6 minutes. Mix in tomato paste, then wine. Bring to boil, scraping up any browned bits. Add broth and sugar, then beef and any accumulated juices. Bring to boil. Reduce heat, cover partially and simmer 1½ hours.

Add potatoes and carrots; simmer uncovered until meat and vegetables are almost tender, about 25 minutes. Add squash; simmer until almost tender, about 10 minutes. Add mushrooms and 3 tablespoons marjoram; simmer until mushrooms are tender, about 5 minutes. Season with salt and pepper. *(Can be made 1 day ahead. Cool slightly. Cover; refrigerate. Before serving, rewarm over medium heat, stirring occasionally.)*

6 SERVINGS

---

◆ ◆ ◆

## FAMILY DINNER FOR SIX

BEEF STEW WITH
SHIITAKE MUSHROOMS AND
BABY VEGETABLES
(AT LEFT; PICTURED OPPOSITE)

FRENCH BREAD

TOSSED GREEN SALAD

DRY RED WINE

VANILLA ICE CREAM AND GINGER
MOLASSES COOKIE SANDWICHES
(PAGE 210)

◆ ◆ ◆

# Grilled Sirloin Steaks with Blue Cheese-Walnut Butter

◆ ◆ ◆

6   ounces blue cheese, crumbled (about 1⅓ cups)
4   tablespoons (½ stick) butter, room temperature
2   tablespoons chopped fresh Italian parsley
¾   teaspoon plus 1 tablespoon dried rosemary, finely crumbled
¼   cup chopped toasted walnuts (about 1 ounce)

6   large garlic cloves, peeled
1½  teaspoons salt
1½  teaspoons ground black pepper
2   1½- to 1¾-pound top sirloin steaks (1 inch thick)

Combine cheese, butter, parsley and ¾ teaspoon rosemary in medium bowl. Stir to blend well. Mix in walnuts. Season to taste with salt and pepper. Transfer blue cheese butter to small bowl. *(Can be prepared 2 days ahead. Cover; chill. Bring to room temperature.)*

Combine 1 tablespoon rosemary, garlic, salt and pepper in processor. Blend until mixture resembles coarse paste. Pat steaks dry. Place in large baking dish. Rub 2 teaspoons of garlic paste on each side of each steak. Cover and let stand 1 hour at room temperature.

Prepare barbecue (medium-high heat). Grill steaks to desired doneness, about 5 minutes per side for medium-rare. Transfer steaks to platter and let stand 5 minutes. Cut each steak into 3 equal portions. Top each portion with a spoonful of blue cheese butter.

6 SERVINGS

# Classic Meat Loaf with Roasted Vegetables

◆ ◆ ◆

4   slices white sandwich bread, crusts trimmed,
    bread torn into bite-size pieces
2   eggs
4   tablespoons Worcestershire sauce
1   cup chopped onion
⅓   cup plus 1 tablespoon ketchup
1   tablespoon garlic powder
½   teaspoon salt
½   teaspoon ground pepper
1½  pounds lean ground beef

1   14½-ounce can beef broth
1   large red-skinned sweet potato (yam), peeled,
    quartered lengthwise
2   russet potatoes, peeled, quartered lengthwise
4   carrots, peeled, halved lengthwise

Preheat oven to 375°F. Mash bread, eggs and 3 tablespoons Worcestershire sauce in large bowl until smooth paste forms. Mix in onion, ⅓ cup ketchup, garlic powder, salt and pepper. Add beef and mix thoroughly. Mound meat mixture in 13 x 9 x 2-inch baking pan, shaping into 8 x 4-inch loaf. Spread 1 tablespoon ketchup over loaf.

Pour broth and remaining 1 tablespoon Worcestershire sauce into pan around meat loaf. Arrange vegetables around meat loaf. Cover pan with foil. Bake 45 minutes. Uncover; bake until vegetables are tender and meat loaf is cooked through, about 35 minutes. Using spatula, transfer meat loaf to platter. Surround with vegetables; spoon some pan juices over.

4 SERVINGS

◆ ◆ ◆

Two kinds of potatoes (sweet and baking) roast alongside the meat loaf in this simple one-pan recipe.

◆ ◆ ◆

## MAGIC FROM MODENA

With its intense sweet-sour tang, balsamic vinegar is remarkably versatile, as flavorful in a vinaigrette as it is reduced to a glaze for steaks (see recipe at right).

Most balsamic vinegar (called *aceto balsamico* in Italy) sold in this country comes from the province of Modena in north-central Italy, where it is produced not from sour wine like most vinegars, but from the juice of local white trebbiano grapes, which is boiled down to a sweet syrup, fermented and then aged in barrels made from a variety of woods. The minimum number of years is 12, but in Italy it is aged—and priced—like fine wine. The best-quality balsamic vinegar will sell for $80 to $100 for a 3.5-ounce bottle.

Italians treasure this flavoring, using it in the smallest amounts. They also drink it as a tonic. Here, we're more inclined to use it in a variety of ways, and less inclined to pay the high price for the real thing. Beware, though, of supermarket balsamic vinegars, which are usually red wine vinegar cut with sugar and water. Instead, look for the aged balsamics available at specialty foods stores and priced $12 to $15 a bottle.

◆ ◆ ◆

# Rib Eye Steaks with Balsamic Vinegar Glaze

◆ ◆ ◆

2   ¾-inch-thick boneless rib eye steaks or other tender beefsteaks (about 6 ounces each)
3   teaspoons olive oil

⅓   cup chopped shallots
2   teaspoons chopped fresh rosemary
3   tablespoons balsamic vinegar

Sprinkle steaks with salt and generous amount of pepper. Rub 1 teaspoon oil over bottom of heavy medium skillet. Heat skillet over medium-high heat. Add steaks to skillet and cook to desired doneness, about 4 minutes per side for rare. Using tongs, transfer steaks to plate; tent with foil to keep warm.

Add remaining 2 teaspoons oil to same skillet. Reduce heat to medium-low. Add shallots and rosemary and cook for 2 minutes, stirring occasionally. Add vinegar and cook until reduced to glaze, stirring up browned bits, about 1 minute. Mix in juices from plate with steaks. Spoon glaze over steaks and serve.

2 SERVINGS

# Steak with Horseradish and Dijon Mustard Crust

◆ ◆ ◆

½    cup chopped fresh horseradish

¾    cup water

6    10-ounce New York sirloin steaks, trimmed of excess fat

6    teaspoons Dijon mustard

1½   cups fresh white breadcrumbs

4    tablespoons vegetable oil

Preheat oven to 350°F. Puree horseradish and water in blender until smooth. Transfer mixture to strainer; drain excess water.

Sprinkle steaks with salt and pepper. Spread 1 teaspoon mustard, then 1 tablespoon horseradish atop each steak. Press ¼ cup breadcrumbs into each steak.

Heat 2 tablespoons oil in heavy large skillet over medium-high heat. Add 3 steaks, crumb side down. Cook until brown, about 4 minutes per side. Transfer steaks to baking sheet, crumb side up. Repeat with remaining 2 tablespoons oil and steaks. Bake steaks in oven until tester inserted into center registers 135°F for medium-rare, about 6 minutes. Serve immediately.

6 SERVINGS

# Sherry-Lemon Veal Medallions

◆ ◆ ◆

| | |
|---|---|
| 1 | pound veal scallops, trimmed |
| ¼ | cup all purpose flour |
| 4 | teaspoons chopped fresh thyme or 1½ teaspoons dried |
| 2½ | teaspoons olive oil |
| ⅔ | cup canned low-salt chicken broth |
| ⅓ | cup dry Sherry |
| 1 | tablespoon fresh lemon juice |
| 1 | garlic clove, minced |

Pound veal between sheets of plastic wrap to ⅛-inch thickness. Cut veal into 16 equal pieces. Sprinkle with salt and pepper. Mix flour and 2½ teaspoons fresh thyme or 1 teaspoon dried thyme in shallow dish. Coat half of veal with flour mixture, shaking off excess. Heat 1 teaspoon oil in large nonstick skillet over high heat. Add veal; sauté until beginning to brown, about 1 minute per side. Place on platter. Repeat with 1 teaspoon oil and remaining veal.

Heat ½ teaspoon oil in same skillet over high heat. Add broth, Sherry, lemon juice and garlic and bring to boil, scraping up browned bits. Add veal; turn to coat. Add remaining 1½ teaspoons fresh thyme or ½ teaspoon dried thyme. Simmer until sauce thickens slightly, about 3 minutes. Season sauce with salt and pepper. Transfer veal and sauce to plates and serve.

4 SERVINGS

## BREADCRUMBS EXPLAINED

There are two types of bread-crumbs—the soft, fresh kind and the dry type. Soft breadcrumbs are better for stuffings and meat loaf and dry breadcrumbs, which are lighter, tend to work better for breading such foods as chicken, veal and fish. Both can easily be made at home.

To make soft breadcrumbs, cut the crusts off slices of one- to two-day-old unsweetened white bread (don't use stale bread or the crumbs will have a stale flavor). (Approximately four to five slices of bread will make one cup of soft breadcrumbs.) Finely grind the bread in a blender or food processor. The crumbs can be stored in a covered container in the refrigerator for two weeks, or frozen for several weeks.

Dry breadcrumbs are made from dry, hard bread or fresh bread toasted in a 300°F oven for 15 minutes per side. They should be prepared the same way as soft breadcrumbs. (Two slices of toasted bread will yield about ⅓ cup breadcrumbs.) The dry kind keep slightly longer than the fresh.

For variety and flavor, make crumbs from whole wheat bread, corn bread or herb bread. You can also add herbs and other seasonings to taste.

◆ ◆ ◆

# Veal Sauté with Caramelized Shallots

◆ ◆ ◆

½    pound veal scallops
1½    tablespoons butter
¼    cup chopped shallots
½    cup dry white wine
1    tablespoon chopped fresh sage or 1 teaspoon dried rubbed sage
1    teaspoon Dijon mustard

Season veal with salt and pepper. Melt ½ tablespoon butter in large nonstick skillet over high heat. Add veal and sauté until cooked through and golden, about 1 minute per side. Using tongs, transfer veal to plate. Add remaining 1 tablespoon butter and shallots to skillet. Reduce heat to medium-low. Cook until shallots soften and brown, stirring frequently, about 3 minutes. Whisk in wine, sage and mustard. Simmer until sauce thickens slightly, about 3 minutes. Season with salt and pepper. Return veal and any collected juices to skillet. Simmer until just heated through, about 1 minute.

2 SERVINGS

# Herbed Veal Chops with Wild Mushroom Sauté

◆ ◆ ◆

1½    cups fresh white breadcrumbs
¼    cup chopped fresh parsley
¼    cup chopped fresh thyme
¼    cup chopped fresh chives
4    teaspoons chopped fresh tarragon
4    8- to 9-ounce veal chops, trimmed
¼    cup Dijon mustard

2    tablespoons (¼ stick) butter
6    tablespoons olive oil
3    tablespoons finely chopped shallots
12    ounces assorted fresh wild mushrooms (such as portobello, chanterelle, oyster and stemmed shiitake), sliced
¼    cup brandy
1    cup canned low-salt chicken broth
½    cup chopped seeded tomato

Preheat oven to 400°F. Mix first 5 ingredients in processor until well combined. Transfer mixture to shallow pan. Sprinkle veal with salt and pepper. Spread mustard over both sides of chops. Coat chops with breadcrumbs. Transfer to plate.

Melt butter with 2 tablespoons oil in heavy large skillet over medium-high heat. Add shallots and sauté until translucent, about 4 minutes. Add mushrooms and sauté until tender, about 4 minutes. Add brandy and simmer until reduced by half, about 2 minutes. Add broth and simmer until most of liquid has evaporated, about 5 minutes. Stir in tomato. Cover and keep warm.

Meanwhile, heat 4 tablespoons oil in heavy large skillet over medium-high heat. Add veal chops to skillet and cook until golden brown, about 2 minutes per side. Transfer chops to baking pan. Roast until cooked as desired, about 8 minutes for medium-rare.

Spoon mushroom mixture over chops. Serve.

4 SERVINGS

# Veal Chops with Balsamic Vinegar

◆ ◆ ◆

6    7- to 8-ounce veal loin chops (about 1 inch thick)
3    garlic cloves, minced
2    tablespoons chopped fresh rosemary or 2 teaspoons dried
2    tablespoons chopped fresh thyme or 2 teaspoons dried

2    tablespoons olive oil
¾    cup balsamic vinegar
1    tablespoon red vermouth or 1 teaspoon sugar
     Additional chopped fresh thyme

Place veal chops in glass baking dish. Rub both sides with garlic, rosemary and 2 tablespoons thyme.

Preheat oven to 450°F. Heat 1 tablespoon oil in each of 2 heavy large ovenproof skillets over high heat. Sprinkle veal with salt and pepper. Add 3 veal chops to each skillet; sear until brown, about 3 minutes per side. Transfer skillets to oven; roast veal about 6 minutes for medium-rare. Transfer veal to platter. Add vinegar to 1 skillet; bring to boil, scraping up any browned bits. Pour mixture into second skillet. Add vermouth and boil until vinegar is reduced to syrup consistency, stirring occasionally and scraping up browned bits, about 3 minutes. Pour over veal. Sprinkle with thyme.

6 SERVINGS

◆ ◆ ◆

These roast veal chops are served with a sauce flavored with balsamic vinegar and vermouth. Try a simple zucchini and fennel sauté alongside.

◆ ◆ ◆

# Grilled Lamb, Potato, Bean and Mushroom Salad

◆ ◆ ◆

¾    cup Dijon mustard

½    cup fresh lemon juice

3    2-ounce cans anchovies, drained, oil reserved, anchovies chopped

1⅓    cups olive oil

1½    cups (packed) chopped fresh basil

1    cup chopped shallots

1    5½-pound leg of lamb, fat trimmed, boned and butterflied (about 3½ pounds boned)

3    pounds small red-skinned potatoes, cut into ¾-inch pieces

2    pounds yellow wax beans, trimmed

1    pound mushrooms, sliced

Spinach leaves
Fresh basil sprigs

Mix mustard and lemon juice in medium bowl. Mix in anchovy oil. Gradually whisk in olive oil. Add anchovies, chopped basil and shallots. Season with salt and pepper. Open lamb in large glass baking dish. Pour 1⅓ cups dressing over, turning to coat. Cover lamb and remaining dressing separately and chill at least 6 hours or overnight. Bring dressing to room temperature before using.

Cook potatoes in large pot of boiling salted water just until tender, about 15 minutes. Drain well. Transfer to large bowl. Add 1½ cups reserved dressing to warm potatoes and toss gently to coat. Cook beans in large pot of boiling salted water until crisp-tender, about 8 minutes. Drain. Rinse with cold water; drain well. Add beans and mushrooms to potatoes. Mix in ½ cup reserved dressing. Season to taste with salt and pepper.

Prepare barbecue (medium-high heat). Sprinkle lamb with salt and pepper. Place lamb on grill and cook until thermometer inserted into thickest part of meat registers 135°F, brushing with remaining marinade from baking dish, about 12 minutes per side for medium-rare. Transfer to platter and let stand at least 15 minutes.

Line large platter with spinach leaves. Mound potato salad in center. Cut lamb across grain in diagonal slices. Arrange sliced lamb around edges of platter. Drizzle lamb with remaining reserved dressing. Garnish salad with fresh basil sprigs and serve.

10 TO 12 SERVINGS

◆ ◆ ◆

## ELEGANT LUNCH FOR TEN

GRILLED PESTO BREADSTICKS
WITH GOAT CHEESE-PESTO
SPREAD
(PAGE 16; PICTURED OPPOSITE)

GRILLED LAMB, POTATO, BEAN
AND MUSHROOM SALAD
(AT LEFT; PICTURED OPPOSITE)

BEAUJOLAIS

FRUIT SHORTCAKES

◆ ◆ ◆

# Braised Lamb Shanks with Caramelized Onions and Shallots

♦ ♦ ♦

| | |
|---|---|
| 4 | tablespoons olive oil |
| 1 | pound onions, sliced |
| 5 | large shallots, sliced (about 1 cup) |
| 2 | tablespoons chopped fresh rosemary or 2 teaspoons dried |
| 6 | ¾- to 1-pound lamb shanks |
| | All purpose flour |
| 2½ | cups dry red wine |
| 2½ | cups canned beef broth |
| 1½ | tablespoons tomato paste |
| 2 | bay leaves |
| | Additional chopped fresh rosemary |

Heat 2 tablespoons olive oil in heavy large Dutch oven over medium-high heat. Add sliced onions and shallots and sauté until brown, about 20 minutes. Mix in 2 tablespoons chopped rosemary. Remove onion mixture from heat.

Sprinkle lamb shanks with salt and pepper; coat lamb with flour. Heat remaining 2 tablespoons olive oil in heavy large skillet

over high heat. Working in batches, add lamb shanks to skillet and cook until brown on both sides, about 10 minutes per batch. Using tongs, transfer lamb shanks to plate. Add 1 cup dry red wine to same skillet and bring to boil, scraping up any browned bits. Pour into Dutch oven with onion mixture. Add remaining 1½ cups red wine, canned beef broth, tomato paste and 2 bay leaves to Dutch oven. Bring to boil, stirring until tomato paste dissolves. Add lamb shanks, turning to coat with liquid.

Bring mixture to boil. Reduce heat, cover and simmer until lamb is almost tender, turning lamb shanks occasionally, about 1½ hours. *(Can be prepared 1 day ahead. Cover and refrigerate.)*

Uncover Dutch oven and boil until liquid is reduced to sauce consistency, stirring and turning lamb shanks occasionally, about 30 minutes. Season with salt and pepper.

Place one lamb shank on each plate. Top with sauce. Sprinkle lamb shanks with additional chopped fresh rosemary and serve.

6 SERVINGS

# Lamb and Rosemary Spiedini

◆ ◆ ◆

5    tablespoons fresh lemon juice
¼    cup olive oil
1    tablespoon chopped fresh rosemary or 1½ teaspoons dried
2    teaspoons grated lemon peel
10   ounces boneless sirloin lamb chops, cut into 1-inch pieces

1    red onion, peeled, cut into 1-inch pieces
½    green bell pepper, cut into 1-inch pieces
½    yellow bell pepper, cut into 1-inch pieces

Prepare barbecue (medium-high heat). Whisk lemon juice, olive oil, rosemary and grated lemon peel in glass pie dish to blend. Sprinkle lamb with salt and pepper; add lamb to marinade and toss to coat. Let mixture stand 10 minutes, tossing occasionally.

Using slotted spoon, transfer lamb to bowl. Add onion, green bell pepper and yellow bell pepper to marinade in pie dish and toss to coat. Thread lamb, onion and bell pepper pieces alternately on 4 skewers. Grill until onion and peppers are slightly charred and lamb is cooked to desired doneness, brushing once with marinade, about 12 minutes for medium. Transfer lamb spiedini to plates and serve.

2 SERVINGS

## SKEWER COOKING

Spearing a few chunks of meat with a sharp stick and cooking them over an open fire must have been one of the first cooking methods known to man. While the herdsmen of the Middle East are said to have invented *shish kebabs*, virtually every culture has its own version of skewer cooking.

In France, meats and vegetables are cooked *en brochette*; in Italy, *spiedini* are both grilled and sautéed; the Greeks have their *souvlakia*, the Russians their *shashlik*; Japanese *kushi yaki* and Indonesian *satay* use richly flavored marinades to flavor thin slices of skewered meat.

In this heyday of grilling—both indoors and out—skewers can take a meal from appetizer to dessert, serving as both cooking and eating utensil for combinations of meats and seafood, vegetables and fruits.

Use thin bamboo or wooden skewers for foods that cook quickly, being sure to soak the skewers in water for 15 minutes to prevent them from burning. Large metal skewers with handles can be used for big chunks of meat. And while long-handled forks make a fine tool for roasting marshmallows, purists still insist on scavenged tree branches—a nod, perhaps, to the ancestral roots of skewer cooking.

◆ ◆ ◆

# Irish Stew

♦ ♦ ♦

5    pounds lamb shoulder chops

20    baby red-skinned potatoes

6    large carrots, peeled, quartered

3    medium onions, quartered

2    medium leeks (white and pale green parts only), split lengthwise, cut into ½-inch-thick slices

⅓    cup chopped fresh parsley

1½    tablespoons chopped fresh thyme

2    cups water

Trim and reserve fat and bones from lamb. Cut meat into 1½-inch pieces. Place fat in heavy large Dutch oven over medium-high heat. Cook fat until 3 tablespoons drippings are rendered, about 5 minutes. Using large spoon, remove any solid fat from pot; discard. Sprinkle lamb with salt and pepper. Working in batches, add lamb to pot; sauté until brown on all sides, about 5 minutes per batch. Using slotted spoon, transfer lamb to plate. Add bones to pot; cook until brown, 5 minutes. Using tongs, transfer bones to plate.

Add vegetables, parsley and thyme to pot; stir to coat with drippings. Return meat and bones to pot. Add 2 cups water and bring to boil. Reduce heat to medium-low. Cover pot tightly; simmer until lamb is tender and vegetables are soft, stirring stew occasionally, approximately 1½ hours.

Discard bones. Place 1 cup vegetables in processor; puree. Add to stew. Season with salt and pepper. *(Can be made 1 day ahead. Cover; chill. Bring to simmer before serving.)*

6 SERVINGS

## Pepita-crusted Lamb with Pomegranate Cream

◆ ◆ ◆

½   cup unsalted shelled pumpkin seeds,* toasted
2   tablespoons all purpose flour
¾   cup fresh white breadcrumbs
2   tablespoons chopped cilantro
1½  teaspoons salt
2   tablespoons milk
1   large egg
2   2¼- to 2⅓-pound racks of lamb, well trimmed

4   cups unsweetened pomegranate juice**
½   cup sour cream

2   tablespoons olive oil

Preheat oven to 400°F. Finely grind pumpkin seeds and flour in processor. Mix with breadcrumbs, cilantro and salt in large bowl. Beat milk and egg in small bowl to blend. Sprinkle lamb with pepper. Brush with egg mixture; press breadcrumb mixture over lamb to coat.

Boil pomegranate juice in heavy medium saucepan until reduced to ¾ cup, about 25 minutes. Transfer syrup to small bowl; cool slightly. Add sour cream; whisk to blend. Season with salt.

Meanwhile, heat oil in heavy large skillet over high heat. Add

---

◆ ◆ ◆

# FUSION COOKING
# FOR SIX

PEPITA-CRUSTED LAMB WITH
POMEGRANATE CREAM
(AT RIGHT; PICTURED AT RIGHT)

WINTER SQUASH AND WHITE BEAN
CHILES RELLENOS
(PAGE 139; PICTURED AT RIGHT)

ZINFANDEL OR MERLOT

CARDAMOM CRÈME BRÛLÉE
(PAGE 205)

◆ ◆ ◆

lamb and cook until brown, about 3 minutes per side. Transfer lamb to baking sheet. Bake until thermometer inserted into center registers 130°F for medium-rare, about 20 minutes. Cut lamb into chops. Divide among 6 plates. Spoon pomegranate cream over.

*Also known as pepitas. Available at Latin American markets, some natural foods stores and many supermarkets.*

**Available at Middle Eastern and natural foods stores.*

6 SERVINGS

# Lamb with Couscous and Minted Fruit Chutney

◆ ◆ ◆

1    tablespoon olive oil (preferably extra-virgin)
4    garlic cloves, minced
1    teaspoon (packed) chopped fresh rosemary or
     ½ teaspoon dried
4    1¼-inch-thick lamb loin chops, trimmed

1¾   cups water
¼    cup dried tart cherries
¼    cup diced dried apricots
¼    cup dried cranberries
¼    cup chopped fresh mint
1    teaspoon balsamic vinegar

1    10-ounce box couscous

Mix oil, garlic and rosemary in 8 x 8 x 2-inch glass baking dish. Add lamb; turn to coat. Cover; refrigerate at least 2 hours and up to 4 hours, turning occasionally.

Mix water, cherries, apricots and cranberries in heavy medium saucepan. Bring to boil. Reduce heat and simmer until water is absorbed and fruits are tender, stirring occasionally, about 20 minutes. Remove from heat. Stir in mint and vinegar. Season to taste with salt and pepper. Cool chutney slightly.

Prepare couscous according to package instructions.

Preheat broiler. Season lamb with salt and pepper. Transfer lamb to broiler pan. Broil lamb chops to desired doneness, about 6 minutes per side for medium-rare.

Transfer lamb to plates. Top with chutney. Spoon couscous alongside. Serve immediately.

4 SERVINGS

◆ ◆ ◆

This one-dish dinner is exotic *and* surprisingly low in fat and calories (12 grams of fat and 535 calories per serving). The chutney would also be good with pork chops.

◆ ◆ ◆

To prepare the butterflied pork roast for stuffing, set it on a work surface atop a large piece of plastic wrap. Unfold both flaps so that the pork resembles an open book.

Spread the stuffing over the pork, then use the plastic to help roll up the pork, enclosing the stuffing.

Using kitchen string, tie the rolled pork at two-inch intervals.

# Roast Stuffed Pork Loin with Applesauce

◆ ◆ ◆

APPLESAUCE

1½   pounds all purpose apples (such as McIntosh), peeled, cored, cut into 2-inch pieces
⅓   cup sugar
2   tablespoons water

STUFFING

3   tablespoons butter, room temperature
1¼  cups chopped onion
2½  cups fresh white breadcrumbs
6   tablespoons mixed chopped fresh herbs (such as parsley, thyme, chives, marjoram and rosemary)

PORK

1   4-pound center-cut boneless pork loin roast, trimmed

GRAVY

2   tablespoons all purpose flour
3   cups canned low-salt chicken broth
2   tablespoons (¼ stick) butter
3   tablespoons mixed chopped fresh herbs

FOR APPLESAUCE: Combine all ingredients in heavy large saucepan. Cover; cook over medium-low heat until apples begin to break down, stirring often, about 20 minutes.

Coarsely mash apples in saucepan to chunky sauce; transfer to medium bowl. *(Can be made 2 days ahead. Cover; chill.)*

FOR STUFFING: Preheat oven to 375°F. Melt butter in heavy large skillet over medium heat. Add onion and sauté until tender, about 5 minutes. Mix in breadcrumbs and fresh herbs. Season stuffing to taste with salt and pepper. Set aside.

FOR PORK: Butterfly pork loin by cutting horizontally almost in half, leaving 1 inch of 1 long side intact. Line work surface with large piece of plastic wrap. Arrange butterflied pork on plastic and open like a book. Top with another large sheet of plastic. Using mallet or rolling pin, pound pork until about ½ inch thick, 10 inches wide and 13 to 14 inches long. Discard top plastic sheet.

Sprinkle pork with salt and pepper. Spread breadcrumb

stuffing evenly over. Starting at 1 long side and using bottom plastic sheet as aid, tightly roll up pork. Discard plastic sheet. Tie pork at 2-inch intervals to hold log shape. Sprinkle pork with salt and pepper. Place rack in large roasting pan. Place pork on rack.

Roast stuffed pork until thermometer inserted into thickest part registers 160°F, about 1 hour 15 minutes. Transfer pork to platter; tent with foil to keep warm. (Do not clean roasting pan.)

FOR GRAVY: Mix butter and flour in small bowl until smooth. Set roasting pan over medium-high heat. Gradually whisk in 3 cups chicken broth and bring mixture to boil, scraping up any browned bits. Whisk in butter-flour mixture and fresh herbs. Boil gravy until thickened to sauce consistency, whisking constantly, about 4 minutes. Season gravy to taste with salt and pepper.

Stir applesauce in saucepan over medium heat until warm.

Cut pork crosswise into ½-inch-thick slices. Place pork slices on plates and top with gravy. Spoon some applesauce alongside.

6 TO 8 SERVINGS

# Wild Rice, Pork and Bean Salad with Cherries and Honey Vinaigrette

♦ ♦ ♦

Cherries, hazelnuts and wild rice are delicious with the pork. A honey and anise vinaigrette is the finishing touch to the salad.

♦ ♦ ♦

| | |
|---|---|
| 3 | tablespoons Dijon mustard |
| 3 | garlic cloves, minced |
| 2 | teaspoons coarsely ground pepper |
| 1 | 1-pound pork tenderloin |
| ½ | pound yellow wax beans, trimmed, cut diagonally into 1½-inch pieces |
| 1 | cup wild rice (about 6½ ounces) |
| 1 | cup coarsely chopped pitted cherries (about 7 ounces) |
| ¾ | cup hazelnuts, toasted, husked, coarsely chopped |
| 3 | tablespoons red wine vinegar |
| 2 | tablespoons honey |
| 1 | tablespoon aniseed, ground in mortar with pestle |
| ½ | cup olive oil |
| 1 | large bunch watercress, trimmed |

Preheat oven to 450°F. Mix mustard, garlic and pepper in small bowl. Rub mixture all over pork tenderloin. Place rack in roasting pan. Place pork on rack in pan. Add enough water to pan to reach just below rack. Roast pork until thermometer inserted into center registers 150°F, about 18 minutes. Transfer pork to plate. Cool 30 minutes. *(Can be prepared 1 day ahead. Cover and chill.)*

Cook wax beans in large pot of boiling salted water until just crisp-tender, about 4 minutes. Using slotted spoon, transfer beans

to large bowl of ice water and cool. Drain well. In same pot of boiling salted water, cook wild rice until tender but not mushy, stirring occasionally, about 50 minutes. Drain and transfer wild rice to large bowl. Pat beans dry. Add beans, cherries and nuts to rice.

Place vinegar, honey and aniseed in medium bowl; whisk to blend. Gradually whisk in oil. Season with salt and pepper. Add to salad and mix gently. Season salad with salt and pepper.

Cut pork into ½-inch slices. Arrange watercress around edge of large platter. Mound salad in center. Arrange sliced pork atop salad.

6 SERVINGS

# Chile Verde Burritos

◆ ◆ ◆

| 2 | cups water |
| 1 | pound tomatillos,* husked, rinsed, halved |
| 4 | garlic cloves, peeled |
| 2 | large jalapeño chilies, halved, with seeds |
| 1 | teaspoon dried oregano |
| 2 | tablespoons vegetable oil |
| 1½ | pounds pork tenderloin, cut into ½-inch cubes |
| ½ | cup chopped onion |
| 2 | garlic cloves, minced |
| ½ | cup finely chopped fresh cilantro |
| ⅓ | cup chopped radish leaves |
| 4 | burrito-size flour tortillas |

Combine first 5 ingredients in heavy large saucepan; bring to boil. Reduce heat to medium. Cover; cook until tomatillos are tender, about 15 minutes. Coarsely puree in batches in blender.

Heat oil in heavy large Dutch oven over medium-high heat. Add pork, onion and minced garlic and sauté 10 minutes. Reduce heat to medium-low. Add tomatillo sauce, cilantro and radish leaves and simmer until pork is tender and sauce thickens, stirring occasionally, about 30 minutes. Season with salt and pepper.

Preheat oven to 350°F. Stack tortillas and wrap in foil. Bake until warm, about 10 minutes. Place 1 tortilla on each of 4 plates. Divide pork mixture among tortillas. Fold in 2 sides, then roll up. Arrange seam side down on plates.

*A green tomato-like vegetable with a paper-thin husk. Available at Latin American markets and some supermarkets.*

MAKES 4

# Pork Tenderloin with Mango Chutney

◆ ◆ ◆

1     tablespoon vegetable oil

½     teaspoon cumin seeds

1     cup chopped onion

1     tablespoon chopped peeled fresh ginger

1     large firm but ripe mango, peeled, pitted, chopped (about 1 cup)

1     tablespoon chopped seeded jalapeño chili

¼     teaspoon ground turmeric

2     tablespoons fresh lime juice

      Nonstick vegetable oil spray

2     12-ounce pork tenderloins, trimmed

1     tablespoon curry powder

2     tablespoons fresh cilantro leaves

Heat oil in large nonstick skillet over medium heat. Add cumin seeds; stir until brown, about 2 minutes. Add onion and ginger to skillet; sauté until onion begins to brown, about 5 minutes. Add mango, jalapeño and turmeric. Stir until mango is heated through, about 3 minutes. Cool slightly. Mix in lime juice. Season chutney with salt and pepper. *(Can be made 6 hours ahead. Cover; chill. Bring to room temperature before serving.)*

Spray barbecue grill with vegetable oil spray. Prepare barbecue (medium-high heat) or preheat broiler. Rub all sides of pork with curry powder; sprinkle with salt and pepper. Grill or broil pork until thermometer inserted into thickest part of pork registers 155°F, turning frequently, about 20 minutes if grilling or 15 minutes if broiling. Transfer pork to work surface. Cut pork crosswise into ½-inch-thick slices. Transfer to plates. Sprinkle with cilantro. Spoon chutney alongside pork and serve.

6 SERVINGS

# Chili-marinated Pork Chops

◆ ◆ ◆

3    dried ancho chilies*

2    tablespoons white distilled vinegar
2    garlic cloves
2    whole cloves
½    teaspoon ground oregano
¼    teaspoon ground cinnamon
¼    teaspoon dried thyme
4    4-ounce boneless pork loin chops

1    tablespoon vegetable oil

Heat heavy large skillet over medium heat; add chilies. Using spatula, press down on chilies until beginning to soften and darken, about 2 minutes per side. Transfer chilies to work surface; cool. Cut chilies in half lengthwise; remove seeds and stems and discard. Cut chilies into small pieces. Place in bowl. Add enough boiling water to cover; let stand until chilies soften, about 1 hour.

Drain chilies, reserving ½ cup soaking liquid. Place chilies in blender. Add vinegar, garlic, cloves, oregano, cinnamon, thyme and reserved soaking liquid. Blend until smooth paste forms, about 2 minutes. Arrange pork in shallow dish. Spoon chili paste over pork; turn to coat. Cover; chill at least 6 hours or overnight.

Heat oil in large nonstick skillet over medium heat. Remove pork from marinade, scraping off excess chili paste. Season pork with salt and pepper. Add pork to skillet; cook until brown and cooked through, about 5 minutes per side.

*Available at Latin American markets and some supermarkets.

4 SERVINGS

## MANY A CHILI

There are hundreds of varieties of chilies, each considerably different than the next. Mexico alone claims some 200 types. Add to that the many forms available—fresh, pickled, canned, dried and crushed—and you have a lot to choose from. Here, ranging from mild to hot, are the most commonly available chilies:

◆ Anaheim: Red or green in color and cone-shaped, this mild to medium-hot chili is stuffed for chiles rellenos and also used in stews and sauces.

◆ Poblano (also called pasilla): Long, fleshy and triangular, this dark green chili is tinged with purple and has a mild to hot flavor. Roasting brings out a rich, smoky taste. When ripened to a deep red-brown and then dried, it becomes an ancho chili. This variety is good in stews, tamales and sauces.

◆ Jalapeño: A smooth and shiny green pepper, the jalapeño is relatively mild in its raw form. When ripened to a red color and smoked, it becomes an extremely hot chipotle chili. Jalapeños can spice up salsas, dips and stews.

◆ Serrano: Ranging in heat from hot to very hot, these small bright green or red chilies give a good salsa its fire. They're also pickled.

◆ ◆ ◆

# Sweet and Spicy Grilled Pork Chops with Vegetable Stir-fry

♦ ♦ ♦

2   large jalapeño chilies, stemmed
2   large garlic cloves, peeled
7   tablespoons olive oil

¼   cup soy sauce
2   tablespoons Dijon mustard
1   tablespoon honey
1   tablespoon oriental sesame oil
1   tablespoon chopped fresh rosemary
2   teaspoons grated lemon peel
4   7- to 8-ounce pork loin chops, about ½ inch thick

10  asparagus spears, trimmed, cut into 1½-inch pieces

3   large garlic cloves, minced
1   medium zucchini, halved lengthwise, cut crosswise
    into ¼-inch-thick diagonal slices
1   yellow summer squash, halved lengthwise, cut crosswise
    into ¼-inch-thick diagonal slices
1   small red bell pepper, seeded, cut into strips

Preheat oven to 350°F. Place chilies and 2 garlic cloves in small baking dish. Spoon 1 tablespoon olive oil over; turn to coat. Roast until chilies and garlic are very soft, turning once, about 40 minutes. Cool. Puree mixture in processor.

Whisk puree, 4 tablespoons olive oil, soy sauce, mustard, honey, sesame oil, rosemary and lemon peel in 13 x 9 x 2-inch glass baking dish. Add pork chops and turn to coat. Cover and chill 1 hour.

Cook asparagus in boiling salted water until crisp-tender, about 1 minute. Drain. Transfer to ice water; cool. Drain.

Prepare barbecue (medium-high heat) or preheat broiler. Remove pork chops from marinade. Sprinkle with salt and pepper. Grill or broil pork chops until no longer pink in center, about 5 minutes per side. Transfer pork chops to platter. Keep warm.

Heat remaining 2 tablespoons oil in heavy large skillet over medium-high heat. Add minced garlic; sauté until golden, about 1 minute. Add zucchini, yellow squash and red bell pepper; sauté until vegetables are crisp-tender, about 2 minutes. Add asparagus; sauté until asparagus is heated through, about 1 minute longer. Season to taste with salt and pepper. Arrange vegetables around pork.

4 SERVINGS

♦ ♦ ♦

# MODERN CHINESE MENU FOR FOUR

STIR-FRIED SHRIMP

SWEET AND SPICY GRILLED PORK CHOPS WITH VEGETABLE STIR-FRY (AT LEFT; PICTURED OPPOSITE)

STIR-FRIED RICE

GEWÜRZTRAMINER OR ZINFANDEL

POACHED ASIAN PEARS WITH STAR ANISE AND TROPICAL FRUIT (PAGE 179; PICTURED OPPOSITE)

♦ ♦ ♦

# Sautéed Chicken Breasts with Curry Sauce

♦ ♦ ♦

| 6 | 4-ounce skinless boneless chicken breast halves |
| 6 | tablespoons all purpose flour |
| 3 | large egg whites |
| 1 | large egg |
| 5½ | teaspoons curry powder |
| ½ | teaspoon salt |
| 5 | teaspons vegetable oil |
| | |
| 2 | garlic cloves, minced |
| 1½ | cups canned low-salt chicken broth |

Place chicken breast halves between layers of plastic wrap and pound to ¼-inch thickness. Place 5 tablespoons flour in pie dish. Whisk egg whites, egg, 4½ teaspoons curry powder and salt in shallow bowl to blend. Heat 2 teaspoons vegetable oil in large non-stick skillet over medium-high heat. Coat 3 chicken breasts with flour, shaking off excess. Dip into egg mixture. Add to skillet and sauté until cooked through, about 2 minutes per side. Transfer to platter. Repeat with 2 teaspoons oil and remaining chicken. Tent chicken with foil to keep warm while preparing sauce.

Heat remaining 1 teaspoon vegetable oil in same skillet over medium-high heat. Add garlic, remaining 1 tablespoon flour and remaining 1 teaspoon curry powder and stir 30 seconds. Gradually whisk in broth. Bring to boil, whisking constantly. Boil until thickened to sauce consistency, about 2 minutes. Season to taste with salt and pepper. Return chicken to skillet and turn to coat with sauce. Transfer chicken to platter. Drizzle with any remaining sauce.

6 SERVINGS

# Lemon-Herb Roast Chicken

♦ ♦ ♦

½    cup (1 stick) butter, room temperature
2    tablespoons chopped fresh rosemary or 2 teaspoons dried
2    tablespoons chopped fresh thyme or 2 teaspoons dried
3    large garlic cloves, minced
1½   teaspoons grated lemon peel

1    6½- to 7-pound roasting chicken

¼    cup dry white wine
1    cup (about) canned low-salt chicken broth
2    tablespoons all purpose flour
     Lemon wedges
     Rosemary sprigs

♦ ♦ ♦

The secret to this savory roast chicken? An herb butter, fragrant with lemon and garlic, gets spread over the breast under the skin and then over the chicken. The bird practically bastes itself while it roasts.

♦ ♦ ♦

Combine butter, rosemary, thyme, garlic and lemon peel in small bowl and stir to blend. Season to taste with salt and pepper. *(Herb butter can be prepared 3 days ahead. Cover and refrigerate. Bring to room temperature before using.)*

Preheat oven to 450°F. Rinse chicken; pat dry. Slide hand under skin of chicken breast to loosen skin from meat. Reserve 2 tablespoons herb butter for gravy. Rub half of remaining herb butter over chicken breast under skin. Spread remaining herb butter over outside of chicken. Season chicken with salt and pepper. Truss chicken.

Place chicken in heavy large roasting pan. Roast 20 minutes. Reduce oven temperature to 375°F. Roast chicken until meat

thermometer inserted into thickest part of inner thigh registers 175°F and juices from thigh run clear when chicken thigh is pierced with skewer, about 1 hour 15 minutes. Lift chicken and tilt slightly, emptying any juices from cavity into roasting pan. Transfer chicken to platter. Tent with aluminum foil to keep warm.

Pour pan juices into large glass measuring cup. Spoon fat off top. Add wine to pan. Place pan over high heat; bring wine to boil, scraping up any browned bits. Pour wine mixture into cup with pan juices. Add enough broth to same cup to measure 2¼ cups liquid. Melt reserved 2 tablespoons herb butter in heavy medium saucepan over medium-high heat. Add flour; whisk until smooth and beginning to color, about 3 minutes. Gradually whisk in pan juices. Boil until thickened to sauce consistency, whisking occasionally, about 7 minutes. Season gravy with salt and pepper. Arrange lemon and rosemary around chicken on platter. Serve with gravy.

4 SERVINGS

# Broiled Chicken with Mango, Ginger and Cilantro

◆ ◆ ◆

2   boneless chicken breast halves with skin

2   teaspoons olive oil
1   tablespoon minced peeled fresh ginger
2   large garlic cloves, minced
¾   cup chopped peeled mango or fresh pineapple
1   tablespoon chopped fresh cilantro
2   teaspoons white wine vinegar

Preheat broiler. Lightly oil broiler pan. Using mallet or rolling pin, pound chicken lightly between sheets of waxed paper to even ½-inch thickness. Season chicken with salt and pepper. Place chicken, skin side up, on prepared pan. Broil until skin is golden brown, about 4 minutes. Turn chicken over and broil until cooked through but still juicy, about 3 minutes longer.

Meanwhile, heat 2 teaspoons oil in heavy small skillet over medium heat. Add ginger and garlic; sauté 2 minutes. Add mango; sauté until beginning to soften, about 3 minutes. Remove from heat. Mix in cilantro and vinegar. Season with salt and pepper.

Place chicken on plates. Top with warm mango mixture and serve.

2 SERVINGS

◆ ◆ ◆

You might add steamed chayote squash and white rice to round out this simple main dish.

# Lebanese Chicken

♦ ♦ ♦

¾   cup fresh lemon juice
8   large garlic cloves, minced
2   tablespoons minced fresh thyme or 2 teaspoons dried
1   tablespoon paprika
1½   teaspoons ground cumin
¾   teaspoon cayenne pepper
2   3-pound chickens, split lengthwise, backbones removed and discarded

Whisk fresh lemon juice, minced garlic, thyme, paprika, cumin and cayenne pepper in small bowl. Place chicken in 13 x 9 x 2-inch glass baking dish. Pour marinade over; turn chicken to coat. Cover and refrigerate at least 6 hours or overnight, turning occasionally.

Preheat oven to 425°F. Transfer chicken and marinade to large roasting pan. Season chicken with salt and pepper. Bake until chicken is cooked through, basting with pan juices, about 50 minutes. Transfer chicken to plates. Pass pan juices separately.

4 SERVINGS

# Chicken Costa del Sol

♦ ♦ ♦

2   large skinless boneless chicken breast halves
3   teaspoons chopped fresh rosemary
2   tablespoons olive oil

1½   cups thinly sliced bell peppers
3   large garlic cloves, chopped
⅓   cup pitted halved brine-cured black olives (such as Kalamata)
4   teaspoons balsamic vinegar

Sprinkle chicken with 1½ teaspoons rosemary, salt and pepper. Heat oil in heavy medium skillet over medium heat. Add chicken; sauté until just cooked through, 10 minutes. Transfer to plate.

Increase heat to medium-high. Add peppers to same skillet; sauté until wilted and beginning to brown, about 3 minutes. Add garlic and remaining 1½ teaspoons rosemary; stir until fragrant, about 30 seconds. Mix in olives and vinegar. Return chicken and any accumulated juices to skillet. Simmer until chicken is heated through, about 2 minutes. Season with salt and pepper. Serve.

2 SERVINGS

♦ ♦ ♦

## MEDITERRANEAN DINNER FOR FOUR

TUNISIAN CARROT SALAD
(PAGE 152; PICTURED OPPOSITE)

PITA BREAD

LEBANESE CHICKEN
(AT LEFT; PICTURED OPPOSITE)

BULGUR PILAF

TURKISH ZUCCHINI PANCAKES
(PAGE 145; PICTURED OPPOSITE)

DRY WHITE WINE

BAKLAVA OR GREEK COOKIES

♦ ♦ ♦

### KIDS' BIRTHDAY PARTY FOR TWELVE

POTATO CHIPS AND DIP

OVEN-BAKED DRUMSTICKS
(AT RIGHT; PICTURED AT RIGHT)

PASTA SALAD

CARROT STRIPS

ORANGE SHERBET PUNCH
(PAGE 38)

BIRTHDAY CAKE

## Oven-baked Drumsticks

◆ ◆ ◆

| | |
|---|---|
| 3 | cups fresh white breadcrumbs |
| 1 | cup freshly grated Parmesan cheese (about 3 ounces) |
| 6 | tablespoons chopped fresh parsley |
| 4 | teaspoons onion powder |
| 1 | tablespoon Hungarian sweet paprika |
| 1 | tablespoon dried oregano |
| 2 | teaspoons salt |
| 1½ | teaspoons pepper |
| 1½ | cups (3 sticks) butter |
| 9 | tablespoons Dijon mustard |
| 24 | chicken drumsticks |

Preheat oven to 350°F. Butter 2 large baking sheets. Combine breadcrumbs, Parmesan cheese, parsley, onion powder, paprika, oregano, salt and pepper in large bowl and stir to blend. Melt butter in small saucepan over medium-low heat. Remove saucepan from heat. Add mustard and whisk to blend. Brush drumsticks generously with butter mixture, then roll in breadcrumb mixture, coating completely. Arrange drumsticks on prepared baking sheets.

Bake drumsticks until golden brown and cooked through, about 1 hour. Serve warm or at room temperature.

12 SERVINGS

# Crunchy Chicken Salad with Spicy Sesame Dressing and Peanuts

◆ ◆ ◆

DRESSING

½   cup plus 1 tablespoon seasoned rice vinegar*

1   tablespoon plus 1½ teaspoons Dijon mustard

½   cup plus 1 tablespoon vegetable oil

¼   cup plus 1½ teaspoons oriental sesame oil

2½   tablespoons soy sauce

12   green onions, chopped

1   teaspoon dried crushed red pepper

SALAD

1   1½-pound head Napa cabbage, sliced

1½   hothouse cucumbers, sliced diagonally

1½   bunches carrots, peeled, sliced diagonally

1   cup chopped fresh mint

6   skinless boneless chicken breast halves

12   fresh shiitake mushrooms, stemmed

1   cup lightly salted dry roasted peanuts, coarsely chopped

FOR DRESSING: Whisk vinegar and mustard in medium bowl. Gradually whisk in both oils, then soy sauce. Mix in green onions and crushed red pepper. Season to taste with salt and pepper.

FOR SALAD: Combine cabbage, cucumbers, carrots and mint in large bowl. Place chicken and mushrooms in large glass baking dish. Pour ½ cup plus 2 tablespoons dressing over and turn to coat. Cover; chill 30 minutes to 1 hour.

Prepare barbecue (medium heat). Remove chicken and mushrooms from marinade; sprinkle with salt and pepper. Grill chicken until cooked through, about 4 minutes per side. Transfer to work surface. Grill mushrooms until tender, about 2 minutes per side. Pour enough dressing over salad to coat and toss gently to blend. Season with salt and pepper. Transfer to large platter. Slice chicken on diagonal and arrange around edge of platter. Halve mushrooms and tuck in among chicken slices. Drizzle chicken with remaining dressing. Sprinkle with nuts and serve.

*Also known as sushi vinegar; available at Asian markets and in the Asian section of some supermarkets.*

6 SERVINGS

◆ ◆ ◆

## SALAD SUPPER FOR SIX

PITA BREAD TRIANGLES
WITH HUMMUS

CRUNCHY CHICKEN SALAD
WITH SPICY SESAME DRESSING
AND PEANUTS
(AT LEFT)

BEER OR FRUITY WHITE WINE

FROZEN FRUIT FANTASY
(PAGE 208)

◆ ◆ ◆

# Chicken, Arugula and
# Red Bell Pepper Sandwiches

◆ ◆ ◆

3    tablespoons low-fat mayonnaise
3    tablespoons nonfat plain yogurt
4    teaspoons Dijon mustard
½    cup chopped fresh arugula

2    large red bell peppers
4    skinless boneless chicken breast halves (each about 4 ounces)
1    teaspoon olive oil

6    5- to 6-inch-long French bread baguette pieces, halved lengthwise
2    large bunches fresh arugula

Mix first 3 ingredients in small bowl. Mix in chopped arugula. Season arugula mayonnaise generously with ground pepper. *(Can be made 1 day ahead. Cover and chill.)*

Char peppers over gas flame or in broiler until blackened on all sides. Place in bag; let stand 10 minutes. Peel and seed bell peppers. Cut into ½-inch-wide strips. Sprinkle chicken with salt and pepper. Heat large nonstick skillet over medium-high heat. Brush skillet with 1 teaspoon oil. Add chicken; sauté until just cooked through, about 4 minutes per side. Transfer to plate; cool. Cut into diagonal slices.

Spread generous 2 teaspoons arugula mayonnaise on each cut side of bread. Cover bottom of bread pieces generously with arugula. Top with sliced chicken, dividing equally. Top with bell pepper strips and generous amount of arugula. Cover with bread tops. *(Can be made 4 hours ahead. Wrap in plastic and chill.)*

6 SERVINGS

# Chicken with Goat Cheese Stuffing, Peppers, Onions and Two Salsas

◆ ◆ ◆

6    large chicken breast halves with skin and bones
1    11-ounce log chilled soft fresh goat cheese (such as Montrachet), cut into eighteen ⅓- to ½-inch-thick rounds

2    tablespoons extra-virgin olive oil
2    medium-size sweet onions (such as Maui), cut into ½-inch-wide slices
2    red bell peppers, cut into 1-inch-wide strips
2    yellow bell peppers, cut into 1-inch-wide strips

     Jalapeño-Cilantro Salsa (see recipe opposite)
     Tomato Salsa (see recipe opposite)
1    bunch fresh chives, finely chopped

Gently slide fingertips between chicken meat and skin along 1 long side of each breast, leaving skin attached on opposite long side. Place 3 goat cheese rounds under skin of each chicken breast. Skewer seams closed with toothpicks. Sprinkle chicken with salt and pepper. *(Can be made 1 day ahead. Cover and chill.)*

Prepare barbecue (medium-high heat) or preheat broiler. Place oil in large bowl. Place onions on baking sheet. Brush with 1 tablespoon oil. Add bell peppers to remaining oil in bowl; toss to coat. Sprinkle onions and peppers with salt and pepper. Grill or broil chicken, skin toward heat, until brown, about 8 minutes. Turn; grill until cooked through, turning occasionally, about 22 minutes. Transfer to baking sheet; tent with foil. Grill or broil onions and peppers until lightly charred, turning occasionally, about 4 minutes.

Remove toothpicks from chicken. Arrange chicken, onions and peppers on plates. Spoon Jalapeño-Cilantro Salsa over chicken. Spoon Tomato Salsa on side. Sprinkle with chives and serve.

6 SERVINGS

## Jalapeño-Cilantro Salsa

| | |
|---|---|
| 4 | large jalapeño chilies |
| ½ | cup extra-virgin olive oil |
| ¼ | cup chopped fresh cilantro |
| 2 | tablespoons fresh lime juice |

Char chilies over gas flame or in broiler until blackened on all sides. Place in paper bag and seal. Let stand 10 minutes. Peel, seed and finely chop chilies. Place chilies in small bowl. Mix in oil and cilantro. *(Can be made 6 hours ahead. Cover; let stand at room temperature.)* Mix lime juice into salsa. Season with salt and pepper.

MAKES ABOUT ½ CUP

## Tomato Salsa

| | |
|---|---|
| 1 | pound tomatoes |
| ⅔ | cup extra-virgin olive oil |
| 3 | tablespoons Sherry wine vinegar |
| 3 | tablespoons thinly sliced fresh basil |
| 1 | shallot, finely chopped |

Bring large pot of water to boil. Add tomatoes and blanch 30 seconds. Drain. Peel, seed and chop tomatoes. Mix tomatoes, olive oil, vinegar, basil and shallot in bowl. Season salsa to taste with salt and pepper. Cover and chill at least 30 minutes and up to 4 hours.

MAKES ABOUT 2 CUPS

◆ ◆ ◆

Easier than its sophisticated title might lead you to believe, this appealing recipe combines chicken breasts (stuffed under the skin with goat cheese), grilled sweet onions and grilled red and yellow peppers. Two different salsas—a jalapeño-cilantro one and a tomato-basil one—are colorful accompaniments.

◆ ◆ ◆

UPDATED DINER
MENU FOR SIX

Turkey Meat Loaf with
Sun-dried Tomatoes
(at right; pictured at right)

Mashed Potatoes and Celery
Root with Blue Cheese
(page 146; pictured at right)

Green Beans

Dinner Rolls

Dry White Wine or
Light Red Wine

Lemon Meringue Pie

# Turkey Meat Loaf with Sun-dried Tomatoes

◆ ◆ ◆

1½  tablespoons olive oil
1   large onion, chopped
3   celery stalks, chopped

1½  pounds ground turkey
1½  cups fresh breadcrumbs made from soft white bread
⅔   cup chopped drained oil-packed sun-dried tomatoes
½   cup milk
2   eggs
2   teaspoons dried rubbed sage
2   teaspoons dried oregano
2   teaspoons salt
2   teaspoons ground pepper
    Ketchup

Preheat oven to 375°F. Grease 9 x 5 x 3-inch glass loaf pan. Heat oil in heavy medium skillet over medium heat. Add onion; sauté 5 minutes. Add celery; sauté until vegetables are very tender, about 15 minutes longer. Transfer to large bowl.

Add all remaining ingredients except ketchup to vegetables in bowl. Mix thoroughly. Transfer to prepared pan. Bake 1 hour. Brush with ketchup and bake until thermometer inserted into center registers 165°F, about 15 minutes longer. Cool 5 minutes.

6 SERVINGS

# Roast Turkey Breast with Sweet Potato-Apple Hash

◆ ◆ ◆

1½   teaspoons olive oil

4   turkey bacon slices, cut into matchstick-size strips

½   cup chopped onion

2   cups diced peeled sweet potatoes

1   cup diced peeled Granny Smith apple

1   cup canned low-salt chicken broth

2   tablespoons Frangelico (hazelnut liqueur)

¼   teaspoon chopped fresh thyme

¼   teaspoon chopped fresh rosemary

1   2-pound boneless turkey breast half, skin and visible fat removed

1   cup plus 2 tablespoons dry Marsala

2   teaspoons minced shallot

½   teaspoon minced garlic

4   cups canned low-salt chicken broth

¼   teaspoon chopped fresh thyme

2   teaspoons arrowroot

Preheat oven to 450°F. Heat 1 teaspoon oil in large nonstick skillet over medium heat. Add bacon and sauté until beginning to brown, about 2 minutes. Add onion and sauté until tender, about 4 minutes. Add sweet potatoes and apple and sauté 2 minutes. Add 1 cup broth and liqueur and bring to boil. Mix in ¼ teaspoon thyme and rosemary. Set hash aside.

Place turkey in large glass baking dish. Rub with ½ teaspoon oil. Sprinkle with salt and pepper. Roast turkey 10 minutes. Spoon hash around turkey and continue roasting until meat thermometer inserted into thickest part of turkey registers 165°F and hash is tender, stirring occasionally, about 25 minutes longer.

Combine 1 cup Marsala, shallot and garlic in heavy large saucepan and boil until reduced by half, about 8 minutes. Add 4 cups broth and boil until reduced by half, about 20 minutes. Mix in ¼ teaspoon thyme. Mix arrowroot and remaining 2 tablespoons Marsala in bowl. Add arrowroot mixture to sauce and bring to boil, stirring. Season sauce with salt and pepper.

Slice turkey and arrange on plates. Spoon hash alongside. Spoon Marsala sauce over turkey and serve.

**4 SERVINGS**

# Tandoori-Style Game Hens with Corn and Cumin-Tomato Sauce

**HENS**

| | |
|---|---|
| 1¼ | cups buttermilk |
| ½ | cup chopped fresh cilantro |
| 4 | teaspoons minced garlic |
| 4 | teaspoons minced fresh ginger |
| 4 | teaspoons chopped serrano chilies |
| 2 | teaspoons turmeric |
| 6 | 1½-pound Cornish game hens |

**SAUCE**

| | |
|---|---|
| 1 | tablespoon olive oil |
| 2 | cups chopped onions |
| 3½ | cups coarsely chopped seeded plum tomatoes (about 2 pounds) |
| ¼ | cup dry white wine |
| 2½ | teaspoons ground cumin |
| 1 | cup whipping cream |

**CORN**

| | |
|---|---|
| 1½ | tablespoons vegetable oil |
| 4½ | cups corn kernels (from 4 ears) |
| 1½ | teaspoons ground cumin |
| ¾ | teaspoon turmeric |
| ½ | cup chopped fresh cilantro |

## FRENCH-INDIAN MENU FOR SIX

ACORN SQUASH VELOUTÉ WITH
GINGER AND MUSTARD SEEDS
(PAGE 28)

TANDOORI-STYLE GAME HENS
WITH CORN AND CUMIN-
TOMATO SAUCE
(AT RIGHT; PICTURED AT RIGHT)

PINOT NOIR

CARDAMOM CRÈME BRÛLÉE
(PAGE 205; PICTURED AT RIGHT)

FOR HENS: Mix first 6 ingredients in medium bowl. Place hens in 15 x 10 x 2-inch glass baking dish. Pour buttermilk mixture over hens. Cover; refrigerate overnight.

Preheat oven to 400°F. Transfer hens to heavy 17 x 11 x 1-inch baking pan. Sprinkle inside and outside of hens with salt and pepper. Pour marinade over. Bake until cooked through, basting occasionally with juices, about 1 hour 10 minutes.

FOR SAUCE: Heat oil in heavy medium saucepan over medium-high heat. Add onions and sauté until golden, about 6 minutes. Add tomatoes, wine and cumin; sauté until tomatoes are tender, about 10 minutes. Puree mixture in blender; return to saucepan. Add cream and simmer until slightly thickened, about 5 minutes. Season with salt and pepper. Keep sauce warm.

FOR CORN: Heat oil in large nonstick skillet over medium-high heat. Add corn, cumin and turmeric; sauté until corn is heated through, 5 minutes. Stir in cilantro. Season with salt and pepper.

Spoon some of sauce onto center of each plate. Place hens atop sauce. Spoon corn onto plates, dividing equally.

6 SERVINGS

# Game Hen with Sherried Gravy

◆ ◆ ◆

6     tablespoons plus ¼ cup canned low-salt chicken broth
1½   cups dry corn bread stuffing mix
2     teaspoons dried rubbed sage
1     1½- to 1¾-pound Cornish game hen, quartered, liver chopped

2     tablespoons dry Sherry

Preheat oven to 475°F. Butter 11 x 7-inch baking pan. Bring 6 tablespoons broth just to simmer in medium saucepan; remove from heat. Mix in stuffing mix and 1 teaspoon sage. Spoon stuffing in 4 mounds in prepared pan. Season hen with 1 teaspoon sage, salt and pepper. Press 1 hen quarter onto each stuffing mound.

Bake until hen is golden brown and juices run clear when hen is pierced with skewer, about 20 minutes. Transfer hen and stuffing to 2 plates; tent with foil to keep warm. Do not clean baking pan.

Place liver and remaining ¼ cup broth in same baking pan. Set pan over medium heat. Boil until slightly thickened, scraping up browned bits, about 2 minutes. Mix in dry Sherry; simmer 1 minute. Spoon gravy over hen pieces and serve immediately.

2 SERVINGS

## BIRDS OF A FEATHER

Game hens, something of a delicacy not long ago, have paved the way for other kinds of birds, both wild and farm-raised. Here's a brief summary of what's available; some you'll find at the local market, others you may have to order from a specialty butcher.

◆ Duck: You can buy both domestic duck and leaner wild duck, though the latter may require a special order. To ensure the most tender meat, ask for a young bird.

◆ Goose: Like duck, there is both domestic and wild goose, the wild kind being richer in taste.

◆ Pheasant: Lean and full-breasted, pheasant is white-fleshed and tastes much like chicken when farm-raised. Wild pheasant has a rich gamey flavor.

◆ Quail: These little birds, often served two per person, have a delicate flavor. Quail is sometimes called partridge.

◆ Squab: Tender, young, farm-raised pigeons, these birds have a dark and flavorful meat and little fat.

◆ Wild Turkey: With a deeper breast and longer legs than its domestic cousin, this big bird has a very distinctive game flavor.

◆ ◆ ◆

# Duck with Wild Mushrooms
## and Fig Sauce

◆ ◆ ◆

| | |
|---|---|
| 30 | dried black Mission figs |
| 2 | cups dry red wine |
| 2¼ | cups canned low-salt chicken broth |
| 2 | cinnamon sticks |
| | |
| 5 | tablespoons butter |
| ⅓ | cup finely chopped shallots |
| 1 | pound assorted fresh wild mushrooms (such as portobello, chanterelle, oyster and stemmed shiitake), thinly sliced |
| 1 | teaspoon finely chopped peeled fresh ginger |
| 3 | tablespoons chopped fresh chives |
| | |
| ¼ | cup honey |
| | |
| 4 | 6-ounce boneless duck breast halves, with skin |
| 1 | tablespoon olive oil |

Cut 14 figs in half lengthwise. Combine cut figs, wine, 2 cups broth and cinnamon in medium saucepan. Simmer over medium-high heat until thickened to sauce consistency, stirring occasionally, about 30 minutes. Strain sauce, pressing on solids to release juices. Discard solids. *(Can be prepared 1 day ahead. Cover and chill.)*

Preheat oven to 450°F. Melt 4 tablespoons butter in heavy large skillet over medium-high heat. Add shallots and sauté until translucent, about 4 minutes. Add mushrooms and ginger; sauté until mushrooms are tender, about 4 minutes. Add remaining ¼ cup broth and simmer until most of liquid is evaporated, about 4 minutes. Stir in chives. Keep warm.

Place remaining 16 figs in small glass baking dish. Drizzle honey over figs. Bake until figs are tender and honey is slightly caramelized, about 12 minutes.

Meanwhile, sprinkle duck breasts with salt and pepper. Melt remaining 1 tablespoon butter with olive oil in another heavy large skillet over medium heat. Add duck breasts, skin side down, and cook 5 minutes. Turn duck breasts over and continue cooking to desired doneness, about 3 minutes for medium-rare.

Spoon mushrooms into center of each plate, dividing equally. Slice duck breasts and arrange atop mushrooms. Rewarm sauce and spoon over duck. Place 4 caramelized figs on each plate.

4 SERVINGS

# Duck with Blackberry Sauce

### ◆ ◆ ◆

3     tablespoons butter

3     tablespoons sugar

⅓     cup dry white wine

⅓     cup orange juice

2     tablespoons raspberry vinegar

1¼    cups frozen blackberries, thawed

1¼    cups canned beef broth

½     cup canned low-salt chicken broth

2     tablespoons Cognac or brandy

1     tablespoon pure maple syrup

4     5- to 6-ounce boneless duck breast halves with skin

Additional blackberries (optional)

Melt 2 tablespoons butter in heavy large nonstick skillet over medium-high heat. Add sugar; stir until sugar dissolves and mixture turns deep amber color, about 5 minutes. Add wine, orange juice and vinegar (mixture will bubble vigorously) and bring to boil, stirring to dissolve caramel. Add 1¼ cups berries and both broths and boil until sauce thickens and is reduced to about 1 cup, stirring occasionally, about 25 minutes. Strain sauce through sieve into heavy small saucepan, pressing on berries with back of spoon. Mix in Cognac and maple syrup. Set sauce aside. *(Can be prepared 1 day ahead. Cover with plastic and refrigerate.)*

Preheat oven to 400°F. Trim any excess fat from duck breasts. Cut three 4-inch-long by ¹⁄₁₆-inch-deep lengthwise slits in skin (not meat) of duck. Season duck with salt and pepper. Heat heavy large ovenproof skillet over high heat until hot. Add duck, skin side down, and sear until brown, about 5 minutes. Turn over; cook 3 minutes. Transfer skillet to oven; continue cooking to desired doneness, about 3 minutes for medium.

Meanwhile, bring sauce to simmer over low heat. Add remaining 1 tablespoon butter and whisk just until melted. Season sauce to taste with salt and pepper.

Spoon sauce onto plates. Slice duck and place atop sauce. Garnish with additional berries, if desired, and serve.

4 SERVINGS

### ◆ ◆ ◆

If you can't find boneless duck breasts, buy two whole ducks and ask the butcher to remove the breasts for you. Freeze the leg and thigh meat to use at another time.

### ◆ ◆ ◆

◆ ◆ ◆

## CASUAL LUNCH
## FOR FOUR

FRESH SALMON BURGERS WITH
TARRAGON MAYONNAISE
(AT RIGHT; PICTURED OPPOSITE)

ASIAN-STYLE COLESLAW
(PAGE 157; PICTURED OPPOSITE)

BAKED POTATOES

FRUITY WHITE WINE

MIXED FRUIT AND COOKIES

◆ ◆ ◆

## ◆ SEAFOOD ◆

# Fresh Salmon Burgers with Tarragon Mayonnaise

◆ ◆ ◆

| | |
|---|---|
| 1 | pound skinless salmon fillet, cut into ¼-inch pieces (about 2¼ cups) |
| 4 | green onions, chopped |
| 1 | tablespoon drained small capers |
| 1 | tablespoon fresh lemon juice |
| 1 | tablespoon chopped fresh tarragon or 1 teaspoon dried |
| 1 | teaspoon Dijon mustard |
| 1 | teaspoon prepared white horseradish |
| ½ | teaspoon salt |
| ½ | teaspoon pepper |
| | Tarragon Mayonnaise (see recipe opposite) |
| ½ | cup dry breadcrumbs |
| 1 | tablespoon butter |
| 8 | slices brioche loaf or egg bread, toasted |
| 4 | large tomato slices |
| 8 | radicchio leaves |

Combine first 9 ingredients in medium bowl. Add 3 tablespoons mayonnaise and mix well. *(Salmon mixture can be prepared 6 hours ahead. Cover and refrigerate.)*

Mix breadcrumbs into salmon mixture. Form into four 1-inch-thick patties. Melt butter in heavy large skillet over medium-high heat. Add salmon patties; cook until just firm to touch and brown and crusty, about 3 minutes per side.

Place 1 slice of toast on each of 4 plates. Top each with burger. Spread burgers generously with mayonnaise. Top each with tomato slice, 2 radicchio leaves and second toast slice. Serve immediately, passing remaining mayonnaise separately.

4 SERVINGS

## Tarragon Mayonnaise

1  cup mayonnaise (regular or low-fat)

¼  cup plain yogurt

4  green onions, chopped

1  tablespoon drained small capers

1  tablespoon fresh lemon juice

1  tablespoon chopped fresh tarragon or 1 teaspoon dried

2  teaspoons Dijon mustard

2  teaspoons prepared white horseradish

Combine mayonnaise, yogurt, green onions, capers, lemon juice, tarragon, mustard and horseradish in small bowl and mix well. Season with salt and pepper. *(Can be prepared 1 day ahead. Cover with plastic wrap and refrigerate.)*

MAKES 1½ CUPS

◆ ◆ ◆

Salmon cakes made with canned salmon, popular in the fifties and sixties, have grown up. In this sophisticated version, they're prepared with fresh salmon, topped with a tarragon mayonnaise and served on toasted, sliced brioche.

◆ ◆ ◆

To help the pecan crust adhere to the fish, first dip the fillets in flour, and brush the flesh side with egg whites. Then press the egg-glazed side of the fish into the ground nuts.

To sauté the trout, melt the butter with olive oil (the oil helps prevent the butter from burning). Cook the fillets, pecan side down, until the crust is golden; then turn them over, and cook until the centers are opaque.

# Pecan-crusted Trout with Orange-Rosemary Butter Sauce

◆ ◆ ◆

TROUT

| 2 | cups pecans (about 8 ounces) |
| 1 | cup all purpose flour |
| 2 | large (12- to 14-ounce) trout, filleted, skin left intact |
| 3 | large egg whites, beaten to blend |

SAUCE

| 1½ | cups fresh orange juice |
| 1 | cup dry white wine |
| ⅔ | cup chopped shallots |
| ¼ | cup white wine vinegar |
| 8 | 5-inch-long fresh parsley stems |
| 1½ | tablespoons fresh lemon juice |
| 1 | large fresh thyme sprig |
| 2 | fresh rosemary sprigs |
| ¼ | cup whipping cream |
| ¾ | cup (1½ sticks) unsalted butter, cut into 12 pieces |

VEGETABLES

| 4 | tablespoons olive oil |
| 1 | carrot, peeled, cut into matchstick-size strips |
| 1 | red bell pepper, thinly sliced |
| 6 | cups thinly sliced savoy cabbage |
| 2 | tablespoons (¼ stick) unsalted butter |

Chopped fresh chives

FOR TROUT: Combine pecans and 1 tablespoon flour in processor. Grind pecans finely; transfer to plate. Place remaining flour on another plate. Sprinkle fish with salt and pepper. Dip 1 fillet into flour to coat; shake off excess. Using pastry brush, brush flesh side with egg whites. Place fillet, egg white side down, onto pecans; press to coat with nuts. Transfer to waxed paper-lined baking sheet, pecan side down. Repeat with remaining 3 fillets; chill.

FOR SAUCE: Combine first 7 ingredients in medium saucepan. Boil 10 minutes; add rosemary. Boil until liquid is reduced to ½ cup,

◆ ◆ ◆

Here, fresh trout is cooked in a pecan crust, then served with an orange-rosemary butter sauce and sautéed vegetables. At the fish market, ask them to remove the head, tail and bones, then to cut each trout into two fillets, leaving the skin intact.

◆ ◆ ◆

about 10 minutes. Strain sauce into another medium saucepan, pressing on solids in sieve. Add cream; bring to boil. Reduce heat to medium-low. Whisk in butter 1 piece at a time (do not boil). Season with salt and pepper. Let stand at room temperature up to 2 hours.

FOR VEGETABLES: Heat 2 tablespoons oil in heavy large Dutch oven over high heat. Add carrot and bell pepper; toss 2 minutes. Add cabbage; toss until cabbage wilts, about 4 minutes. Season with salt and pepper. Remove from heat.

Melt 1 tablespoon butter with 1 tablespoon oil in heavy large skillet over medium-high heat. Place 2 fillets, pecan side down, into skillet. Cook until crust is golden and crisp, about 2 minutes. Using spatula, turn fillets. Cook until just opaque in center, 2 minutes. Transfer to plate. Repeat with remaining butter, oil and fish.

Whisk sauce over low heat to rewarm (do not boil). Divide vegetables among plates. Top with fish. Spoon sauce around fish and vegetables. Sprinkle with chopped chives and serve.

4 SERVINGS

# Salmon with Watercress Sauce

◆ ◆ ◆

4    tablespoons (½ stick) butter
½    cup finely chopped shallots
2    large bunches watercress, tough ends trimmed
1½   cups whipping cream

8    8-ounce salmon fillets with skin

Additional watercress

Melt butter in heavy large skillet over medium-low heat. Add shallots and sauté until beginning to soften, about 3 minutes. Add watercress and stir until wilted and still bright green, about 3 minutes. Add cream. Increase heat to high and bring to boil. Remove from heat. Puree hot sauce in blender until almost smooth. Transfer to heavy small saucepan. Season with salt and pepper. *(Can be made 8 hours ahead. Refrigerate.)*

Butter 2 steamer racks and place in 2 large saucepans over simmering water. Season salmon fillets with salt and pepper. Place salmon, skin side down, on steamer racks. Cover saucepans and steam until salmon is just opaque in center, about 10 minutes.

Whisk sauce over low heat to rewarm. Transfer salmon to platter. Spoon some of sauce over salmon. Garnish with additional watercress. Serve, passing remaining sauce separately.

8 SERVINGS

◆ ◆ ◆

## IRISH COUNTY HOUSE DINNER FOR EIGHT

TWICE-BAKED
GOAT CHEESE SOUFFLÉS
(PAGE 22; PICTURED OPPOSITE)

SALMON WITH WATERCRESS SAUCE
(AT RIGHT; PICTURED OPPOSITE)

STEAMED NEW POTATOES

VEGETABLE STIR-FRY

BEAUJOLAIS

RHUBARB TART
(PAGE 174; PICTURED OPPOSITE)

◆ ◆ ◆

# Wheat Berry, Tuna and Asparagus Salad

### ◆ ◆ ◆

1   pound asparagus, trimmed
1½  cups wheat berries (about 10½ ounces)*
2   cups minced green onions (about 12)
1   small bunch radishes, trimmed, quartered

¼   cup chopped peeled fresh ginger
3   tablespoons rice vinegar
2   tablespoons soy sauce
3   garlic cloves, minced
1   teaspoon garlic chili sauce**
½   cup plus 1 tablespoon peanut oil
¼   cup oriental sesame oil

2   8-ounce tuna steaks (about ¾ inch thick)

Cilantro sprigs

Cook asparagus in large pot of boiling salted water until just crisp-tender, about 2 minutes. Using tongs, transfer asparagus to bowl of ice water and cool. Drain. Add wheat berries to same pot of boiling water; gently boil, uncovered, until tender but not mushy, stirring occasionally, about 55 minutes. Drain. Transfer wheat berries to large bowl. Pat asparagus dry with paper towels. Cut diagonally into ½-inch pieces. Mix asparagus, green onions and radishes into wheat berries in large bowl.

Combine ginger, vinegar, soy sauce, garlic and garlic chili sauce in medium bowl. Gradually whisk in ½ cup peanut oil and sesame oil. Season vinaigrette to taste with salt and pepper.

Heat remaining 1 tablespoon peanut oil in heavy medium skillet over high heat. Sprinkle tuna with salt and pepper; add to skillet. Cook tuna until brown but still pink in center, about 3 minutes per side. Transfer tuna to plate; let cool 15 minutes.

Cut tuna into ½-inch pieces. Add to wheat berry salad. Mix in enough vinaigrette to coat evenly. Season with salt and pepper. Garnish salad with cilantro sprigs.

*Also known as wheat kernels or whole grain wheat; available at most natural foods stores across the country.*

** *Available at Asian markets and in some supermarkets.*

6 SERVINGS

# Swordfish with Orange, Honey and Soy Sauce

◆ ◆ ◆

½   cup orange juice
¼   cup honey
¼   cup soy sauce
2   tablespoons fresh lemon juice
1   teaspoon garlic powder
½   teaspoon ground ginger
4   6-ounce swordfish steaks (each about ¾ inch thick)

Cooked white rice

Combine orange juice, honey, soy sauce, lemon juice, garlic powder and ginger in 8 x 8 x 2-inch glass baking dish and stir. Add fish and turn to coat. Let fish marinate at room temperature for 1 hour, turning occasionally.

Preheat broiler. Remove fish from marinade; place on broiler rack. Transfer marinade to small saucepan and boil 1 minute. Broil fish until just opaque in center, basting occasionally with marinade, about 4 minutes per side. Transfer fish to plates and serve with rice.

4 SERVINGS

## GREAT GRAINS

Once the specialized domain of health food stores, whole grains have gained new popularity in recent times. People are becoming more aware of the nutritional benefits of grains, which are not only a good source of protein, vitamins, minerals and fiber, but also a high-energy way to introduce taste and texture into dishes.

◆ Barley: The most common kind, pearl, is polished; unpolished is available and more nutritious. Good in soups and stews.

◆ Brown rice: With its bran and nutrients intact, brown rice is a good substitute for white in most recipes, but takes longer to cook.

◆ Bulgur: Cooked cracked wheat, this grain cooks quickly and is good in salads and pilafs.

◆ Kasha: These whole wheat groats from Russia have an earthy flavor and soft texture. A good addition to vegetable dishes.

◆ Quinoa: Pronounced keen-wa, this ancient, extra-nutritious grain from the Andes has a nutty whole-grain flavor and light texture. It can be used much as rice is.

◆ Wheat berries: Unprocessed whole wheat kernels, these have a hearty flavor and chewy texture. Soak overnight and add to salads.

◆ ◆ ◆

# Swordfish with Pasta and Provençal Red Wine Sauce

◆ ◆ ◆

| | |
|---|---|
| 4 | tablespoons olive oil |
| 2 | large onions, chopped |
| 1 | large shallot, chopped |
| 2 | large garlic cloves, minced |
| 5 | large tomatoes, coarsely chopped |
| ¼ | teaspoon dried crushed red pepper |
| 1 | 750-ml bottle dry red wine |
| 3 | fresh parsley sprigs |
| 2 | fresh marjoram sprigs |
| 2 | fresh thyme sprigs |
| 2 | bay leaves |
| 1 | teaspoon sugar |
| 1½ | cups Kalamata olives, pitted, coarsely chopped |
| 3 | tablespoons drained capers |
| 2 | tablespoons chopped fresh marjoram |
| 2 | tablespoons chopped fresh thyme |
| 6 | 5-ounce swordfish or tuna steaks |
| 12 | ounces fettuccine |

Heat 2 tablespoons oil in heavy large saucepan over medium-high heat. Add onions and shallot and sauté until translucent, about 5 minutes. Add garlic and sauté until vegetables begin to brown, about 5 minutes longer. Add tomatoes and dried red pepper and sauté 1 minute. Add wine, herb sprigs, bay leaves and sugar. Increase heat and boil until sauce is thick, stirring occasionally, about 1 hour.

Working in batches, puree sauce in blender. Strain sauce into medium saucepan. Mix in olives, capers, chopped marjoram and chopped thyme. Season with salt and pepper. *(Sauce can be made 1 day ahead. Cover; chill. Bring to simmer before using.)*

Preheat boiler. Brush fish with 2 tablespoons oil. Sprinkle with salt and pepper. Broil until just opaque in center, about 8 minutes.

Meanwhile, cook pasta in large pot of boiling salted water until just tender. Drain well. Return pasta to same pot.

Add sauce to pasta and stir to coat. Transfer pasta to plates. Top with fish and serve immediately.

6 SERVINGS

◆ ◆ ◆

## PROVENÇAL DINNER FOR SIX

CRUDITÉS WITH AIOLI

SWORDFISH WITH PASTA AND PROVENÇAL RED WINE SAUCE
(AT LEFT; PICTURED OPPOSITE)

GRILLED EGGPLANT AND ZUCCHINI STRIPS

GREEN SALAD

CÔTES DU RHÔNE OR GIGONDAS

LEMON AND HONEY TART WITH WALNUT CRUST AND HONEYED FIGS
(PAGE 177; PICTURED OPPOSITE)

◆ ◆ ◆

# Tuna Steaks with Olive Salad

◆ ◆ ◆

SALAD

⅔  cup (4 ounces) cracked green olives, pitted, coarsely chopped

⅔  cup (4 ounces) brine-cured black olives (such as Kalamata), pitted, coarsely chopped

⅔  cup (4 ounces) Niçoise olives,* pitted, coarsely chopped

⅓  cup finely chopped red onion

¼  cup chopped fresh basil

¼  cup finely chopped red bell pepper

3  tablespoons fresh lemon juice

2  tablespoons chopped fresh mint

1  tablespoon finely chopped garlic

1  tablespoon grated lemon peel

1  tablespoon olive oil

TUNA

6  tablespoons olive oil

¼  cup fresh lemon juice

3  tablespoons finely chopped garlic

2  teaspoons dried oregano

6  7-ounce tuna steaks (¾ inch thick)

FOR SALAD: Combine all ingredients in medium bowl. Season to taste with salt and pepper. Let stand 20 minutes. *(Can be prepared 1 day ahead. Cover and refrigerate.)*

FOR TUNA: Combine oil, lemon juice, garlic and oregano in 13 x 9 x 2-inch glass baking dish. Whisk to blend. Season to taste with salt and pepper. Add tuna and turn to coat. Cover and refrigerate at least 30 minutes and up to 4 hours, turning occasionally.

Prepare barbecue (medium-high heat). Grill tuna until just opaque in center, about 4 minutes per side. Transfer tuna to plates. Spoon salad atop tuna and serve.

*Small brine-cured black olives, available at specialty foods stores and in some supermarkets nationwide.*

6 SERVINGS

# Smoked Salmon Sandwiches with Capers and Red Onion Relish

◆ ◆ ◆

1    cup finely chopped red onion
1    tablespoon sugar
1    tablespoon rice vinegar

4    ounces cream cheese, room temperature
3    tablespoons chopped chives
2    tablespoons crème fraîche or sour cream
1    tablespoon chopped fresh dill or
     1 teaspoon dried dillweed
1    tablespoon drained capers
12   slices thin Danish-style pumpernickel bread*
     (each about 3¾ x 3¾ x ¼ inches)
6    ounces thinly sliced smoked salmon

Mix onion, sugar and vinegar in bowl. Let stand 10 minutes. Meanwhile, mix cream cheese, chives, crème fraîche, dill and capers in another small bowl. Spread each bread slice with about 1 tablespoon cheese mixture to cover. Divide salmon among 8 bread slices. Sprinkle about 1 tablespoon red onion mixture atop salmon on each bread slice. Top each of 4 salmon-topped bread slices with another salmon-topped bread slice, salmon side up. Top each stack with 1 cheese-covered bread slice, cheese side down, forming a total of 4 three-layer sandwiches. Cut each sandwich into 4 triangles.

*Available in the refrigerated deli section of supermarkets.*

4 SERVINGS

◆ ◆ ◆

These would make an ideal afternoon tea sandwich, pretty as they are, but you could also enjoy them at lunch or as a starter.

◆ ◆ ◆

# MEXICAN MENU
# FOR FOUR

COLD AVOCADO SOUP
(PAGE 32; PICTURED OPPOSITE)

GRILLED SHRIMP, CORN AND
BLACK BEAN TOSTADA SALAD
(AT RIGHT; PICTURED OPPOSITE)

BEER

MEXICAN BROWNIES
(PAGE 216; PICTURED OPPOSITE)

# Grilled Shrimp, Corn and
# Black Bean Tostada Salad

◆ ◆ ◆

DRESSING

5   tablespoons fresh lime juice
¾   cup olive oil
6   tablespoons chopped fresh cilantro
1½   tablespoons minced seeded jalapeño chili (preferably red)
1   tablespoon ground cumin

SALAD

3   cups chopped seeded tomatoes
1   15-ounce can black beans, rinsed, drained
1   cup chopped green onions
¾   cup chopped fresh cilantro
¾   cup chopped red onion

6   cups shredded iceberg lettuce (about 1 head)
2   ears corn, husked
24   large shrimp (about 1½ pounds), peeled
    (tails left intact), deveined

24   large tortilla chips
    Additional chopped fresh cilantro (optional)

FOR DRESSING: Place lime juice in bowl. Gradually whisk in oil. Mix in cilantro, jalapeño and cumin. Season with salt and pepper.

FOR SALAD: Combine tomatoes, beans, green onions, ¾ cup cilantro and red onion in large bowl. *(Dressing and salad can be prepared 6 hours ahead. Cover dressing and let stand at room temperature. Cover salad and refrigerate.)*

Prepare barbecue (medium-high heat). Mix lettuce into salad. Pour ¼ cup dressing into small bowl. Reserve remainder for salad. Brush corn with dressing from bowl. Grill corn until beginning to brown, turning often, about 5 minutes. Brush shrimp with dressing from bowl and grill until opaque in center, turning occasionally, 5 minutes.

Cut kernels from corn and add to salad. Toss salad with enough dressing to coat. Season with salt and pepper. Top with shrimp. Garnish with tortilla chips and additional cilantro.

4 SERVINGS

# Asian Risotto with Pancetta and Mussels

◆ ◆ ◆

1½  cups hot water
1    ounce dried shiitake mushrooms

3    cups bottled clam juice
2    cups water

1    tablespoon vegetable oil
¼  pound pancetta,* chopped
2    tablespoons minced peeled fresh ginger
1    bunch green onions, chopped
1½  pounds mussels, scrubbed, debearded

2    cups ¼-inch-thick slices bok choy stems
2    cups arborio or medium-grain rice
½  cup dry vermouth

2    cups chopped bok choy leaves
½  pound snow peas, stringed, thinly sliced lengthwise
¼  cup chopped fresh cilantro

Fresh cilantro sprigs

Combine 1½ cups hot water and shiitake mushrooms in small bowl. Let stand until mushrooms soften, about 30 minutes. Remove mushrooms from water and squeeze excess liquid back into bowl. Cut out hard stems and discard. Thinly slice mushrooms.

Pour mushroom soaking liquid into large saucepan, leaving any sediment in bottom of bowl. Add clam juice and 2 cups water. Bring to simmer. Reduce heat to very low and keep liquid hot.

Heat oil in heavy large Dutch oven over medium-high heat. Add pancetta, ginger and half of green onions; stir until aromatic, about 2 minutes. Add mussels, cover and cook until mussels open, about 6 minutes. Using tongs, transfer mussels to large bowl (discard any that do not open). Cover bowl with foil.

Add sliced mushrooms and bok choy stems to Dutch oven; stir over medium-high heat 2 minutes. Add rice; stir 1 minute. Add vermouth; stir until absorbed, about 2 minutes. Add 1 cup hot liquid; adjust heat so that rice simmers slowly. Cook rice until liquid is absorbed, stirring often, about 5 minutes. Continue cooking until rice is almost tender, adding 1 cup liquid every 5 minutes and stirring often, about15 minutes longer.

Mix bok choy leaves and snow peas into risotto and continue cooking until rice is just tender and mixture is creamy, adding hot liquid ½ cup at a time and stirring often, about 10 minutes longer. Mix in chopped cilantro and remaining chopped green onions. Season risotto with salt and pepper.

Transfer risotto to large bowl. Arrange mussels around edge of bowl. Garnish with cilantro sprigs and serve.

*Pancetta, Italian bacon cured in salt, is available at Italian markets, some specialty foods stores and some supermarkets.*

4 SERVINGS

# Scallops with Vegetables, Ginger and Cream

◆ ◆ ◆

| 4 | tablespoons (about) butter |
| 1 | turnip, peeled, cut into matchstick-size strips |
| 1 | large red bell pepper, cut into matchstick-size strips |
| 1 | large carrot, peeled, cut into matchstick-size strips |
| 1 | tablespoon minced peeled fresh ginger |
| 1 | large zucchini, cut into matchstick-size strips |
| 20 | large sea scallops |
| ¾ | cup whipping cream |

Melt 2 tablespoons butter in heavy large skillet over medium heat. Add turnip, bell pepper, carrot and ginger. Cover and cook 3 minutes. Add zucchini and sauté uncovered until vegetables are crisp-tender, about 3 minutes. Season to taste with salt and pepper.

Melt 1 tablespoon butter in another heavy large skillet over medium-high heat. Working in batches, add scallops; sauté until cooked through, adding more butter as needed, about 2 minutes per side. Transfer scallops to plate; tent with foil. Add cream to skillet. Increase heat; boil until reduced to sauce consistency, about 3 minutes. Season with salt and pepper.

Divide vegetables among 4 plates, mounding in center. Place scallops around vegetables. Spoon sauce over.

4 SERVINGS

# Spicy Shrimp Tacos with Tomatillo Salsa

◆ ◆ ◆

CHILI SOUR CREAM

2   cups sour cream

2   teaspoons chili powder

½   teaspoon cayenne pepper

SALSA

¾   pound tomatillos,* husks removed, rinsed, quartered (about 3 cups)

½   cup coarsely chopped unpeeled green apple (such as Granny Smith)

2   tablespoons coarsely chopped fresh basil

2   tablespoons coarsely chopped fresh mint

SHRIMP

1½  teaspoons chili powder

1½  teaspoons paprika

2   pounds uncooked medium shrimp, peeled, deveined

2   tablespoons olive oil

1   tablespoon minced garlic

16  purchased taco shells

1   large bunch watercress, trimmed

2   avocados, peeled, pitted, cubed

FOR SOUR CREAM: Whisk all ingredients in medium bowl to blend. Season with salt. *(Can be made 1 day ahead. Chill.)*

FOR SALSA: Finely chop tomatillos, apple, basil and mint in food processor. Transfer to small bowl. Season to taste with salt. *(Can be prepared 6 hours ahead. Let stand at room temperature.)*

FOR SHRIMP: Combine chili powder and paprika in large bowl. Add shrimp; toss to coat. Let stand 5 minutes. Heat oil in heavy large skillet over high heat. Add garlic and sauté until fragrant, about 1 minute. Add shrimp; sauté until opaque in center, about 5 minutes. Season with salt and pepper. Transfer to small bowl.

Preheat oven to 350°F. Arrange taco shells on heavy large baking sheet. Bake until hot, about 8 minutes. Place shells in napkin-lined basket. Arrange half of watercress on platter. Top with shrimp. Chop remaining watercress. Place in small bowl. Place sour cream, salsa, avocados and watercress in separate bowls.

*A green tomato-like vegetable with a paper-thin husk. Available at Latin American markets and some supermarkets.*

8 SERVINGS

◆ ◆ ◆

## SOUTHWESTERN SUPPER FOR EIGHT

SPICY SHRIMP TACOS WITH
TOMATILLO SALSA
(AT LEFT; PICTURED OPPOSITE)

MANGO, JICAMA AND CORN SALAD
(PAGE 154; PICTURED OPPOSITE)

BLACK BEAN AND
BELL PEPPER SALAD
(PAGE 151; PICTURED OPPOSITE)

CORN BREAD

MARGARITAS AND LEMONADE

CHEESECAKE

◆ ◆ ◆

Pour the egg, vegetable and cheese mixture into a nonstick ovenproof skillet. Arrange the potato slices and bell pepper strips on top.

Cook the frittata over direct heat just until the sides begin to set, then transfer the frittata—skillet and all— to the oven to finish cooking.

Run a spatula around one edge of the frittata to loosen it from the skillet. Slide the frittata out onto a platter.

# ◆ MEATLESS ◆

# Vegetable Frittata with Herbs and Goat Cheese

◆ ◆ ◆

VEGETABLES

1   tablespoon olive oil
2   medium-size red-skinned potatoes (about 9 ounces total), sliced crosswise into ⅛-inch-thick rounds
1   medium onion, halved, thinly sliced
1   red bell pepper, cut into ⅓-inch-wide strips
1   yellow bell pepper, cut into ⅓-inch-wide strips
1   tablespoon chopped fresh marjoram or 1 teaspoon dried
2   teaspoons minced fresh rosemary or ¾ teaspoon dried
½   teaspoon salt
¼   teaspoon dried rubbed sage

FRITTATA

9   large eggs
1   tablespoon chopped fresh dill or 1 teaspoon dried dillweed
¾   teaspoon salt
½   teaspoon pepper
4   ounces chilled soft fresh goat cheese (such as Montrachet), crumbled (about 1 cup)

2   teaspoons olive oil

    Fresh herb sprigs and chopped fresh herbs (such as rosemary, dill and marjoram; optional)

FOR VEGETABLES: Heat oil in 12-inch-diameter nonstick ovenproof skillet over medium-low heat. Add potatoes, onion, bell peppers, marjoram, rosemary, salt and sage. Cook 5 minutes, stirring occasionally. Cover and cook until potatoes are tender, stirring occasionally, about 15 minutes. Cool mixture in skillet 5 minutes. *(Can be prepared 2 hours ahead. Let stand at room temperature.)*

FOR FRITTATA: Preheat oven to 350°F. Whisk eggs, dill, salt and pepper in large bowl to blend. Mix in 3 ounces cheese. Transfer several potato slices and bell pepper strips to small dish and reserve. Stir remaining vegetable mixture into egg mixture.

Wipe same 12-inch skillet clean. Add oil; heat over medium-high heat, tilting skillet to coat bottom with oil. Pour egg-and-vegetable mixture into skillet, stirring vegetables to distribute. Arrange reserved vegetables on top in attractive pattern; sprinkle with 1 ounce cheese. Cook until sides begin to set, about 2 minutes. Transfer skillet to oven; bake until set in center, about 15 minutes.

Run spatula around edge of frittata to loosen from skillet. Slide out onto platter. Serve hot, or cover loosely with foil and let stand at room temperature up to 2 hours.

Garnish frittata with herb sprigs and chopped herbs, if desired. Cut frittata into wedges and serve.

6 SERVINGS

# Mixed Vegetable Curry

◆ ◆ ◆

The evaporated skim milk imparts
a rich creaminess with almost no fat.
The result is a delicious dish that contains a mere three grams of fat and
425 calories per serving.

◆ ◆ ◆

| | |
|---|---|
| 1 | teaspoon vegetable oil |
| ¾ | cup chopped onion |
| 2½ | teaspoons curry powder |
| 1 | teaspoon ground cumin |
| | Generous pinch of dried crushed red pepper |
| 1 | cup evaporated skim milk |
| 2 | cups 1-inch cubes peeled potatoes |
| 2 | cups chopped seeded plum tomatoes |
| 2 | cups broccoli florets |
| 2 | cups thin diagonal carrot slices |
| 1 | cup cauliflower florets |
| | |
| 4 | cups hot cooked rice (preferably basmati) |
| ¼ | cup cilantro leaves (optional) |

Heat oil in large nonstick skillet over medium-low heat. Add
onion; cook until tender, stirring occasionally, about 10 minutes. Add
curry powder, cumin and crushed red pepper; stir until fragrant,
about 1 minute. Add milk; bring to boil. Add potatoes and 1 cup
tomatoes. Cover; simmer until potatoes are almost tender, stirring
occasionally, about 15 minutes. Add broccoli, carrots and cauliflower.

Cover; simmer until all vegetables are tender, stirring occasionally, about 7 minutes. Season with salt and pepper.

Divide rice among 4 plates. Top with curry. Sprinkle with remaining 1 cup tomatoes and garnish with cilantro leaves.

4 SERVINGS

# Black Bean and Vegetable Burritos

◆ ◆ ◆

4    9- to 10-inch-diameter flour tortillas

¾    cup chopped onion
2    teaspoons vegetable oil
½    teaspoon ground cumin
½    teaspoon chili powder
1    cup chopped red bell pepper
⅔    cup frozen corn kernels, thawed
1    medium carrot, coarsely grated
1⅔    cups canned black beans, rinsed, drained
½    cup drained canned Mexican-style stewed tomatoes
2    teaspoons minced seeded jalapeño chili

8    tablespoons grated Monterey Jack cheese (about 2 ounces)
4    tablespoons nonfat sour cream
4    tablespoons chopped fresh cilantro

Preheat oven to 350°F. Wrap tortillas in foil. Warm in oven until heated through, about 15 minutes.

Meanwhile, combine onion and oil in large nonstick skillet. Stir over medium-high heat until onion is golden, about 6 minutes. Add cumin and chili powder; stir 20 seconds. Add bell pepper, corn and carrot; sauté until almost tender, about 5 minutes. Add beans, tomatoes and jalapeño; bring to simmer. Season with salt and pepper. Remove filling from heat.

Place warm tortillas on work surface. Spoon filling down center, dividing equally. Top each with 2 tablespoons cheese, then 1 tablespoon each of sour cream and cilantro. Fold sides of tortillas over filling, forming packages. Turn each package, seam side down, onto plate.

4 SERVINGS

# MEXICAN FOOD LIGHTENS UP

One of the most popular choices for a quick and inexpensive meal, Mexican food has gotten an unfair reputation for also being one of our most fattening. True, it is often loaded with irresistible and highly caloric extras like guacamole, sour cream, cheese and deep-fried tortilla chips; but in reality, authentic Mexican cooking is based on the same sort of healthful diet that distinguishes most peasant cuisines. It's an ideal diet, one that emphasizes beans, rice and corn, with helpings of fresh fruits and vegetables and judicious additions of chicken and fish, pork and beef.

A growing number of Mexican restaurants are now offering lighter fare based on traditional Mexican cooking and regional specialties. Featured on their menus are such delicious alternatives as vegetable tostadas, grilled fish and chicken, and soft tacos topped with salsas.

At home, you can follow their lead by cooking nutritious Mexican dishes that trim the fat but not the flavor. Focus on complex carbohydrates and flavorful vegetables, grilled meats and seafood. Create your own salsas and experiment with seasonings such as cilantro and chilies.

◆ ◆ ◆

# Grilled Vegetable Salad with Greens, Tomatoes, Herbs, Olives and Cheese

◆ ◆ ◆

¾ cup olive oil

¼ cup balsamic vinegar

1 large red onion, cut into ¾-inch-thick rounds

12 baby beets, stems trimmed to 1 inch, peeled, halved lengthwise

3 small zucchini, each cut lengthwise into 4 slices

3 Japanese eggplants, each cut lengthwise into 4 slices

2 large red bell peppers, cut into 1-inch-wide strips

6 slices country-style French bread
   Additional olive oil

10 cups mixed baby greens

4 large tomatoes, sliced

3 tablespoons chopped fresh basil

2 tablespoons chopped fresh chives or green onions

1 tablespoon chopped fresh marjoram

¾ cup chilled fresh mild goat cheese (such as Montrachet), crumbled (about 3 ounces)

½ cup freshly grated Pecorino Romano cheese (about 2 ounces)

¾ cup brine-cured black olives (such as Kalamata)

Prepare barbecue (medium-high heat). Whisk ¾ cup oil and vinegar in medium bowl to blend. Place onion, beets, zucchini, eggplants and red bell peppers on baking sheet. Brush both sides with some of vinaigrette. Sprinkle vegetables with salt and pepper. Grill vegetables until just cooked through, about 10 minutes per side for beets, 6 minutes per side for onion and 4 minutes per side for zucchini, eggplants and peppers. *(Vegetables can be grilled 1 hour ahead. Let stand at room temperature.)* Brush bread with additional olive oil; sprinkle with pepper. Grill bread until beginning to brown, about 2 minutes per side. Set bread aside.

Arrange greens on large platter. Overlap tomatoes atop greens in center. Sprinkle tomatoes with salt and pepper. Arrange grilled vegetables atop greens around edge. Drizzle remaining vinaigrette over tomatoes and grilled vegetables. Sprinkle tomatoes and vegetables with herbs. Sprinkle tomatoes with goat cheese. Sprinkle Romano cheese over all. Garnish with olives. Serve with bread.

*6 SERVINGS*

◆ ◆ ◆

## WARM-WEATHER DINNER PARTY FOR SIX

DEVILED EGGS WITH RADISHES, CHIVES AND THYME
(PAGE 13; PICTURED OPPOSITE)

GRILLED VEGETABLE SALAD WITH GREENS, TOMATOES, HERBS, OLIVES AND CHEESE
(AT LEFT; PICTURED OPPOSITE)

SAUVIGNON BLANC

COUNTRY-STYLE PLUM TART
(PAGE 175; PICTURED OPPOSITE)

◆ ◆ ◆

# Cheese and Chili Strata

◆ ◆ ◆

1   cup milk
2   large eggs
½   teaspoon salt
½   teaspoon pepper
1   cup (packed) grated Monterey Jack cheese
3   tablespoons sliced green onion
2   teaspoons minced jalapeño chili
2   cups cubed white sandwich bread (about 3 slices)

½   cup bottled chunky salsa
2   tablespoons chopped fresh cilantro

Preheat oven to 400°F. Lightly butter 9-inch-diameter glass pie plate. Whisk milk, eggs, salt and pepper in medium bowl to blend. Mix in cheese, green onion and chili. Add bread and stir until moistened. Transfer mixture to prepared pie dish. Let stand until bread absorbs most of custard, pressing several times to submerge cubes, about 5 minutes.

Bake strata uncovered until light brown around edges, top is crusty and knife inserted into center comes out clean, 20 minutes.

Combine salsa and chopped fresh cilantro in small bowl. Cut strata into wedges. Serve with salsa.

2 SERVINGS

◆ ◆ ◆

A strata is a savory bread pudding of bread cubes and cheese baked in custard—real comfort food. Here, the traditional recipe is given a spicy edge with green onions and jalapeño.

◆ ◆ ◆

# Barley, Beet and Feta Cheese Salad with Fennel Vinaigrette

◆ ◆ ◆

6    medium-size red beets, trimmed

¼   cup balsamic vinegar
3    garlic cloves, minced
2    teaspoons fennel seeds
¾   cup walnut oil or olive oil
¼   cup olive oil

4    cups canned low-salt chicken broth
1½  cups pearl barley (about 10 ounces)

3    cups crumbled feta cheese (about 12 ounces)
1½  cups walnuts, toasted (about 6 ounces), coarsely chopped
2    large bunches arugula, cut into 1-inch pieces

Place beets in large saucepan. Add enough water to cover. Bring to boil. Reduce heat to medium-high; boil beets until tender when pierced with fork, about 50 minutes. Drain and cool to lukewarm. Peel beets. Cut beets into thin wedges. Transfer beets to large bowl.

Combine vinegar, garlic and fennel seeds in medium bowl. Gradually whisk in ¾ cup walnut oil and ¼ cup olive oil. Season to taste with salt and pepper. Add 3 tablespoons vinaigrette to beets; toss to coat. Season to taste with salt and pepper.

Bring 4 cups chicken broth to boil in heavy large saucepan. Add barley; return to boil. Reduce heat, cover and simmer until barley is just tender and liquid is absorbed, stirring occasionally, about 40 minutes. Remove from heat, uncover and let barley stand 10 minutes. Transfer barley to large bowl. Fluff with fork, then cool to room temperature. *(Can be prepared 8 hours ahead. Cover and refrigerate beets, remaining vinaigrette and barley separately. Let stand at room temperature 1 hour before continuing.)*

Add cheese, walnuts, arugula and ⅔ cup vinaigrette to barley and mix gently to combine. Season to taste with salt and pepper. Mound barley salad onto large platter; arrange beets atop salad. Serve, passing remaining vinaigrette separately.

6 SERVINGS

◆ ◆ ◆

Even people who are not crazy about beets will warm up to this main-course salad. Walnuts, feta and arugula add more flavor and crunch.

◆ ◆ ◆

♦ ♦ ♦

# VEGETARIAN
# DINNER PARTY
# FOR SIX

Sherried Winter Squash Bisque
(page 31)

Modern Waldorf Salad
(page 159)

Vegetable Pot Pie with Wine
Sauce and Polenta Crust
(at right; pictured above)

Chardonnay and
Sparkling Water

Low-Fat Orange and Almond
Cream Cheese Pie
(page 171)

♦ ♦ ♦

# Vegetable Pot Pie with Wine Sauce and Polenta Crust

♦ ♦ ♦

FILLING

15    pearl onions

2     large carrots
2     russet potatoes (about 8 ounces each), peeled
2     rutabagas (about 6 ounces each), peeled
1     red bell pepper, seeded
1     leek (white and pale green parts only), chopped
10    ounces mushrooms, coarsely chopped
2     tablespoons olive oil
1½    teaspoons dried herbes de Provence*
1     cup frozen peas, thawed

1     cup canned vegetable broth
1     cup dry red wine
1     tablespoon cornstarch

POLENTA
2     cups canned vegetable broth
1     cup water
¾     cup cornmeal
½     teaspoon salt
1     tablespoon freshly grated Romano cheese

FOR FILLING: Preheat oven to 425°F. Blanch pearl onions in large pot of boiling water 2 minutes. Drain onions and cool. Peel onions.

Cut carrots, potatoes, rutabagas and bell pepper into ½-inch pieces. Place in heavy large baking pan with onions, leek and mushrooms. Add olive oil and herbes de Provence and toss to coat. Roast until vegetables are tender, stirring occasionally, about 1 hour. Transfer vegetables to 8-inch square glass baking dish. Stir in peas. Season vegetables to taste with salt and pepper. *(Can be prepared 1 day ahead. Cover tightly and refrigerate.)*

Reduce oven temperature to 350°F. Mix 1 cup vegetable broth and ¾ cup dry red wine in heavy small saucepan over medium heat. Bring to simmer. Stir remaining ¼ cup red wine and 1 tablespoon cornstarch in small bowl until smooth. Add to broth mixture and simmer until sauce thickens slightly, stirring occasionally, about 4 minutes. Pour sauce over roasted vegetables.

FOR POLENTA: Combine vegetable broth and 1 cup water in

heavy medium saucepan over medium heat. Bring to boil. Gradually stir in cornmeal and salt. Cook until polenta thickens and pulls away from sides of pan, stirring constantly, about 10 minutes. Pour warm polenta over vegetable mixture. Using spatula, smooth top, covering vegetables completely. Sprinkle polenta with cheese.

Bake pot pie until polenta is firm to touch and vegetable mixture is heated through, about 15 minutes. Preheat broiler. Broil pot pie until polenta is golden, about 4 minutes. Spoon pot pie onto plates.

*A dried herb mixture available at specialty foods stores and some supermarkets. A combination of dried thyme, basil, savory and fennel seeds can be used instead.*

6 SERVINGS

# Quick Moroccan Vegetable Couscous

◆ ◆ ◆

⅓    cup sliced almonds
1    tablespoon olive oil
3    cups mixed cut-up vegetables (such as red onion, carrots, zucchini and cauliflower)
1½    teaspoons ground cumin
1½    teaspoons ground coriander
1    cup dry white wine
⅓    cup golden raisins
¾    cup canned vegetable broth

1    5- to 7-ounce box couscous and lentil mix or other couscous blend

Place almonds in heavy medium skillet. Stir over medium heat until almonds are pale golden, about 4 minutes. Transfer almonds to bowl. Add oil to same skillet. Increase heat to medium-high. Add vegetables, cumin and coriander; sauté until vegetables just begin to soften, about 3 minutes. Add wine and raisins. Boil until wine is reduced by half, about 3 minutes. Add broth. Partially cover skillet; simmer until vegetables are tender, about 6 minutes. Season with salt and pepper.

Meanwhile, prepare couscous according to package directions.

Mound couscous on platter. Spoon vegetable topping and juices over. Sprinkle with almonds and serve.

2 SERVINGS

◆ ◆ ◆

EASY MEATLESS
SUPPER FOR
TWO

QUICK MOROCCAN
VEGETABLE COUSCOUS
(AT LEFT)

SLICED TOMATO AND CUCUMBER
SALAD

WARM PITA BREAD

BEER

PISTACHIO ICE CREAM ON
ORANGE SEGMENTS

◆ ◆ ◆

# Whole Wheat Crepes with Corn, Bell Pepper and Cheese Filling

◆ ◆ ◆

CREPES

1      cup low-fat (1%) milk
2      large eggs
⅓      cup water
½      teaspoon salt
⅔      cup whole wheat pastry flour*
⅓      cup unbleached all purpose flour

2      tablespoons (¼ stick) butter, melted

FILLING

1      tablespoon olive oil
1      cup chopped onion
1¼     cups finely diced red bell pepper
2      teaspoons minced garlic
1¾     cups fresh corn kernels
1      teaspoon chopped fresh rosemary or ½ teaspoon dried
1      teaspoon chopped fresh thyme or ½ teaspoon dried

1      cup nonfat cottage cheese
⅓      cup (about 2 ounces) soft fresh goat cheese (such as Montrachet)
3      tablespoons grated Pecorino Romano cheese
2      large egg whites (unbeaten)

     Red Bell Pepper Puree (see recipe opposite)

FOR CREPES: Blend milk, eggs, water and salt in blender. With machine running, add both flours in 4 additions total. Blend 1 minute. Transfer batter to medium bowl. Refrigerate 2 hours.

Heat medium nonstick skillet with 6½-inch-diameter bottom over medium-high heat. Lightly brush bottom of pan with some of melted butter. Whisk batter to blend well. Add 2 tablespoons batter to pan and swirl pan to coat bottom thinly. Cook until edges are brown and crepe lifts easily, about 45 seconds. Loosen edges of crepe gently with spatula. Carefully turn crepe over; cook until beginning to brown in spots, about 20 seconds. Turn crepe out onto plate. Place paper towel atop crepe. Repeat with remaining crepe batter, using 2 tablespoons per crepe, brushing pan with melted butter as needed and covering each crepe with paper towel. *(Can be made 1 day ahead. Wrap crepes layered between paper towels in foil and chill.)*

FOR FILLING: Heat oil in large nonstick skillet over medium heat. Add onion and sauté until tender, about 4 minutes. Add bell pepper and garlic; sauté until bell pepper is tender, about 5 minutes. Add corn kernels, rosemary and thyme; sauté until corn is heated through, 5 minutes longer. Season with salt and pepper. Cool.

Blend cottage cheese and goat cheese in processor until smooth. Transfer to large bowl. Stir in corn mixture and Romano cheese. Season filling to taste with salt and pepper. Mix in egg whites. *(Can be prepared 3 hours ahead; chill.)*

Preheat oven to 400°F. Lightly butter 13 x 9 x 2-inch glass baking dish. Spoon generous 2 tablespoons filling down center of each crepe. Roll up crepes. Arrange crepes, seam side down, in prepared baking dish. Cover with foil. Bake until heated through, about 20 minutes. Spoon Red Bell Pepper Puree over crepes and serve.

*\*Also called whole grain pastry flour. Available at most natural foods stores and some supermarkets.*

6 SERVINGS

## Red Bell Pepper Puree

5    red bell peppers (about 2 pounds)

1    tablespoon olive oil
2    garlic cloves, minced
2    tablespoons low-fat buttermilk
¼    teaspoon sugar

Preheat oven to 450°F. Place bell peppers on baking sheet. Bake until puffed and blackened on all sides, turning every 10 minutes, about 30 minutes. Transfer to large bowl; cover with plate. Let stand 30 minutes. Peel, stem and seed peppers over medium bowl to collect juice. Transfer peppers to processor. Strain accumulated bell pepper juice into small bowl; reserve.

Heat oil in small nonstick skillet over medium-low heat. Add garlic; sauté until just golden, about 30 seconds. Transfer garlic and oil to processor with peppers. Puree. Add buttermilk and sugar. Season with salt and pepper; thin with reserved bell pepper juice, if desired. Transfer to small bowl; serve warm or at room temperature. *(Can be made 1 day ahead. Cover bell pepper puree and refrigerate. Bring to room temperature before serving.)*

MAKES ABOUT 2 CUPS

# Potato and Wild Mushroom Lasagna

❖ ❖ ❖

| | |
|---|---|
| 2 | large russet potatoes (11 to 12 ounces each), peeled |
| 2 | tablespoons (¼ stick) butter |
| | |
| 2 | teaspoons vegetable oil |
| 6 | ounces portobello mushrooms, stemmed, thinly sliced |
| 12 | ounces fresh shiitake mushrooms, stemmed, caps thinly sliced |
| 4 | ounces fresh oyster mushrooms, thinly sliced |
| 5 | ounces fresh chanterelle mushrooms, thinly sliced |
| ½ | cup dry white wine |
| ½ | cup canned vegetable broth |
| ½ | cup finely chopped shallots |
| | |
| ½ | cup cubed seeded tomatoes |
| 3 | tablespoons chopped fresh parsley |

Preheat oven to 350°F. Line large baking sheet with parchment paper. Trim russet potatoes to form 4 x 2-inch rectangular blocks. Using large sharp knife, carefully cut each potato block lengthwise into ⅛-inch-thick rectangles. Melt 1 tablespoon butter in large nonstick skillet. Brush parchment lightly with half of melted butter. Sprinkle salt and pepper over parchment. Arrange 16 of the most uniform potato rectangles in single layer on parchment (reserve remaining potato rectangles and trimmings for another use). Brush potatoes with remaining butter. Sprinkle with salt and pepper. Cover potatoes with another sheet of parchment. Bake until tender, 12 minutes.

Melt remaining 1 tablespoon butter with vegetable oil in same skillet over medium-high heat. Add portobello mushrooms; sauté until almost soft, about 2 minutes. Add shiitake mushrooms and sauté until almost soft, about 2 minutes. Add oyster and chanterelle mushrooms and sauté until almost soft, about 2 minutes. Add white wine, vegetable broth and chopped shallots and simmer until shallots are translucent, about 4 minutes. Season mushrooms to taste with salt and pepper. Strain, reserving mushroom broth.

Arrange 4 potato rectangles on clean baking sheet, spacing apart. Top each rectangle with 3 tablespoons mushroom mixture. Place another potato rectangle atop each. Repeat layering with 3 tablespoons mushroom mixture, 1 potato rectangle and 3 tablespoons mushroom

❖ ❖ ❖

This low-cal (255 calories per serving), low-fat (nine grams per serving) take on lasagna uses potato slices in place of pasta and a sauté of wild mushrooms instead of the traditional meat and cheese filling. (Be sure to buy very large potatoes to make it easier to cut the rectangles, and to use a variety of mushrooms to give this elegant main course additional flavor and textural contrast.)

❖ ❖ ❖

mixture on each lasagna. Top each lasagna with 1 potato rectangle. Place another baking sheet atop lasagnas to compress. Let stand at room temperature at least 1 hour and up to 2 hours. Remove top baking sheet. *(Can be made 8 hours ahead. Cover lasagnas and broth separately and refrigerate.)*

Preheat oven to 350°F. Bake lasagnas on baking sheet until heated through, about 8 minutes.

Meanwhile, boil reserved mushroom broth in small saucepan until reduced to ½ cup, about 4 minutes.

Using metal spatula, place 1 lasagna in center of each plate. Spoon 2 tablespoons of mushroom broth over and around each lasagna. Sprinkle tomatoes and parsley over and around each.

4 SERVINGS

# Fettuccine with Swordfish and Sugar Snap Peas

◆ ◆ ◆

12 ounces sugar snap peas, trimmed
2 medium carrots, peeled, cut into matchstick-size strips (about 2 cups)

8 ounces fettuccine

2 teaspoons olive oil
1 pound skinless swordfish steaks, cut into ¾-inch cubes
3 tablespoons chopped fresh parsley
1 tablespoon all purpose flour
½ cup bottled clam juice
½ cup canned low-salt chicken broth
½ cup dry white wine
1½ tablespoons fresh lemon juice

4 green onions, thinly sliced
½ teaspoon paprika
Lemon wedges

Blanch peas in medium saucepan of boiling salted water 1 minute. Add carrots and blanch 1 minute longer. Drain. Rinse under cold water. Drain well.

Cook fettuccine in large pot of boiling salted water until pasta is tender but still firm to bite.

Meanwhile, heat oil in large nonstick skillet over high heat. Sprinkle fish with salt and pepper. Add fish to skillet and sauté until golden brown and almost cooked through, about 2 minutes. Using slotted spoon, transfer fish to plate. Tent with foil to keep warm. Add parsley and flour to skillet; stir 30 seconds. Add clam juice, broth, wine and lemon juice. Simmer until sauce thickens, stirring, about 2 minutes. Add peas and carrots; stir 1 minute. Add fish; stir gently until heated through, 1 minute. Season with salt and pepper.

Drain pasta. Divide among 4 plates. Spoon fish, vegetables and sauce over. Sprinkle with onions, paprika. Serve with lemon.

4 SERVINGS

---

◆ ◆ ◆

## LIGHT AND EASY DINNER FOR FOUR

CELERY WITH
RICOTTA-BASIL SPREAD

FETTUCCINE WITH SWORDFISH AND
SUGAR SNAP PEAS
(AT RIGHT; PICTURED OPPOSITE)

CHERRY TOMATOES WITH
FRESH HERBS
(PAGE 141; PICTURED OPPOSITE)

SAUVIGNON BLANC OR
PINOT GRIGIO

LEMON CUSTARD PHYLLO CUPS
(PAGE 200; PICTURED OPPOSITE)

◆ ◆ ◆

# Farfalle with Sun-dried Tomatoes and Arugula

♦ ♦ ♦

| | |
|---|---|
| 6 | ounces farfalle (butterfly- or bow-tie-shaped pasta) |
| ½ | cup chopped drained oil-packed sun-dried tomatoes (about one 7½-ounce jar), 1 tablespoon oil reserved |
| 1 | large garlic clove, chopped |
| ⅔ | cup dry white wine |
| 4 | cups coarsely chopped arugula (about 4 large bunches) |
| 6 | tablespoons grated Parmesan cheese |

Cook pasta in pot of boiling salted water until just tender but still firm to bite. Drain well; reserve ¼ cup cooking liquid.

Meanwhile, heat oil from tomatoes in heavy large skillet over medium-high heat. Add garlic and stir until fragrant, about 30 seconds. Add chopped tomatoes and white wine. Boil until wine is reduced slightly, about 3 minutes. Add arugula; toss until wilted, 1 minute.

Add pasta and 4 tablespoons Parmesan cheese to sauce in skillet. Toss until well blended. Moisten pasta with reserved cooking liquid, if desired. Season pasta to taste with salt and pepper. Sprinkling with remaining Parmesan and serve.

2 SERVINGS

# Linguine with Chicken and Spicy Pesto Sauce

◆ ◆ ◆

2    tablespoons olive oil
1    pound skinless boneless chicken breasts, cut into ⅓-inch-wide strips
3    green onions, thinly sliced
⅓    cup chopped fresh cilantro
⅓    cup chopped pecans, toasted
1    tablespoon minced garlic
2    teaspoons minced seeded jalapeño chili
¼    teaspoon dried crushed red pepper
½    cup purchased pesto

12    ounces linguine

     Additional chopped fresh cilantro
     Freshly grated Parmesan cheese

Heat oil in heavy large skillet over medium-high heat. Season chicken with salt and pepper. Add chicken to skillet and sauté until cooked through and beginning to brown, about 3 minutes. Using slotted spoon, transfer chicken to bowl. Add green onions, ⅓ cup cilantro, pecans, garlic, jalapeño and dried red pepper to same skillet. Sauté until green onions wilt, about 2 minutes. Add pesto, chicken and any accumulated juices; stir to blend. Remove from heat.

Meanwhile, cook linguine in pot of boiling salted water until tender but still firm to bite. Drain, reserving ¼ cup cooking liquid.

Bring sauce to simmer. Add linguine and reserved cooking liquid to sauce and toss to coat. Season to taste with salt and pepper. Transfer to large bowl. Sprinkle with additional cilantro. Serve, passing Parmesan cheese separately.

4 SERVINGS

◆ ◆ ◆

Purchased pesto takes a Southwestern turn in this flavorful pasta dish, with the addition of cilantro, pecans and jalapeño chili.

◆ ◆ ◆

# Southwest Fusilli with Tomatoes, Garlic and Chilies

◆ ◆ ◆

| | |
|---|---|
| 2¾ | pounds plum tomatoes |
| ⅓ | cup olive oil |
| 2 | tablespoons plus 2 teaspoons minced garlic |
| ⅔ | cup chopped fresh cilantro |
| ⅓ | cup chopped red onion |
| 2 | tablespoons plus 2 teaspoons fresh lime juice |
| 4 | teaspoons minced seeded serrano or jalapeño chilies |
| 4 | teaspoons tomato paste |
| 2¾ | teaspoons chili powder |
| 12 | ounces fusilli or other corkscrew pasta |
| 1⅓ | cups (about 6 ounces) crumbled feta cheese |
| ¼ | cup chopped fresh cilantro |

Bring medium pot of water to boil. Fill medium bowl with cold water and place on work surface close to pot. Cut shallow X through skin at bottom of tomatoes. Working in batches, add tomatoes to boiling water and cook 30 seconds to blanch. Using slotted spoon, transfer each batch of tomatoes to cold water to cool quickly.

Using small sharp knife as aid and starting at X on bottom, pull skin off tomatoes. Using same knife, make neat cone-shaped incision around core at stem end of each tomato; remove cores. Cut tomatoes in half crosswise; squeeze out seeds. Cut tomatoes into small dice and place in large bowl. Season with salt.

Heat oil in heavy medium skillet over high heat. Add garlic and sauté just until fragrant, about 30 seconds. Pour garlic oil over tomatoes and toss to blend. Mix in ⅔ cup cilantro, onion, lime juice, chilies, tomato paste and chili powder. *(Can be prepared 2 hours ahead. Let sauce stand at room temperature.)*

Cook fusilli in large pot of boiling salted water until just tender but still firm to bite, stirring occasionally. Drain fusilli well. Add fusilli and half of cheese to tomato sauce; toss to blend. Season pasta to taste with salt and pepper. Transfer pasta to large shallow serving bowl. Sprinkle with remaining cheese. Garnish pasta with ¼ cup chopped cilantro and serve.

4 SERVINGS

Begin the peeling and seeding process by blanching the tomatoes in boiling water. Leave them in just long enough for the skin to loosen, but not so long that they start to cook.

Grasp the curled tomato skin between a small knife and your thumb, and pull it off in sections.

Core the tomatoes, then cut them in half crosswise. The separate chambers of seeds are now easy to see. Gently squeeze out the seeds.

# Crab and Salmon Ravioli

◆ ◆ ◆

RAVIOLI

All purpose flour

⅓ cup chopped peeled carrot

1½ teaspoons finely chopped peeled fresh ginger

3 ounces skinless salmon fillet

3 tablespoons chilled whipping cream

1 tablespoon egg white

4 ounces fresh crabmeat

1 green onion, chopped

½ celery stalk, finely diced

2 teaspoons chopped fresh cilantro

1½ teaspoons fresh lemon juice

⅛ teaspoon salt

⅛ teaspoon pepper

32 gyoza (potsticker) wrappers*

VINAIGRETTE

1 cup olive oil

¼ cup white wine vinegar

¼ cup fresh lemon juice

2 tomatoes, peeled, seeded, diced

3 ounces snow peas, cut into strips

1 celery stalk, cut into strips

3 tablespoons minced fresh chives

FOR RAVIOLI: Lightly sprinkle large baking sheet with flour. Bring medium saucepan of water to boil. Add carrot and ginger and blanch 1 minute. Drain and cool.

Remove any bones from salmon. Chop salmon coarsely. Transfer to processor. Add cream and egg white; puree. Transfer to bowl. Mix in carrot, ginger, crab, onion, celery, cilantro, lemon juice, salt and pepper. Place 1 gyoza wrapper on work surface. Place 1 level tablespoon filling in center. Brush edges with water. Cover with another gyoza wrapper and press firmly around edges to seal. Transfer to prepared sheet. Repeat with remaining gyoza wrappers and filling. *(Can be made 8 hours ahead. Cover and chill.)*

Bring large saucepan of water to boil. Add ravioli in batches and cook until tender, about 3 minutes per batch. Using slotted spoon, transfer ravioli to another baking sheet. Cover with foil.

◆ ◆ ◆

This wonderful ravioli recipe is made easy with storebought *gyoza* wrappers used in place of homemade pasta. Look for them in the refrigerated section of your local grocery store or at an Asian market.

MEANWHILE, PREPARE VINAIGRETTE: Combine oil, vinegar and lemon juice in large skillet. Stir over medium heat until warm. Add tomatoes, snow peas and celery; stir just until heated through, about 2 minutes. Add chives. Divide vinaigrette between plates. Place ravioli atop vinaigrette. Serve immediately.

*Gyoza *wrappers are available at Asian markets and in the refrigerated section of many supermarkets.*

2 SERVINGS

# Rice Noodles with Cilantro, Mint and Peanuts

◆ ◆ ◆

| ¼ | cup rice vinegar |
| 1 | tablespoon sugar |
| ½ | sweet onion (such as Vidalia), thinly sliced, separated into rings |
| 8 | ounces firm dried rice noodles* |
| ¼ | cup fresh lime juice |
| 2 | teaspoons vegetable oil |
| ½ | teaspoon dried crushed red pepper |
| ⅓ | cup chopped fresh mint |
| ⅓ | cup chopped fresh cilantro |
| 1 | large cucumber, peeled, halved lengthwise, seeded, thinly sliced |
| 4 | green onions, thinly sliced |
| 3 | fresh plum tomatoes, seeded, chopped |
| 2 | tablespoons chopped lightly salted cocktail peanuts |

◆ ◆ ◆

Inspired by Vietnamese cuisine, this pasta dish would make a satisfying meatless lunch. You could also serve it as a side dish in most any Asian-themed meal.

◆ ◆ ◆

Whisk vinegar and sugar in medium bowl to blend. Add onion rings and toss to coat. Cover and let stand at least 30 minutes and up to 4 hours. Drain, reserving 2 tablespoons vinegar mixture.

Cook noodles in large pot of boiling water until tender but still firm to bite, 2 minutes. Drain. Rinse under cold water. Drain well.

Whisk lime juice, oil and crushed red pepper in small bowl to blend. Stir in mint and cilantro. Using kitchen shears, cut noodles into 3- to 4-inch-long sections. Place handful of noodles in large bowl. Drizzle with reserved 2 tablespoons vinegar mixture and toss to coat. Add remaining noodles, cucumber, green onions, tomatoes and marinated onions. Drizzle lime juice mixture over and toss gently. Season to taste with salt and pepper. Sprinkle with peanuts and serve.

*Available at Asian markets and in many supermarkets.*

2 SERVINGS

# Wild Mushroom Frittata with Onions and Pancetta

◆ ◆ ◆

3 ounces angel hair pasta

12 ounces fresh chanterelles or other fresh wild mushrooms (such as oyster or stemmed and sliced shiitake)

4 ounces thinly sliced pancetta or other bacon, chopped

1 garlic clove, chopped

1½ cups thinly sliced sweet onion (such as Maui)

½ cup dry white wine

12 large eggs

3 tablespoons chopped fresh parsley

½ teaspoon salt

½ teaspoon ground pepper

1 tablespoon olive oil

1 garlic clove, halved

Onion, Tomato and Arugula Relish (see recipe opposite)
Freshly grated Parmesan cheese

Cook pasta in large pot of boiling salted water until tender but still firm to bite. Drain. Rinse under cold water. Cut into 3-inch

lengths. Cool completely. *(Can be prepared 1 day ahead. Toss with oil to prevent sticking. Cover and refrigerate.)*

Heat large nonstick skillet over medium-high heat. Add mushrooms and sauté until brown and any exuded liquid evaporates, about 7 minutes. Transfer to plate and cool.

Sauté pancetta and chopped garlic in same skillet over medium-high heat until pancetta is almost crisp, about 3 minutes. Add onion; sauté until light golden, about 3 minutes. Add wine; simmer until liquid evaporates, about 3 minutes. Cool completely.

Preheat broiler. Whisk eggs in large bowl to blend. Add pasta, mushrooms, onion mixture, parsley, salt and pepper; stir to blend. Heat oil in 12-inch-diameter nonstick broilerproof skillet over medium heat. Add halved garlic; sauté until golden, about 3 minutes. Using slotted spoon, remove garlic. Add egg mixture to skillet. Cook until bottom is set, lifting edge of cooked egg mixture and tilting skillet to allow uncooked egg to flow under, about 8 minutes. Cover skillet and cook until eggs are almost set in center, about 5 minutes. Uncover skillet. Transfer to broiler; cook until eggs are set and frittata is golden, about 4 minutes.

Slide rubber spatula around sides of frittata to loosen. Slide frittata onto platter. Cut into wedges and serve with Onion, Tomato and Arugula Relish and Parmesan cheese.

6 SERVINGS

# Onion, Tomato and Arugula Relish

2  medium-size sweet onions (such as Maui), quartered
4  tablespoons olive oil

1⅓ cups chopped seeded tomatoes
¾  cup coarsely chopped arugula
2  teaspoons balsamic vinegar
2  teaspoons rice vinegar

Preheat oven to 450°F. Grease large baking sheet; arrange onions on sheet. Drizzle with 2 tablespoons oil. Bake until golden and tender, turning occasionally, about 30 minutes. Cool. Chop.

Mix onions, tomatoes and arugula in medium bowl. Whisk balsamic vinegar, rice vinegar and 2 tablespoons oil in small bowl. Add to onion mixture; toss to coat. Season with salt and pepper. Cover and refrigerate relish at least 2 hours or overnight. Bring relish to room temperature before serving.

MAKES ABOUT 2 CUPS

◆ ◆ ◆

## SUNDAY BRUNCH FOR SIX

CHAMPAGNE COCKTAILS

WILD MUSHROOM FRITTATA WITH
ONIONS AND PANCETTA
(AT LEFT; PICTURED OPPOSITE)

ONION, TOMATO AND
ARUGULA RELISH
(AT LEFT; PICTURED OPPOSITE)

GRILLED ITALIAN SAUSAGES

PINOT GRIS

BAKED PEARS

BISCOTTI

GRAPPA

COFFEE

◆ ◆ ◆

# Pappardelle with Portobello Mushrooms, Spinach and Pine Nuts

### ◆ ◆ ◆

This earthy pasta dish can be made with the wide, long noodles called *pappardelle,* or with thinner, more readily available fettuccine.

### ◆ ◆ ◆

1   teaspoon plus 6 tablespoons extra-virgin olive oil
½   cup pine nuts

2   10-ounce packages ready-to-use spinach leaves
6   large garlic cloves (unpeeled)

12   ounces pappardelle or fettuccine

6   medium portobello mushrooms, stems trimmed

½   cup freshly grated Parmesan cheese (about 1½ ounces)
    Additional freshly grated Parmesan cheese

Heat 1 teaspoon oil in heavy medium skillet over medium heat. Add pine nuts and sauté until golden brown, about 7 minutes. Transfer pine nuts to small bowl.

Bring large pot of water to boil. Add spinach and cook until just wilted, about 20 seconds. Using tongs, transfer to bowl of ice water. Return water in pot to boil. Add garlic and boil 1 minute. Drain and cool. Peel garlic and slice thinly. Drain spinach. Squeeze out any excess moisture from spinach. *(Can be prepared 1 day ahead. Store pine nuts in airtight container at room temperature. Cover and refrigerate spinach and garlic separately.)*

Preheat broiler. Bring large pot of salted water to boil. Add pasta; boil until tender but still firm to bite, stirring occasionally.

Meanwhile, place mushrooms on baking sheet. Brush with 4 tablespoons oil. Sprinkle with salt and pepper. Broil mushrooms until lightly charred and tender, about 5 minutes per side. Transfer to cutting board. Cut each mushroom into 4 wedges. Set aside.

Drain pasta, reserving ½ cup cooking liquid. Heat 2 tablespoons oil in heavy large skillet over high heat. Add blanched garlic and sauté until golden, about 2 minutes. Add spinach and mushrooms; sauté until heated through, about 2 minutes. Add pasta and ½ cup cheese to spinach mixture; toss well. Add enough reserved pasta cooking liquid to moisten pasta, if necessary. Season with salt and pepper. Sprinkle with pine nuts. Serve, passing additional cheese separately.

2 TO 3 SERVINGS

# Taglierini with Roasted Asparagus, Tomatoes and Fennel

◆ ◆ ◆

3    tablespoons olive oil (preferably extra-virgin)
3    large garlic cloves, minced
5    small plum tomatoes (about ¾ pound), cored, halved lengthwise
½    pound asparagus, trimmed
2    small fresh fennel bulbs, trimmed, each cut into 8 wedges

½    pound taglierini or fettuccine
½    cup dry white wine
3    tablespoons minced fresh chives

Preheat oven to 500°F. Mix oil and garlic in small bowl. Arrange tomatoes, asparagus and fennel in single layer on large baking sheet with rim. Brush vegetables with 1 tablespoon garlic oil. Roast vegetables 5 minutes. Turn vegetables over; brush with additional 1 tablespoon garlic oil. Roast vegetables 5 minutes. Transfer asparagus to plate. Return tomatoes and fennel to oven; roast until softened and tinged with brown, about 10 minutes. Cut asparagus on diagonal into 1½-inch pieces.

Meanwhile, cook pasta in large pot of boiling salted water until just tender but still firm to bite. Drain pasta; return to pot. Add wine and 1 tablespoon garlic oil. Simmer over medium-low heat until liquid is slightly reduced, about 2 minutes.

Add roasted vegetables and 2 tablespoons chives to pasta. Toss to combine. Season to taste with salt and pepper. Transfer to large bowl. Sprinkle with remaining 1 tablespoon chives.

2 SERVINGS

◆ ◆ ◆

Sprinkle this colorful pasta dish with grated Parmesan cheese. Add a salad of bitter greens (like arugula, endive and radicchio) tossed with balsamic vinaigrette to make it a meal.

◆ ◆ ◆

# ITALIAN MENU FOR SIX

ANTIPASTO PLATTER

BREADSTICKS

PERCIATELLI WITH MEATBALLS
AND TOMATO-PORCINI SAUCE
(AT RIGHT; PICTURED OPPOSITE)

CHIANTI

CANNOLI

◆ ◆ ◆

# Perciatelli with Meatballs and Tomato-Porcini Sauce

◆ ◆ ◆

2    ounces dried porcini mushrooms*
2    cups hot water

SAUCE
3    tablespoons olive oil
1½   large onions, chopped
3    garlic cloves, chopped
1    tablespoon chopped fresh rosemary
¼    teaspoon dried crushed red pepper
1½   28-ounce cans crushed tomatoes with
     added puree (about 4½ cups )

MEATBALLS
4    slices English muffin toasting bread or white
     sandwich bread with crusts, torn into pieces
2    cups milk
¾    pound ground veal
¾    pound sweet Italian sausages, casings removed
¾    cup freshly grated Pecorino Romano cheese
3    eggs
1    tablespoon chopped fresh rosemary or 1 teaspoon dried
1    teaspoon salt
1    teaspoon freshly ground pepper

     Olive oil (for frying)

1¼   pounds perciatelli or spaghetti
     Additional freshly grated Pecorino Romano cheese

Place mushrooms in small bowl. Pour 2 cups hot water over; soak 30 minutes to soften. Remove mushrooms from water; squeeze liquid back into bowl. Chop mushrooms; reserve liquid.

FOR SAUCE: Heat oil in heavy large Dutch oven over medium-high heat. Add onions and garlic; sauté until tender, about 8 minutes. Add rosemary and crushed red pepper; stir 30 seconds. Add tomatoes and 1 cup chopped porcini. Pour in mushroom liquid, leaving sediment in bowl. Bring to boil. Reduce heat; simmer 20 minutes.

MEANWHILE, PREPARE MEATBALLS: Place bread in medium bowl. Pour milk over. Let stand until bread is very soft, about 15 minutes. Squeeze milk from bread; place bread in large bowl. Add veal, sausage, ¾ cup cheese, eggs, rosemary, salt, pepper and remaining porcini mushrooms. Using hands, blend veal mixture thoroughly.

Pour oil into heavy large skillet to depth of ¼ inch; heat over medium-high heat. Working in batches, form veal mixture into 1½-inch balls; add to skillet. Cook until brown, about 4 minutes. Using slotted spoon, transfer meatballs to paper towels; drain.

Add meatballs to tomato sauce. Simmer until sauce thickens and meatballs are just cooked through, about 10 minutes. Season to taste with salt and pepper. *(Can be prepared 1 day ahead. Cover and refrigerate. Before using, bring to simmer, stirring frequently.)*

Cook pasta in pot of boiling salted water until just tender but still firm to bite, stirring occasionally. Drain. Transfer to platter. Spoon sauce and meatballs over. Serve, passing additional cheese separately.

*\*Porcini are available at Italian markets, specialty foods stores and many supermarkets nationwide.*

6 SERVINGS

◆ ◆ ◆

This upmarket rendition of spaghetti and meatballs features *perciatelli,* long hollow pasta. The noodles are topped with a rich tomato and porcini mushroom sauce, and meatballs made with ground veal, Italian sausage and more porcini.

◆ ◆ ◆

# Presto Pesto Pizza

◆ ◆ ◆

1½   cups (packed) stemmed spinach leaves
½   cup (packed) fresh basil leaves (about 1 bunch)
1½   tablespoons oil from oil-packed sun-dried tomatoes or olive oil
1   large garlic clove

1   1-pound loaf frozen bread dough, thawed, room temperature
⅓   cup sliced drained oil-packed sun-dried tomatoes
2   cups (packed) grated mozzarella cheese (about 8 ounces)
1   cup grated Parmesan cheese

Blend first 4 ingredients in processor to coarse puree.

Preheat oven to 375°F. Spray 12-inch-diameter pizza pan with vegetable oil spray. Using moistened fingertips, press out dough on prepared pan to cover completely (if dough shrinks, let stand 5 minutes and press out again). Spread all of pesto over dough. Sprinkle with sun-dried tomatoes, then cheeses. Bake pizza until crust browns and cheeses melt, about 35 minutes.

4 TO 6 SERVINGS

◆ ◆ ◆

Just four ingredients to a quick, homemade pesto sauce. You can make it a day ahead, but be sure to press a piece of plastic wrap directly onto the surface of the pesto sauce to cover it, then refrigerate.

◆ ◆ ◆

# Grilled Scampi Pizza

◆ ◆ ◆

1   12-inch-diameter baked cheese pizza crust (such as Boboli)
4   tablespoons olive oil

¼   cup (½ stick) butter
1   large garlic clove, minced
10   ounces uncooked large shrimp, peeled, deveined
2   tablespoons dry white wine
1   tablespoon chopped fresh parsley

2   tomatoes (about 10 ounces), seeded, chopped
2   tablespoons chopped leek (white and pale green parts only)
2   tablespoons chopped green onion
1   tablespoon chopped fresh chives or green onion
¼   cup shredded sharp white cheddar cheese (about 2 ounces)
¼   cup shredded mozzarella cheese (about 2 ounces)
¼   cup shredded Parmesan cheese (about 1 ounce)

Prepare barbecue (medium heat) or preheat broiler. Brush top of crust with 1 tablespoon olive oil. Grill or broil crust, oiled side toward

heat, until brown spots appear, rotating frequently, about 1 minute. Brush bottom of crust with 1 tablespoon oil. Turn over and grill until beginning to crisp, about 1 minute. Transfer to baking sheet.

Preheat oven to 425°F. Melt butter in heavy large skillet over medium-high heat. Add garlic and stir 30 seconds. Add shrimp and sauté 1 minute. Add wine and parsley and cook until shrimp are almost cooked through, stirring occasionally, about 1 minute. Using slotted spoon, transfer shrimp to large bowl. Boil cooking liquid 30 seconds. Pour liquid over shrimp.

Mix tomatoes, leek, green onion and chives in medium bowl. Stir in remaining 2 tablespoons oil. Season with salt and pepper. Spoon vegetable mixture over crust. Top with shrimp and any juices from bowl. Sprinkle cheeses over.

Bake pizza until cheeses melt and shrimp are cooked through, about 7 minutes. Cut into wedges and serve.

4 SERVINGS

# Pizza with Sautéed Endive, Bacon and Fontina

◆ ◆ ◆

1    teaspoon olive oil
2    bacon slices, cut into ¼-inch pieces
6    medium-size heads Belgian endive, cut crosswise
     into ½-inch-thick slices (about 6 cups)
3    tablespoons freshly grated Parmesan cheese
1    teaspoon fresh lemon juice

1    12-inch-diameter baked cheese pizza crust
1½   cups grated Fontina cheese (about 5 ounces)

Heat olive oil in heavy large skillet over medium-high heat. Add bacon and sauté until crisp, about 3 minutes. Add endive and sauté until endive is golden, about 5 minutes. Reduce heat to medium and cook until endive is tender, about 5 minutes. Transfer to bowl. Stir in Parmesan and lemon juice. Season with salt and pepper.

Preheat oven to 500°F. Place crust on large baking sheet. Spoon topping over crust, leaving 1-inch border around edge. Sprinkle Fontina over topping. Bake pizza until cheese melts and crust is crisp, about 8 minutes. Cut pizza into wedges.

MAKES ONE 12-INCH PIZZA

## ENDIVE GOES MAINSTREAM

For many years Belgian endive, that elegant vegetable with the crisp, slightly bitter-tasting leaves, was a rarity on American tables. Its short season and elaborate growing process made it a hard-to-find and expensive treat. While the process—which involves forcing the shoots in the dark to keep them from turning green and bitter—hasn't changed, endive is more widely cultivated and so more easily available and affordable.

Belgian endive's true name is witloof chicory, and in Belgium it is known as *witloof*. In many parts of Europe (and occasionally in this country) it is called chicory, and its delicate white shoots, or *chicons*, are the most commonly used winter salad greens in France.

When choosing Belgian endive, look for firm, crisp heads with pale leaves (the paler the better). You will often find them wrapped in paper to protect them from exposure to sunlight, too much of which causes them to darken and turn bitter.

As for uses, endive lends itself to a variety of different techniques, and is as wonderful raw in a salad as it is cooked—in the pizza here for example.

◆ ◆ ◆

# ·On the Side·

A good side dish never draws attention away from the main course it accompanies. Rather it heightens the taste of the other dishes on the plate, making the entire dining experience even more satisfying. In this respect, any delicious vegetable, salad or bread recipe acts as a sort of secret weapon for the cook. Easily made, side dishes offer a big payback for the small amount of effort actually put into them.

The recipes in this chapter show just how easily a few simple twists can transform old favorites into dishes guaranteed to enliven any meal. Consider, for example, what sweet, rich-tasting parsnips and rutabagas do for humble spuds in the Potato and Root Vegetable Mash (page 148). Or look at how always-popular corn muffins gain exciting new flavor from the addition of green onions and sesame seeds (page 162).

The ease with which these subtle changes to the recipes can be accomplished is evident in recipes like Asian-Style Coleslaw (page 157), in which seasoned rice vinegar and ground ginger enliven the dressing; or Sesame Asparagus (page 141), a low-fat dish that gets a punch of flavor from just a half a teaspoon of oriental sesame oil. The effort it takes to make these side dishes is minimal; the results, nothing short of magical.

*Grilled Vegetables with Lemon, Thyme and Mustard Basting Sauce (page 140)*

# Apple-glazed Carrots

◆ ◆ ◆

◆ ◆ ◆

Baby carrots sautéed in apple juice and honey and garnished with minced green onion make a simple accompaniment for roast chicken.

◆ ◆ ◆

1     tablespoon butter
1     16-ounce package peeled trimmed baby carrots
1     cup unsweetened apple juice
1     teaspoon honey
1     tablespoon minced green onion tops

Melt butter in large nonstick skillet over medium-high heat. Add carrots and sauté until carrots begin to brown slightly, about 8 minutes. Add apple juice and honey and bring to boil. Reduce heat and simmer until carrots are tender and liquid is reduced to glaze, stirring occasionally, about 15 minutes. Season to taste with salt and pepper. Transfer to bowl. Sprinkle with green onion tops and serve.

4 SERVINGS

# Winter Squash and White Bean Chiles Rellenos

◆ ◆ ◆

1   2-pound acorn squash, halved, seeds and fibers discarded
2   tablespoons canned chicken broth
1   cup drained canned Great Northern beans

1   teaspoon corn oil
⅔   cup chopped onion
½   cup finely chopped peeled carrot
2   bacon slices, chopped
2   large garlic cloves, chopped
1   tablespoon chopped fresh thyme
¼   cup dry white wine

12   medium-large poblano chilies*

Preheat oven to 350°F. Place squash halves, cut side down, on baking sheet. Bake until just tender, about 30 minutes. Cool 1 squash half. Continue baking second squash half until very soft, about 30 minutes. Peel first squash half and cut into ¼-inch pieces. Scrape flesh from second squash half into processor; add chicken broth and puree until smooth. Season with salt and pepper. Combine squash puree, squash pieces and beans in large bowl.

Heat oil in heavy large skillet over medium heat. Add onion, carrot, bacon, garlic and thyme; sauté until onion is translucent, about 5 minutes. Add wine and simmer 2 minutes. Add squash mixture and stir to blend flavors. Cool. Season with salt and pepper. Chill.

Preheat oven to 350°F. Brush 15 x 10 x 2-inch glass baking dish with oil. Char chilies over gas flame or in broiler until blackened on all sides. Wrap in paper bag and let stand 10 minutes. Peel chilies, keeping chilies intact. Starting just below stem, cut lengthwise slit down 1 side of each chili, almost to tip, creating pocket. Remove seeds from each chili, leaving stem intact.

Fill each chili with ⅓ cup squash filling. Fold cut ends over to enclose filling. Arrange chilies in prepared baking dish. *(Can be made 6 hours ahead. Chill.)* Cover baking dish with foil. Bake chilies until hot, about 30 minutes. Serve.

*\*A fresh green chili, often called a* pasilla, *available at Latin American markets and many supermarkets.*

MAKES 12

## SQUASH FOR ALL SEASONS

While all squash are basically just gourds with seeds, we split them up into two varieties—summer and winter. Summer squash are picked when immature and firm, with edible skins and seeds; winter squash are picked when mature, with hard tough skins and large seeds. Though both kinds are now available year-round, they have become known by these seasonal distinctions.

The most popular summer squash are zucchini, dark green and oblong in shape; yellow crookneck, bright yellow with a bulbous base and narrow curved neck; and small, green, scalloped-edged patty pan squash.

There is an amazing variety of winter squash available: huge orange pumpkins; banana and Hubbard squash; small, individual-sized acorn squash. And then there is spaghetti squash, which began as a seed catalog novelty and has become a popular, no-calories foil for pasta sauces (once cooked, its flesh scrapes out of the shell to resemble linguine).

Although squash is an ancient food, new varieties are being introduced all the time. Look for Australian Blue, Honey Delight, Cushaw and Sweet Dumpling.

◆ ◆ ◆

# Grilled Vegetables with Lemon, Thyme and Mustard Basting Sauce

◆ ◆ ◆

◆ ◆ ◆

Grilling vegetables is surprisingly easy, and a great way to showcase the best of the season's produce (experiment with what's available in the markets). Conveniently, the vegetables can be thrown on the grill alongside whatever main course you're cooking, be it chicken, steak or fish.

◆ ◆ ◆

BASTING SAUCE

½   cup (1 stick) butter, diced
⅓   cup chopped shallots
¼   cup olive oil
3   tablespoons Dijon mustard
2   tablespoons fresh lemon juice
2   tablespoons chopped fresh thyme
1   tablespoon grated lemon peel

VEGETABLES

2   large ears fresh corn, husked, each cut crosswise into 4 pieces
1   small eggplant (about 1 pound), cut crosswise into ½-inch-thick rounds
1   large red onion, cut into ¾-inch-thick wedges
1   large red bell pepper, seeded, cut lengthwise into 6 strips
1   large yellow or green bell pepper, seeded, cut lengthwise into 6 strips
1   large zucchini, trimmed, quartered lengthwise
8   asparagus spears, trimmed
1   large carrot, peeled, cut on deep diagonal into ¼-inch-thick slices

Fresh herb sprigs
Lemon wedges

FOR BASTING SAUCE: Combine all ingredients in heavy medium saucepan. Whisk over medium heat until butter melts and sauce is well blended. Season to taste with salt and pepper.

FOR VEGETABLES: Arrange corn pieces, eggplant rounds and onion wedges in single layer on large baking sheet. Arrange bell pepper strips, zucchini spears, asparagus spears and carrot slices in single layer on another large baking sheet. Transfer ½ cup sauce to small saucepan and reserve for dipping. Brush both sides of vegetables lightly with some of remaining basting sauce.

Prepare barbecue (medium-high heat). Grill corn, eggplant and onion until tender and lightly charred, brushing occasionally with basting sauce and turning with tongs, about 6 minutes. Transfer to small platter as vegetables finish grilling.

Grill bell peppers, zucchini, asparagus and carrot until tender and lightly charred, brushing occasionally with basting sauce and turning with tongs, about 6 minutes. Transfer vegetables to same platter, arranging alongside other vegetables. Season all vegetables with salt and pepper. Garnish with fresh herb sprigs and lemon.

Place pan with reserved ½ cup sauce over low heat or at edge of barbecue and whisk sauce until warmed through. Transfer to small bowl. Serve vegetables, passing warm dipping sauce separately.

4 SERVINGS

# Sesame Asparagus

◆ ◆ ◆

1    pound fresh asparagus, ends trimmed,
     each stalk cut diagonally into thirds

½    teaspoon vegetable oil
½    cup finely diced red bell pepper
1    tablespoon low-sodium soy sauce
½    teaspoon oriental sesame oil
2    teaspoons sesame seeds, toasted

Cook asparagus in large pot of boiling salted water until crisp-tender, about 3 minutes. Drain. Rinse under cold water. Drain.

Heat vegetable oil in large nonstick skillet over medium-high heat. Add bell pepper and stir 1 minute. Add asparagus and sauté until heated through, about 2 minutes. Add soy sauce and sesame oil; toss until asparagus and bell pepper are coated, about 1 minute. Transfer to platter. Sprinkle with sesame seeds.

4 SERVINGS

# Cherry Tomatoes with Fresh Herbs

◆ ◆ ◆

1    12-ounce basket cherry tomatoes

1½   teaspoons olive oil
4    teaspoons chopped mixed fresh herbs (such as oregano and thyme)

Blanch tomatoes in medium pot of boiling water 30 seconds. Drain. Rinse under cold water. Drain. Peel tomatoes.

Heat oil in heavy skillet over high heat. Add herbs and tomatoes and stir until tomatoes are coated with herbs, about 1 minute. Remove from heat. Season to taste with salt and pepper. Serve.

4 SERVINGS

## A LITTLE LEFTOVER

It's good to experiment, to try out new ingredients when you cook. But what do you do with those bottles and jars of unusual sauces and seasonings after you've made that particular dish? Here are a few ideas for what to do when you have a little left of...

◆ Clam juice: Simmered with white wine, chopped onion and fresh parsley, clam juice makes a good substitute for fish stock.

◆ Fresh ginger: Finely minced ginger can add a spark of flavor to sweet marinades and barbecue sauces, glazed carrots, cooked sweet potatoes and squash. Ginger can be frozen for several months.

◆ Oriental sesame oil: Use this strong-flavored oil sparingly, with a milder oil in salad dressings, and with steamed or blanched vegetables.

◆ Pesto: This fresh basil-garlic sauce is wonderful over hot or cold pasta. Be creative and try it tossed in a warm potato salad, spread on small baked eggplant halves, sandwiches or pizza, tucked under the skin of roast chicken or blended with butter to serve with grilled fish.

◆ Rice vinegar: Sprinkle this light vinegar on fruit salad, steamed vegetables or shredded cabbage.

◆ ◆ ◆

# Vegetables Glazed with Balsamic Vinegar

◆ ◆ ◆

2   tablespoons olive oil
1   red bell pepper, cut into ¼-inch-wide strips
1   yellow bell pepper, cut into ¼-inch-wide strips
1   small onion, thinly sliced
2   zucchini, trimmed, cut crosswise into ½-inch-thick rounds
2   yellow summer squash, trimmed, cut crosswise
     into ½-inch-thick rounds
2   tablespoons balsamic vinegar

Heat oil in heavy large nonstick skillet over medium-high heat. Add peppers and onion. Sauté until beginning to soften, about 4 minutes. Add zucchini and yellow squash and sauté until tender, about 8 minutes. Add vinegar to skillet and boil until liquid is reduced to glaze and coats vegetables, about 2 minutes. Season to taste with salt and pepper. Transfer to platter and serve.

4 SERVINGS

◆ ◆ ◆

Chopped fresh mint enlivens this Thai-inspired stir-fry of carrots, red pepper, broccoli and red cabbage.

◆ ◆ ◆

# Five-Vegetable Stir-fry

◆ ◆ ◆

     Nonstick vegetable oil spray
2   teaspoons vegetable oil
4   medium carrots, peeled, cut diagonally into ¼-inch-thick slices
1   large onion, cut into 1-inch pieces
1   large red bell pepper, cut into
     1-inch triangular pieces
3   cups small broccoli florets
3   cups sliced red cabbage
½   cup canned low-salt chicken broth
3   tablespoons chopped fresh mint

Spray large nonstick skillet with vegetable oil spray. Heat 1 teaspoon oil in skillet over medium-high heat. Add carrots, onion and bell pepper. Sauté 6 minutes. Add 1 teaspoon oil, broccoli and cabbage. Add broth; stir-fry until cabbage wilts and vegetables are crisp-tender, about 8 minutes. Stir in chopped mint. Season vegetables with salt and pepper and serve.

6 SERVINGS

# Artichokes with Lemon-Garlic Butter

◆ ◆ ◆

4   fresh artichokes

¼   cup olive oil
6   large garlic cloves, minced
4   teaspoons minced fresh thyme or 2 teaspoons dried
½   cup fresh lemon juice
½   cup (1 stick) butter

Place steamer rack in large pot. Fill pot with enough water to come just to bottom of rack. Cut stems and top 1½ inches from artichokes. Cut away first outside row of artichoke leaves. Using scissors, cut off pointed tips of leaves. Arrange artichokes on rack. Bring water to boil. Cover pot; steam artichokes until knife pierces base easily, adding more water if necessary, about 45 minutes.

Meanwhile, heat oil in heavy medium saucepan over medium heat. Add garlic and thyme; cook 1 minute. Add lemon juice and butter; whisk until butter melts. Season with salt and pepper. Serve artichokes warm with seasoned butter.

4 SERVINGS

# Asparagus with
# Tomato-Bell Pepper Salsa

◆ ◆ ◆

¾   pound tomatoes
1   cup finely chopped yellow bell pepper
¾   cup chopped green onions
2   tablespoons chopped fresh cilantro
1   tablespoon fresh lime juice
1   tablespoon olive oil
1   garlic clove, minced

2   pounds fresh asparagus, tough ends trimmed

Blanch tomatoes in pot of boiling water for 20 seconds. Drain. Peel tomatoes. Cut in half; squeeze out seeds. Chop tomatoes. Place in medium bowl. Mix in bell pepper, green onions, cilantro, lime juice, oil and garlic. Season with salt and pepper.

Steam asparagus until crisp-tender, about 5 minutes. Transfer to bowl filled with ice water; cool. Drain and pat dry. *(Asparagus and salsa can be prepared 4 hours ahead. Cover separately and chill.)*

Arrange asparagus on platter. Top with salsa and serve.

8 SERVINGS

# Turkish Zucchini Pancakes

◆ ◆ ◆

1     pound zucchini, trimmed, coarsely grated

2     cups chopped green onions

4     eggs, beaten to blend

½     cup all purpose flour

⅓     cup chopped fresh dill or 1½ tablespoons dried dillweed

⅓     cup chopped fresh parsley

2     tablespoons chopped fresh tarragon or 2 teaspoons dried

½     teaspoon salt

½     teaspoon ground pepper

½     cup crumbled feta cheese (about 3 ounces)

⅔     cup chopped walnuts (about 3 ounces)

    Olive oil

Place zucchini in colander. Sprinkle zucchini with salt and let stand 30 minutes to drain. Squeeze zucchini between hands to remove liquid, then squeeze dry in several layers of paper towels.

Combine zucchini, chopped green onions, 4 eggs, flour, chopped dill, parsley, tarragon, ½ teaspoon salt and pepper in medium bowl. Mix well. Fold in crumbled feta cheese. *(Zucchini mixture can be prepared 3 hours ahead. Cover tightly and refrigerate. Stir to blend before continuing.)* Fold chopped walnuts into zucchini mixture.

Preheat oven to 300°F. Place baking sheet in oven. Cover bottom of large nonstick skillet with olive oil. Heat skillet over medium-high heat. Working in batches, drop zucchini mixture into skillet by heaping tablespoonfuls. Fry until pancakes are golden brown and cooked through, about 3 minutes per side. Transfer to baking sheet in oven to keep warm. Serve pancakes hot.

MAKES ABOUT 20

## VEGETABLE PANCAKES

Vegetable pancakes—grated vegetables pressed into patties and quickly fried in a hot, oiled pan—are a versatile and delicious side dish that is showing up on menus across the country. While Jewish latkes, or potato pancakes, are probably the best-known type, the new pancakes take this recipe beyond its humble origins with vegetables of all kinds.

Crisp vegetables, including carrots, winter squash and zucchini, work especially well. Root vegetables, such as turnips, parsnips, sweet potatoes and Jerusalem artichokes, also make delicious crunchy pancakes. Green onions, herbs, even kasha and tiny noodles can be added to the mix, which is bound together with egg, flour or breadcrumbs and sometimes a little whipping cream.

The secret to crisp vegetable pancakes is removing as much liquid as possible from the vegetables, particularly when using moisture-rich potatoes and zucchini. Spread the shredded vegetables on a kitchen towel, roll up and squeeze tightly. Then proceed with the recipe. As for serving ideas, applesauce or sour cream flavored with herbs make good accompaniments.

◆ ◆ ◆

# Fried Rice with Bok Choy, Green Onions and Mushrooms

◆ ◆ ◆

2  ounces dried shiitake mushrooms
4  cups hot water

4  baby bok choy

6  tablespoons vegetable oil
8  green onions, chopped
2  tablespoons minced peeled fresh ginger
4  cups cooked long-grain white rice, cold (about 1½ cups raw)

Place mushrooms in medium bowl. Pour 4 cups hot water over; let stand 30 minutes to soften. Drain. Cut off mushroom stems and discard. Thinly slice mushroom caps. Set aside.

Blanch bok choy in medium saucepan of boiling water 15 seconds. Drain and cool. Cut each bok choy lengthwise in half. Cut crosswise into 1-inch pieces. Drain on paper towels. Set aside.

Heat oil in wok or heavy large skillet over high heat. Add green onions and ginger and stir-fry until fragrant, about 1 minute. Add mushrooms and stir-fry until tender, about 2 minutes. Add rice; stir-fry until hot, about 4 minutes. Add bok choy; stir-fry 30 seconds. Season with salt. Serve immediately.

4 SERVINGS

# Mashed Potatoes and Celery Root with Blue Cheese

◆ ◆ ◆

4  large russet potatoes, peeled, cut into 1½-inch pieces
1  celery root, peeled, cut into 1-inch pieces
⅓  pound Maytag blue cheese, crumbled
2  tablespoons (¼ stick) butter
⅓  cup milk

Cook vegetables in saucepan of boiling salted water until tender, about 20 minutes. Drain. Transfer to heavy-duty mixer fitted with whisk attachment. Beat potatoes and celery root until mashed. Add cheese and butter; beat until butter melts. Mix in milk. Season with salt and pepper. Serve immediately.

6 SERVINGS

# Stilton Potato Gratin

### ◆ ◆ ◆

2½  pounds russet potatoes (about 5 medium), peeled, thinly sliced
8    ounces Stilton cheese or other blue cheese, crumbled
1⅓  cups canned low-salt chicken broth
2    tablespoons (¼ stick) butter, cut into small pieces

Preheat oven to 350°F. Butter 13 x 9 x 2-inch glass baking dish. Arrange ⅓ of potato slices in bottom of pan, overlapping slightly. Sprinkle half of cheese over potatoes. Sprinkle with salt and pepper. Arrange half of remaining potatoes slices over cheese. Pour broth over. Sprinkle with salt and pepper. Dot top with butter.

Bake potatoes until top is golden brown, potatoes are tender and liquid thickens, tilting pan occasionally to baste top layer of potatoes with broth mixture, about 1 hour 40 minutes.

Transfer pan to rack and let stand 5 minutes. Serve hot.

6 SERVINGS

# Chive Jive New Potatoes

### ◆ ◆ ◆

3    cups canned low-salt chicken broth
1½  pounds small red-skinned potatoes, rinsed
2    bay leaves
¼   cup dry white wine

½   cup chopped fresh chives or green onions

Combine broth, potatoes and bay leaves in heavy large saucepan. Bring to boil. Reduce heat, cover partially and simmer until potatoes are tender, about 15 minutes. Using slotted spoon, transfer potatoes to large bowl. Add wine to broth and boil until reduced to ⅓ cup, about 12 minutes. Discard bay leaves. Return potatoes to pot. *(Can be prepared 1 day ahead. Cover and refrigerate.)*

Stir potatoes over medium heat until heated through, about 4 minutes. Stir in chives. Season to taste with salt and pepper. Transfer potatoes to bowl and serve.

4 SERVINGS

## THE CHEESE KING

In England, a land noted for its lush dairylands, cheese is one of its most beloved products. Certainly Stilton, known as the king of British cheeses, has ardent admirers.

The noble Stilton is produced only in the counties of Derbyshire, Leicestershire and Nottingham north of London. A firm, creamy cheese with blue-green veins, it is usually made in 16-pound rounds, but is also available in five-pound wheels and in decorative half-pound jars. Whether you buy it by the wheel or by the slice, a perfect Stilton is creamy ivory in color with a concentration of blue veins near the center, changing to a brownish yellow color near the crust.

In days gone by, diners would scoop out helpings with a spoon, but cheese experts now suggest carefully slicing off the top of a round of Stilton, then cutting thin, level wedges across the surface. Its delicate flavor makes the cheese an ideal companion for the traditional glass of Port, slices of apple or pear or a chunk of crusty bread. Stilton is also delicious crumbled in a salad, grilled in a sandwich or added to a savory tart or gratin.

### ◆ ◆ ◆

## ROOT VEGETABLES: BEYOND CARROTS

Many common root vegetables— potatoes, onions and carrots, included—have become year-round standbys in the kitchen. Other, less common kinds are beginning to show up more often in everday cooking. Here are some to look for:

◆ Celeriac: A knobbly cousin of celery, celeriac (or celery root) has a celery flavor with a hint of sweetness and a texture similar to that of a potato.

◆ Parsnip: This creamy-colored root vegetable is high in protein and has a sweet, nutty flavor.

◆ Rutabaga: A cross between a cabbage and a turnip, the large, yellow-orange rutabaga has a sweet yet strong and earthy flavor. Peel off the thick brown skin to get to the dense, moist, nutritious interior.

◆ Sweet potato: There are two types of sweet potato—the orange, moist-fleshed "yam" (which isn't really a yam, however, as the true yam is a different vegetable alto- gether, and available only in Latin markets), and the smaller, yellow, dry-fleshed sweet potato.

◆ Turnip: Best when harvested young, the turnip is small and ten- der, with a purple top and firm white flesh. Be sure to peel it before using, as the skin is bitter.

◆ ◆ ◆

# Potato and Root Vegetable Mash

◆ ◆ ◆

3  large russet potatoes (about 2½ pounds), peeled, cut into 2-inch pieces
3  rutabagas (about 1¾ pounds), peeled, halved, thinly sliced
6  small parsnips (about 14 ounces), peeled, cut into 1-inch pieces

3  tablespoons olive oil

Bring large pot of salted water to boil. Add potatoes, rutabagas and parsnips. Boil until tender, about 30 minutes. Drain.

Return vegetables to same pot. Mash until coarse puree forms. Mix in 3 tablespoons olive oil. Season vegetables to taste with salt and pepper. *(Vegetable mash can be prepared 2 hours ahead. Let stand at room temperature. Rewarm over low heat, stirring fre- quently.)* Transfer vegetables to bowl and serve.

6 SERVINGS

# Grilled Potato and Onion Packages

◆ ◆ ◆

⅔  cup olive oil
1  tablespoon Dijon mustard
2  tablespoons chopped fresh thyme or 1 tablespoon dried
1  teaspoon salt
1  teaspoon ground black pepper

2  pounds white-skinned potatoes (about 4 large), peeled, sliced ¼ inch thick
2  large red onions, halved, sliced ½ inch thick
   Nonstick vegetable oil spray

   Fresh thyme sprigs (optional)

Combine oil, mustard, thyme, salt and pepper in large bowl. Whisk to blend well. *(Can be prepared 6 hours ahead. Cover and let stand at room temperature.)*

Prepare barbecue (medium-high heat). Add potatoes and onions to mustard oil. Toss to coat. Set six 18 x 9-inch sheets of heavy-duty aluminum foil on work surface. Spray foil with nonstick vegetable oil spray. Divide vegetables among foil sheets, placing in center of left half of each. Sprinkle with salt and pepper. Fold right half of foil over vegetables. Fold edges together to seal tightly.

Place packages on grill. Grill until potatoes are tender and golden brown, turning occasionally, about 25 minutes. Remove packages from grill. Slit top of foil and fold back. Garnish potatoes with thyme sprigs, if desired.

6 SERVINGS

# Mixed Grains Provençale

◆ ◆ ◆

5 cups water
¾ cup long-grain brown rice
¾ cup pearl barley

1 tablespoon vegetable oil
2 medium zucchini, trimmed, diced
1 tablespoon minced garlic
6 large plum tomatoes, cored, seeded, diced
1 cup fresh corn kernels or frozen, thawed
½ cup canned low-salt chicken broth
½ cup chopped fresh basil
¼ cup chopped fresh Italian parsley
2 tablespoons pine nuts, toasted

Combine 5 cups water and brown rice in heavy medium saucepan. Bring to boil. Reduce heat to medium-low; cover and simmer 10 minutes. Add barley; cover and simmer until rice and barley are tender, about 25 minutes. Drain and cool. *(Can be made 1 day ahead; cover and chill.)*

Heat oil in large nonstick skillet over medium-high heat. Add zucchini and garlic; sauté until beginning to brown, about 3 minutes. Mix in tomatoes and corn. Mix in cooked grains, broth, basil and parsley. Simmer until liquid is absorbed, about 5 minutes. Season with salt and pepper. Transfer to bowl. Sprinkle with pine nuts.

8 SERVINGS

◆ ◆ ◆

A perfect idea for a cookout. And if there are kids around, you might let them in on the fun by having them make the foil packages. To check the potatoes for doneness, carefully remove one package from the grill, and unfold the foil.

◆ ◆ ◆

## AN ORCHARD OF PEARS

Here's a guide to the different pear varieties found in most markets.

*Anjou.* Available October through June. Large and egg-shaped with thin green-yellow skin and juicy medium-grain to coarse texture. Excellent for cooking and eating fresh.

*Bartlett.* Available July through December. Bell-shaped fruit with light green-yellow skin; sweet juicy flesh. When firm but ripe, Bartlett pears are good for baking, poaching, and home canning.

*Bosc.* Available late August through May. Distinctive dull russet-gold skin and a slender form. Creamy flesh and nutty flavor make this one ideal for baking and eating fresh.

*Comice.* Available August through March. Predominantly green when under-ripe; medium yellow with areas of light green when ripe. With its fine texture, Comice is nice for use in salads. Delicious eaten fresh.

*Seckel.* Available August through January. A thick-skinned, small, juicy pear. Medium-green to russet-colored skin. Its firm, fine-grain texture and sweet-spicy flavor make it good for eating fresh, poaching, and canning.

# ◆ SALADS ◆

# Pear Salad with Feta, Bacon, Hazelnuts and Shallot Vinaigrette

◆ ◆ ◆

| | |
|---|---|
| 1 | tablespoon plus ½ cup olive oil |
| ¾ | cup thinly sliced shallots |
| 8 | bacon slices |
| 5 | tablespoons Sherry wine vinegar |
| 8 | cups loosely packed and trimmed watercress (about 2 large bunches) |
| 2 | heads Belgian endive, trimmed, sliced crosswise |
| 3 | ripe pears, halved, cored, thinly sliced |
| ¾ | cup crumbled feta cheese |
| ⅓ | cup husked toasted hazelnuts, coarsely chopped |

Heat 1 tablespoon oil in large nonstick skillet over medium heat. Add shallots; sauté until tender and golden, about 8 minutes. Transfer to small bowl; cool. Cook bacon in same skillet until crisp. Transfer to paper towels; drain. Crumble bacon into small pieces. Whisk vinegar and remaining ½ cup oil in medium bowl to blend. Stir in shallots. Season dressing generously with salt and pepper.

Combine watercress, endive and pears in large bowl. Pour dressing over salad and toss to coat. Sprinkle with feta cheese, hazelnuts and bacon and serve.

8 SERVINGS

# Black Bean and Bell Pepper Salad

◆ ◆ ◆

VINAIGRETTE

½    cup water

16   dates (about 4 ounces), pitted, finely chopped

½    cup fresh lime juice
6    tablespoons extra-virgin olive oil
2    tablespoons dried oregano
4    teaspoons honey
4    teaspoons ground cumin
4    teaspoons ground coriander

SALAD

4    15-ounce cans black beans, rinsed, drained
½    cup chopped red bell pepper
½    cup chopped yellow bell pepper
½    cup chopped green bell pepper
½    cup chopped red onion
½    cup chopped fresh parsley

FOR VINAIGRETTE: Boil water and dates in small saucepan 2 minutes. Remove from heat; cover and let stand 1 hour to soften.

Transfer date mixture to blender. Add lime juice, oil, oregano, honey, cumin and coriander and puree. Season to taste with salt and pepper. *(Can be made 1 day ahead. Cover and refrigerate. Let stand 1 hour at room temperature before using.)*

FOR SALAD: Combine black beans, chopped bell peppers, onion and parsley in large bowl. Toss salad with enough vinaigrette to coat. Season with salt and pepper. *(Can be made 6 hours ahead. Let salad stand at room temperature until ready to serve.)*

8 SERVINGS

◆ ◆ ◆

Black beans teamed with the red, yellow and green bell peppers provide an interesting contrast in color and texture. And the unusual dressing combines dates (for sweetness) and lime juice (for tang), with spice added in the form of cumin and coriander.

◆ ◆ ◆

# Broccoli and Cherry Tomato Salad

◆ ◆ ◆

4     cups broccoli florets
1     1-pint basket cherry tomatoes, halved
2     teaspoons Dijon mustard
3     tablespoons seasoned rice vinegar*
1     tablespoon olive oil
2     tablespoons chopped fresh oregano or 2 teaspoons dried

Steam broccoli until just crisp-tender, about 3 minutes. Transfer to large bowl and cool. Add tomatoes. Place mustard in small bowl. Gradually whisk in vinegar, then oil. Mix in oregano. Add to salad and toss to coat. Season with salt and pepper. *(Can be made 6 hours ahead. Cover; refrigerate.)*

*\*Also known as sushi vinegar; available at Asian markets and in the Asian section of many supermarkets.*

6 SERVINGS

# Tunisian Carrot Salad

◆ ◆ ◆

1½   pounds carrots, peeled, cut into ¼-inch-thick rounds

3     tablespoons olive oil
2¼   teaspoons ground cumin
¼     teaspoon cayenne pepper
½     cup water
3     tablespoons white wine vinegar
⅓     cup chopped fresh cilantro

Cook carrots in medium saucepan of boiling salted water until crisp-tender, about 8 minutes. Drain well.

Stir oil, cumin and cayenne in heavy large skillet over medium heat until aromatic, about 30 seconds. Add carrots, then ½ cup water and vinegar. Simmer over medium heat until liquid is absorbed, stirring often, about 5 minutes. Season with salt and pepper. Remove from heat. Cool. Mix in cilantro. *(Can be made 1 day ahead. Cover and chill. Bring to room temperature before serving.)*

4 SERVINGS

◆ ◆ ◆

It's been a long time since *salad* meant a wedge of iceberg with Thousand Island dressing. As the definition of the term becomes broader, salads get more and more creative—like this exotically spiced carrot version without a shred of lettuce.

◆ ◆ ◆

# Caesar Salad with
# Portobello Mushrooms

◆ ◆ ◆

| | |
|---|---|
| 9 | drained canned anchovy fillets, minced |
| 3 | tablespoons fresh lemon juice |
| 1½ | tablespoons Dijon mustard |
| 2 | garlic cloves, minced |
| ½ | cup plus 3 tablespoons olive oil |
| 1 | medium head romaine lettuce, cut into bite-size pieces |
| 1 | large head radicchio, cut into bite-size pieces |
| 4 | garlic cloves, flattened, peeled |
| 3 | large portobello mushrooms (about ¾ pound), stems discarded, caps sliced crosswise into ⅜-inch-thick strips |
| ¼ | cup chopped fresh parsley |
| 1⅓ | cups coarsely grated Asiago or Parmesan cheese (about 4 ounces) |

Combine minced anchovy fillets, fresh lemon juice, Dijon mustard and minced garlic in small bowl. Gradually whisk in ½ cup olive oil. Combine romaine lettuce and radicchio in large bowl.

Heat remaining 3 tablespoons oil in heavy large skillet over medium heat. Add flattened garlic to skillet and cook until brown, about 4 minutes. Discard garlic. Increase heat to medium-high. Add mushrooms and sauté until brown, 4 minutes per side. Remove from heat. Season with salt and pepper. Sprinkle with parsley.

Add dressing to salad and toss to coat. Mix in cheese. Season salad to taste with salt and pepper. Divide salad among plates. Top with mushrooms and serve immediately.

6 SERVINGS

◆ ◆ ◆

In the world of food, the giant portobello mushroom—whether grilled, broiled or sautéed—was one of last year's signature ingredients. Caesar salad, which was *Bon Appetit*'s "food of the year" in the January 1994 issue, has only continued to gain popularity. Here, the two are combined in a real crowd-pleaser.

◆ ◆ ◆

# Mango, Jicama and Corn Salad

◆ ◆ ◆

6    ears fresh corn
6    small mangoes, peeled, pitted, coarsely chopped
2    pounds jicama, peeled, chopped
1    cup chopped red onion
½    cup chopped fresh cilantro
½    cup fresh lime juice

Cook corn in pot of boiling salted water 2 minutes. Drain and cool corn. Cut off enough kernels to measure 4 cups (reserve remaining corn for another use). Place corn in medium bowl. Add mangoes, jicama, red onion, cilantro and lime juice. Toss to combine. Season to taste with salt and pepper. Cover and refrigerate until cold. *(Can be prepared 3 hours ahead. Keep refrigerated.)* Serve cold.

8 SERVINGS

# Mixed Greens and Walnuts with Buttermilk Dressing

◆ ◆ ◆

1    tablespoon fresh lime juice
1    tablespoon balsamic vinegar
½    teaspoon Dijon mustard
⅓    cup low-fat buttermilk
1    tablespoon walnut oil or olive oil

8    ounces mixed baby greens
¼    cup walnut pieces, toasted
3    tablespoons chopped fresh parsley

Whisk lime juice, vinegar and mustard in medium bowl to blend. Gradually whisk in buttermilk, then oil. Season with salt and pepper. *(Can be prepared 6 hours ahead. Cover and chill.)*

Combine greens, walnuts and parsley in large bowl. Toss with enough dressing to coat. Season with salt and pepper and serve.

6 SERVINGS

◆ ◆ ◆

This delicious all-purpose buttermilk dressing works with almost any mix of greens, its special tang enlivening the everyday salad.

◆ ◆ ◆

# Sweet Orange, Mint and Olive Salad

◆ ◆ ◆

½   teaspoon coriander seeds
½   teaspoon cumin seeds
⅓   cup brine-cured black olives (such as Kalamata), pitted
¼   cup fresh orange juice
¼   cup chopped fresh mint
3   green onions, chopped
¼   teaspoon sugar

5   medium navel oranges, peel and white pith removed

Romaine lettuce leaves

Toast coriander seeds and cumin seeds in medium skillet over medium heat just until fragrant, about 2 minutes. Transfer spices to a heavy small plastic bag. Using flat side of knife, press on spices to crush coarsely. Transfer spices to large bowl. Add olives, orange juice, mint, green onions and sugar; stir to blend.

Cut oranges into ⅓-inch-thick rounds. Add orange rounds to olive mixture and stir gently to coat. Season to taste with salt and pepper. *(Can be prepared 1 hour ahead. Cover and refrigerate.)*

Arrange lettuce leaves on platter. Arrange orange mixture decoratively atop lettuce and serve.

6 SERVINGS

# Potato-Cauliflower Salad with Marinated Red Onions

◆ ◆ ◆

9    tablespoons olive oil
5    tablespoons prepared cream-style white horseradish
3    tablespoons white wine vinegar
1    8-ounce red onion, peeled, halved, thinly sliced

3    cups small cauliflower florets (about 10 ounces)
2    pounds small red-skinned potatoes (about 20)

½    cup (about 2 ounces) crumbled blue cheese

Whisk olive oil, horseradish and white wine vinegar in medium bowl to blend. Mix in onion. Season generously with salt and pepper. Let stand 2 hours at room temperature or cover and refrigerate up to 1 day, tossing occasionally.

Steam cauliflower until just tender, about 4 minutes. Cool 5 minutes, then add to red onion mixture. Steam potatoes until just tender, about 20 minutes. Cool 15 minutes.

Slice potatoes thickly. Place in large bowl. Add onion mixture to potatoes. Add blue cheese; toss gently to blend. Season to taste with salt and pepper. *(Can be prepared 2 hours ahead. Cover and let stand at room temperature.)*

6 SERVINGS

◆ ◆ ◆

Blue cheese and horseradish make this take on classic potato salad extra special. Try it with grilled steaks or burgers for a great casual meal.

◆ ◆ ◆

# Watercress, Melon and Almond Salad

◆ ◆ ◆

3   tablespoons fresh lime juice
1   teaspoon sugar
1   teaspoon minced peeled fresh ginger
¼   cup vegetable oil
2   large bunches watercress (about 10 ounces total), tough ends trimmed, sprigs torn in half
2½  cups ½-inch pieces watermelon
2½  cups ½-inch pieces cantaloupe
⅓   cup sliced almonds, toasted

Whisk lime juice, sugar and ginger in large bowl to blend. Gradually whisk in oil. Season dressing with salt and pepper. Add watercress, watermelon and cantaloupe to dressing and toss to coat. Transfer salad to plates. Sprinkle with sliced almonds.

4 SERVINGS

# Asian-Style Coleslaw

◆ ◆ ◆

2½  cups thinly sliced cabbage
½   head radicchio, thinly sliced
1   large carrot, peeled, cut into matchstick-size strips
3   ounces snow peas, stringed, thinly sliced lengthwise

4   teaspoons seasoned rice vinegar
1   teaspoon dried mustard
1   teaspoon ground ginger
2   tablespoons vegetable oil
1   tablespoon oriental sesame oil
2   teaspoons soy sauce

Combine first 4 ingredients in large bowl. *(Can be prepared 6 hours ahead. Cover and refrigerate.)*
Combine vinegar, mustard and ginger in small bowl; stir until mustard and ginger dissolve. Gradually mix in both oils and soy sauce. Pour dressing over salad; toss to blend. Season with salt.

4 SERVINGS

◆ ◆ ◆

Thinly sliced radicchio, carrot and snow peas—plus the traditional cabbage—make this take on coleslaw colorful and tasty. Rice vinegar, sesame oil and ground ginger add Asian nuances to the dressing.

◆ ◆ ◆

## NUTRITIOUS NUTS

Many of us have been avoiding nuts because of their high-fat reputation. But the truth of the matter is that, although nuts are at least 50 percent fat, the oils they contain are good for you and may actually work to keep you healthy, much as is the case with olive oil.

Many nuts are high in essential vitamins and minerals, such as thiamin, niacin, magnesium and phosphorus. Almonds, for instance, are a good source of protein and vitamin E, while chestnuts (which contain only one to three percent fat) are very high in vitamin C. Walnuts have large amounts of omega-3 fatty acids, which fight heart disease.

In addition to all these nutritional benefits, nuts contribute terrific flavor and crunch to many of the foods we eat. Beyond their typical use in cookies and breads, nuts are also great sprinkled in a salad, added to stuffings or rice dishes, and as a topping for casseroles and desserts. Toasting them brings out their flavor.

Because of their high fat content, nuts last longer and taste better when stored in a tightly sealed container or bag in the freezer.

◆ ◆ ◆

# Green Bean Salad with Cilantro and Soy-glazed Almonds

◆ ◆ ◆

¼ cup whole almonds (about 1½ ounces)
4 teaspoons low-sodium soy sauce

1 pound green beans, trimmed, cut into 1-inch pieces

2 tablespoons rice vinegar
1 tablespoon vegetable oil
1 large garlic clove, pressed
1 teaspoon minced peeled fresh ginger
2 tablespoons thinly sliced green onions
⅓ cup fresh cilantro leaves

Place almonds in small nonstick skillet. Stir over medium heat until almonds are lightly toasted, about 5 minutes. Increase heat to medium-high. Add 3 teaspoons soy sauce and stir until soy sauce evaporates and coats almonds, about 1 minute. Transfer to plate and cool. Chop almonds.

Cook beans in large pot of boiling salted water until just tender, about 5 minutes. Drain. Rinse beans under cold water. Drain well. *(Almonds and beans can be prepared 6 hours ahead. Cover almonds and store at room temperature. Cover and refrigerate beans; bring to room temperature before continuing.)*

Whisk vinegar, oil, garlic, ginger and remaining 1 teaspoon soy sauce in large bowl to blend. Add beans and toss to coat. Season to taste with salt and pepper. Sprinkle green onions, cilantro and almonds over salad and serve.

4 SERVINGS

# Modern Waldorf Salad

◆ ◆ ◆

¼  cup low-fat mayonnaise

¼  cup nonfat plain yogurt

2  tablespoons orange juice

2  teaspoons grated orange peel

½  teaspoon Cajun seasoning*

1  head romaine lettuce

1  grapefruit

1  firm but ripe Bosc pear, peeled, cored, diced

1  tart green apple (such as Pippin), peeled, cored, diced

1  cup seedless grapes, halved

⅓  cup chopped dates

¼  cup pine nuts, toasted

The traditional apple, walnut and celery salad is updated with a yogurt and low-fat mayonnaise citrus dressing, pine nuts and Cajun seasoning.

◆ ◆ ◆

Mix mayonnaise, yogurt, orange juice, orange peel and Cajun seasoning in small bowl to blend. *(Dressing can be prepared 1 day ahead. Cover and refrigerate.)*

Line large bowl with large outer leaves of lettuce. Chop enough remaining leaves into bite-size pieces to measure 6 cups (reserve remaining lettuce for another use). Place chopped lettuce in another large bowl. Using small sharp knife, cut off peel and white pith from grapefruit. Cut between membranes to release grapefruit segments. Cut segments in half. Place in bowl with chopped lettuce. Add diced pear, diced apple, halved grapes and chopped dates. Add dressing to salad and toss to coat.

Transfer salad to leaf-lined bowl. Sprinkle salad with pine nuts.

*Available in the spice section of most supermarkets.*

6 SERVINGS

# Spinach Salad with Grilled Red Onions and Tahini Vinaigrette

◆ ◆ ◆

Tahini, a creamy sesame seed paste available at Middle Eastern markets, natural foods stores and some supermarkets, adds a nice twist to the dressing for this salad.

◆ ◆ ◆

VINAIGRETTE

½   cup water
¼   cup white wine vinegar
3   tablespoons tahini (sesame seed paste)*
2   tablespoons coarse-grained mustard
1   teaspoon honey
1   small garlic clove, minced
¾   cup vegetable oil

SALAD

2   large red onions

12  cups (packed) baby spinach, trimmed
10  large radicchio leaves

FOR VINAIGRETTE: Combine all ingredients except oil in blender and blend well. Gradually blend in oil. Season with salt and pepper.

FOR SALAD: Cut onions lengthwise into ½-inch-thick wedges, leaving root ends intact. Place onions in 15 x 10-inch glass baking dish. Pour 1 cup vinaigrette over onions, coating evenly. Let marinate 3 hours. Refrigerate remaining dressing. *(Can be made 1 day ahead. Refrigerate onions.)*

Prepare barbecue (medium-high heat) or preheat broiler. Sprinkle onions with salt and pepper. Grill or broil onions until golden, turning occasionally, about 12 minutes. *(Can be made 6 hours ahead. Let stand at room temperature.)*

Place spinach in large bowl. Toss with enough vinaigrette to coat. Season with salt and pepper. Fill radicchio leaves with spinach. Top with grilled onions. Pass remaining dressing separately.

*\*Tahini (sesame seed paste) is available at Middle Eastern and natural foods stores and some supermarkets.*

10 SERVINGS

# Two-Bean Salad with Balsamic Vinaigrette

◆ ◆ ◆

1    14- to 16-ounce can garbanzo beans (chickpeas), rinsed, drained
1    14- to 16-ounce can black beans, rinsed, drained
⅔    cup chopped red onion
¼    cup chopped fresh parsley
3    tablespoons olive oil
2    tablespoons balsamic vinegar or red wine vinegar
3    garlic cloves, finely chopped

Combine all ingredients in medium bowl. Toss to blend well. Season with salt and pepper. *(Can be prepared 1 day ahead. Cover and chill. Let stand at room temperature 30 minutes before serving.)*

4 TO 6 SERVINGS

# Warm Lentil Salad with Jicama

◆ ◆ ◆

2    cups (about 13 ounces) lentils

¼    cup olive oil
1    tablespoon chopped garlic
2½   cups diced seeded tomatoes
2    cups diced peeled jicama
1½   cups chopped green onions
1    cup corn kernels (from 1 large ear)
¼    cup plus 2 tablespoons thinly sliced fresh basil
3    tablespoons fresh lemon juice

Cook lentils in large pot of boiling water until just tender, about 20 minutes. Drain thoroughly.

Heat oil in large Dutch oven over medium heat. Add garlic; sauté until golden, about 2 minutes. Mix in 2 cups tomatoes, jicama, onions, corn, ¼ cup basil and lemon juice. Add lentils; stir until mixture is just heated through, about 6 minutes. Season generously with salt and pepper. *(Can be made 3 hours ahead. Let stand at room temperature. Rewarm over medium heat.)* Stir in 2 tablespoons basil. Mound salad in large serving bowl. Sprinkle ½ cup diced tomatoes around edge of salad and serve.

6 TO 8 SERVINGS

# Green Onion and Sesame Corn Muffins

◆ ◆ ◆

6 tablespoons (¾ stick) butter
1 bunch green onions, thinly sliced

1 cup yellow cornmeal
1 cup all purpose flour
⅓ cup sugar
¼ cup sesame seeds, toasted
2 teaspoons baking powder
1½ teaspoons salt
½ teaspoon baking soda
1 cup buttermilk
1 egg, beaten to blend

Additional sesame seeds, untoasted

Preheat oven to 425°F. Line 12 muffin cups with foil muffin liners. Melt 2 tablespoons butter in heavy small skillet over medium heat. Add green onions and sauté until beginning to soften, about 1 minute. Add remaining 4 tablespoons butter and stir until just melted. Remove onion mixture from heat.

Mix cornmeal, flour, sugar, ¼ cup toasted sesame seeds, baking powder, salt and baking soda in large bowl. Make well in center. Add buttermilk, beaten egg and onion mixture to well in center. Mix into dry ingredients.

Divide batter among prepared muffin cups. Sprinkle with additional sesame seeds. Bake until golden and firm to touch, about 20 minutes. Transfer to rack. Serve warm or at room temperature.

MAKES 12

◆ ◆ ◆

## SOUP AND BREAD SUPPER FOR SIX

CLASSIC CLAM CHOWDER
(PAGE 26)

PICKLED BEET, SHREDDED CARROT AND LETTUCE SALAD

GREEN ONION AND SESAME CORN MUFFINS
(AT RIGHT)

BEER OR LEMONADE

APPLE PIE WITH CHEDDAR CHEESE

◆ ◆ ◆

# Currant Scones

◆ ◆ ◆

3   cups all purpose flour
3   tablespoons sugar
1   teaspoon baking soda
½   teaspoon salt
6   tablespoons (¾ stick) chilled unsalted butter, cut into pieces
⅓   cup dried currants
1   egg, beaten to blend
¾   cup plus 3 tablespoons (about) buttermilk

1   tablespoon milk
    Butter or whipped cream
    Assorted jams

Preheat oven to 425°F. Lightly flour large baking sheet. Mix 3 cups flour, sugar, baking soda and salt in large bowl. Add butter and rub in with fingertips until mixture resembles fine meal. Mix in currants. Mix in egg and enough buttermilk to form soft dough. Turn dough out onto floured surface. Pat dough into ¾-inch-thick round. Cut out rounds, using 2½-inch round cookie cutter. Gather scraps, press together and pat out to ¾-inch-thick round. Cut out rounds.

Transfer scones to prepared baking sheet. Brush tops with milk. Bake until scones are golden brown and cooked through, about 18 minutes. Serve warm with butter or whipped cream and jam.

MAKES ABOUT 15

# Grilled Bread with Olive Oil

◆ ◆ ◆

1   French bread baguette, cut into 1-inch diagonal slices
¼   cup extra-virgin olive oil

Prepare barbecue (medium-high heat). Brush both sides of bread generously with oil; season with salt and pepper. Grill until golden, about 1 minute per side.

6 SERVINGS

◆ ◆ ◆

In this recipe, for a change of pace from plain olive oil, try any of the oils currently on the market that are flavored with garlic, basil or rosemary.

◆ ◆ ◆

# Olive Bread

1   cup warm water (105°F to 115°F)
1   tablespoon sugar
1   teaspoon all purpose flour
2   envelopes dry yeast

6   tablespoons olive oil
1   teaspoon salt
½   cup rye flour
½   cup whole wheat flour
2¼  cups (about) bread flour

¾   cup coarsely chopped pitted brine-cured black olives
    (such as Kalamata)

Combine water, sugar and all purpose flour in large bowl. Sprinkle yeast over. Stir to blend. Cover and let stand until very spongy, about 15 minutes.

Whisk oil and salt into yeast mixture. Stir in rye flour, whole wheat flour, then 2 cups bread flour. Turn out onto floured surface. Knead until smooth and silky, adding more bread flour if dough is sticky to touch, about 10 minutes.

Oil clean large bowl. Add dough and turn to coat. Cover bowl with plastic wrap and towel. Let dough rise in warm draft-free area until doubled in volume, about 45 minutes.

Turn dough out onto floured board; knead gently to deflate. Sprinkle olives over; knead to incorporate (dough will become slightly moist and sticky). Let dough rest 10 minutes.

Flour baking sheet. Divide dough into 2 equal pieces. Shape each piece into 10-inch-long by 2-inch-wide loaf. Place on baking sheet. Using sharp knife, cut several shallow diagonal slashes about 2 inches apart in top of each loaf. Cover with towel. Let rise in warm draft-free area until almost doubled in volume, about 30 minutes.

Preheat oven to 425°F. Bake bread until loaves are crusty and sound hollow when tapped on bottom, rotating sheet after 15 minutes for even baking, about 25 minutes. Transfer loaves to wire racks; cool completely.

MAKES 2 LOAVES

◆ ◆ ◆

Olive breads are everywhere lately—in restaurants, at bakeries, in grocery stores. For those who have become fans of these rustic loaves, here's an easy, very tasty version.

◆ ◆ ◆

# Anadama Rolls with Mixed Seeds

### ◆ ◆ ◆

1½ cups milk (do not use low-fat or nonfat)

⅓ cup mild-flavored (light) molasses

2 tablespoons (¼ stick) unsalted butter

2 teaspoons salt

¼ cup warm water (105° to 115°F)

2 envelopes dry yeast

¾ cup yellow cornmeal

1½ cups whole wheat flour

2¾ cups (about) bread flour

Additional yellow cornmeal

1 egg, beaten to blend (glaze)
   Assorted seeds (such as fennel, anise, celery and/or caraway)

Mix milk, molasses, butter and salt in small saucepan. Bring to simmer. Pour milk mixture into bowl of heavy-duty mixer fitted with paddle attachment. Cool to 115°F, about 30 minutes.

Meanwhile, place ¼ cup warm water in measuring cup. Sprinkle yeast over and stir to blend. Let stand until yeast dissolves, about 10 minutes. Stir yeast mixture into milk mixture. Mix in ¾ cup cornmeal. Mix in whole wheat flour. Mix in enough bread flour, ½ cup at a time, to form slightly sticky dough. Turn dough out onto floured surface. Knead until smooth and elastic, adding more bread flour if dough is too sticky, about 8 minutes. Form into ball.

Butter large bowl. Place dough in bowl; turn to coat. Cover bowl with plastic, then towel. Let rise until doubled, about 1½ hours.

Sprinkle 2 heavy large baking sheets generously with cornmeal. Punch down dough. Turn out onto floured surface and knead until smooth, about 3 minutes. Divide dough into 16 equal portions. Roll each portion between palms and work surface to 8-inch-long rope about ¾ inch thick. Grasping 1 rope at both ends, tie into loose knot. Repeat with remaining ropes. Place on prepared baking sheets, spacing 2 inches apart. Cover with towels. Let rise in warm area until almost doubled, about 45 minutes.

Position 1 rack in center and 1 rack in top third of oven and preheat to 375°F. Brush rolls with egg glaze. Sprinkle with seeds. Bake until rolls are golden and sound hollow when tapped, switching and rotating baking sheets halfway through baking, about 20 minutes. Transfer to racks. Serve warm or at room temperature.

MAKES 16

Anadama bread recipes, which date back to pre-Revolutionary New England, all call for molasses and cornmeal for substantial—and delicious results. This contemporary rendition is no exception.

### ◆ ◆ ◆

## ALL ABOUT CORNMEAL

Used by the Indians for centuries, cornmeal was introduced to Europe by the early explorers of the Americas. Colonial cooks, taking advantage of less-expensive cornmeal, substituted it for flour in many of their recipes, and such down-home classics as johnnycake, spoon bread, corn pone, grits and hasty pudding became part of our culinary heritage.

Water-ground cornmeal retains the vitamin-rich germ of the corn kernal; commercially ground meal is made only from the starchy part of the kernal. Grinds range from coarse to fine: Coarse is ideal for polenta, while fine grinds are best for muffins and breads. Cornmeal also comes in different colors, depending on the color of the corn; but there is not much difference in taste between white and yellow, or even blue cornmeal.

Cornmeal is more popular now than ever, turning up in everything from polenta to pancakes. There is corn bread, of course, and tamales, where cornmeal is the main ingredient; but, used in smaller amounts, it can also add sweetness and texture to cakes, cookies and puddings. It can thicken a soup and add crunch to coatings for fried chicken and fish.

◆ ◆ ◆

# White Soda Bread

◆ ◆ ◆

3½ cups all purpose flour
2 tablespoons caraway seeds (optional)
1 teaspoon baking soda
¾ teaspoon salt
1½ cups (about) buttermilk

Preheat oven to 425°F. Lightly flour baking sheet. Mix flour, caraway seeds, if using, baking soda and salt in large bowl. Mix in enough buttermilk to form moist clumps. Gather dough into ball. Turn out onto lightly floured surface and knead just until dough holds together, about 1 minute. Shape dough into 6-inch-diameter by 2-inch-high round. Place on prepared baking sheet. Cut 1-inch-deep X across top of bread, extending almost to edges. Bake until bread is golden brown and sounds hollow when tapped on bottom, about 35 minutes. Transfer bread to rack and cool completely.

8 SERVINGS

# Boston Brown Bread

◆ ◆ ◆

1 cup (packed) dried currants (about 5 ounces)
⅓ cup brandy

1 cup whole wheat flour
1 cup unbleached all purpose flour
¾ cup whole-grain rye flour*
¾ cup yellow cornmeal
2 teaspoons baking soda
1½ teaspoons salt
½ teaspoon ground ginger
1¾ cups buttermilk
2 large eggs
¼ cup pure maple syrup
¼ cup mild-flavored (light) molasses
2 tablespoons unsalted butter, melted, cooled

Nonstick vegetable oil spray

Maple-Molasses Butter (see recipe opposite)

Combine currants and brandy in small bowl. Let mixture stand until currants plump slightly, about 45 minutes.

Generously butter four 14½-to 16-ounce cans. Place rack in bottom of heavy large pot. Pour enough water into pot to reach depth of 3 inches. Bring water to boil.

Mix whole wheat flour and next 6 ingredients in large bowl. Whisk buttermilk, eggs, syrup, molasses and melted butter in medium bowl to blend. Mix into dry ingredients. Stir in currant mixture.

Divide batter among prepared cans. Cut out four 12 x 6-inch pieces of foil. Fold foil crosswise in half, forming 6-inch squares. Spray foil with vegetable oil spray. Cover tops of cans with foil, sprayed side down, leaving 2-inch-high space above cans so that bread can rise. Secure foil tightly with heavy rubber bands or string just below rims of cans.

Place cans on steamer rack in pot; pour additional water into pot to bring water two-thirds up sides of cans. Bring water to boil. Cover pot; reduce heat to medium-low and simmer until wooden skewer inserted into center of bread comes out clean, occasionally adding more hot water to pot, about 45 minutes.

Using tongs, transfer cans to rack. Let cool 10 minutes. Remove rubber bands and foil. Run small knife around sides of breads to loosen. Gently shake to remove breads from cans. *(Can be made 1 day ahead. Cool completely. Return breads to cans. Wrap breads tightly with foil. Steam cans, covered with foil and secured with heavy rubber bands, on rack set over simmering water until heated through, about 15 minutes.)* Cut breads into ½-inch-thick slices. Serve warm with Maple-Molasses Butter.

*Available at natural foods stores and some supermarkets.

MAKES 4 SMALL LOAVES

## Maple-Molasses Butter

1   cup (2 sticks) unsalted butter, room temperature
¼   cup pure maple syrup
2   tablespoons mild-flavored (light) molasses

Mix all ingredients in small bowl until well blended. *(Can be prepared 2 days ahead. Cover and refrigerate. Bring butter to room temperature before serving.)*

MAKES ABOUT 1 CUP

# · Desserts ·

For many good cooks, dessert is the key to successful enter-taining. They know that a truly impressive dessert makes the entire meal memorable.

That does not mean, however, that you must put a lot of work into your menu's final course. As the recipes in this chapter demonstrate, some of the best desserts take very little time to pre-pare—provided, that is, you know all the necessary shortcuts.

Take Grilled Pound Cake with Sour Cherry and Pecan Ice Cream (page 187) or Vanilla Ice Cream and Ginger Molasses Cookie Sandwiches (page 210). Both start with store-bought vanilla ice cream, cutting preparation time at least in half. Along the same lines, Frozen Fruit Fantasy (page 208) uses so many con-venient ingredients that it requires absolutely no cooking.

Ease enters into these fabulous dessert recipes in other ways as well. Champagne Zabaglione with Fresh Fruit Compote (page 196), for example, offers an ingenious way to make this frothy Ital-ian dessert ahead. Tropical Fruit Granita (page 213) and Kir Royale Sorbet (page 209) yield frozen sweets without need of an ice cream maker. And Old-fashioned Apple Cake (page 189) reveals a time-honored trick for quickly decorating a dessert: The result looks so pretty your guests will wonder just how you did it. Now, it's your secret.

*Chocolate Strawberry Shortcake (page 194) and Lemon and Blueberry Shortcakes (page 188)*

# Apple and Blackberry Pie

◆ ◆ ◆

A wonderfully homespun dessert, this pie is simple and delicious. The crust has a nice biscuit-like texture.

◆ ◆ ◆

CRUST

2    cups self-rising flour

9    tablespoons sugar

¾    cup (1½ sticks) chilled unsalted butter, cut into pieces

1    large egg, beaten to blend

2    tablespoons (about) ice water

FILLING

2    pounds tart green apples (such as Granny Smith), peeled, quartered, cored, cut into ¼-inch-thick slices

1½    cups frozen unsweetened blackberries, unthawed

⅓    cup plus 2 teaspoons sugar

2    tablespoons all purpose flour

Milk

Sweetened whipped cream

FOR CRUST: Combine flour and sugar in medium bowl. Add butter and rub in with fingertips until coarse crumbs form. Mix in beaten egg. Mix in enough ice water by tablespoonfuls to form moist clumps. Divide dough in half. Gather dough into 2 balls; flatten into disks. Wrap each disk in plastic and refrigerate until firm enough to roll out, about 30 minutes. *(Can be made 1 day ahead. Soften slightly at room temperature before rolling out.)*

FOR FILLING: Preheat oven to 375°F. Mix apples, blackberries, ⅓ cup sugar and flour in large bowl.

Roll out 1 dough disk on floured surface to 12-inch round. Transfer to 9-inch-diameter glass pie dish.

Spoon filling into crust. Roll out second dough disk on floured surface to 12-inch round. Place dough atop filling. Fold top crust edge under bottom edge and pinch to seal. Crimp edges decoratively. Brush crust with milk. Sprinkle with remaining 2 teaspoons sugar. Cut several slits in top of pie.

Bake pie until crust is golden brown and fruit is tender, covering edges of pie with aluminum foil if browning too quickly, about 55 minutes. Cool on rack 30 minutes. Serve warm with whipped cream.

6 TO 8 SERVINGS

# Low-Fat Orange and Almond Cream Cheese Pie

◆ ◆ ◆

CRUST

Nonstick vegetable oil spray

1¾   cups low-fat granola

½    cup blanched slivered almonds (about 2 ounces)

¼    cup plus 1 tablespoon orange juice

1    tablespoon honey

FILLING

½    cup orange juice

1    envelope unflavored gelatin

1    16-ounce container nonfat cottage cheese

4    ounces nonfat cream cheese, room temperature

¼    cup canned evaporated skim milk

3    tablespoons sugar

2    tablespoons honey

½    teaspoon almond extract

    4 oranges

¼    cup apricot preserves

1    tablespoon sliced almonds, toasted

FOR CRUST: Preheat oven to 400°F. Spray 9-inch diameter springform pan with nonstick vegetable oil spray. Coarsely grind granola and blanched slivered almonds in processor. Transfer mixture to medium bowl. Stir in orange juice and honey. Press mixture onto bottom of prepared springform pan. Bake until crust is set and beginning to color, 10 minutes. Transfer pan to rack and cool.

FOR FILLING: Stir orange juice and gelatin in heavy small saucepan over low heat until gelatin dissolves, about 3 minutes. Remove from heat. Puree cottage cheese, cream cheese, evaporated milk, sugar, honey and almond extract in blender until very smooth. Transfer to large bowl. Stir in gelatin. Pour filling into crust. Cover and chill overnight. *(Can be prepared 1 day ahead.)*

Cut peel and white pith from oranges. Cut oranges crosswise into ¼-inch-thick rounds. Cut each round in half. Drain orange pieces on several layers of paper towels. Arrange oranges decoratively over top of cheese pie. Stir apricot preserves in heavy small saucepan over low heat until melted. Brush oranges with apricot glaze. Sprinkle pie with toasted almonds and serve.

10 SERVINGS

◆ ◆ ◆

This tastes indulgent, but it's made with nonfat cottage cheese, nonfat cream cheese and evaporated skim milk. The result is 247 calories and six grams of fat per serving.

# EXOTIC FRUITS

The exotic tropical fruits of ten years ago—kiwi, papaya and mango—are now almost as common as apples and bananas. Even the creamy-fleshed cherimoya and whimsically shaped star fruit have become familiar to many of us. So what qualifies as exotic these days? According to Frieda's, Inc., the leading California-based marketer of specialty produce, these are the up-and-coming fruits.

◆ Feijoa: Also called pineapple guava, this large, rough-skinned kiwi-like fruit has a soft, custardy flesh with a tangy, pineapple-spearmint flavor. Peel and slice into fruit salads.

◆ Kiwano: The green flesh and edible seeds of this large, yellow spiced melon (it's also called a horned melon) have a distinctive cucumber-banana-lime flavor. Scoop it out with a spoon to eat.

◆ Lychee: With a rough, leathery brown skin on the outside, this smooth, round white fruit has a delicate grape-like sweetness. It is good in salads and fruit desserts and with poultry.

◆ Tamarillo: This sweet-tart red fruit is rich in flavor and is delicious eaten on its own or paired with other fruits in salads. It also makes good jam or jelly. Peel before using.

◆ ◆ ◆

# Tropical Fruit Tart

◆ ◆ ◆

CRUST

1¾ cups all purpose flour
¼ cup sugar
¼ teaspoon salt
10 tablespoons (1¼ sticks) chilled unsalted butter, cut into small pieces
1 large egg yolk
3 tablespoons whipping cream
½ teaspoon vanilla extract

FILLING

1 cup milk (do not use low-fat or nonfat)
3 large egg yolks
⅓ cup sugar
2 tablespoons cornstarch
2 tablespoons minced crystallized ginger

⅔ cup ginger preserves*
2 tablespoons Cognac or brandy
3 kiwis, peeled, thinly sliced
1 papaya, seeded, peeled, thinly sliced
1 ripe mango, pitted, peeled, thinly sliced
Fresh mint sprigs

FOR CRUST: Mix flour, sugar and salt in processor. Add butter and cut in, using on/off turns, until mixture resembles coarse meal. Whisk egg yolk, cream and vanilla in small bowl. Add to flour mixture; process until moist clumps form. Gather dough into ball. Flatten into disk. Wrap in plastic; refrigerate 4 hours.

FOR FILLING: Pour milk into heavy medium saucepan. Bring just to simmer. Whisk yolks, sugar and cornstarch in medium bowl to blend. Gradually whisk in hot milk. Return mixture to same saucepan. Whisk over medium heat until mixture thickens and comes to boil. Boil 1 minute. Pour pastry cream into medium bowl. Stir in minced ginger. Press plastic onto surface of pastry cream. Cover; chill until cold, about 4 hours. *(Dough and pastry cream can be made 1 day ahead. Keep chilled separately. Let dough soften slightly at room temperature before pressing into pan.)*

Preheat oven to 375°F. Press dough onto bottom and up sides of 11 x 7½-inch rectangular or 11-inch round tart pan with removable bottom. Line crust with foil. Fill with dried beans or pie weights. Bake

until sides of crust are set, about 15 minutes. Remove foil and beans. Bake until crust is golden, piercing with fork if bubbles form, about 15 minutes. Transfer pan to rack and cool crust completely. Remove sides from pan.

Combine preserves and Cognac in small saucepan. Stir over medium heat until preserves melt and mixture is thick, about 2 minutes. Strain syrup into another small saucepan; discard solids. Brush half of syrup onto bottom of crust. Let stand at room temperature until set, about 5 minutes. Spread pastry cream evenly over. Arrange fruit over pastry cream. Rewarm ginger syrup. Brush over fruit. *(Can be made 2 hours ahead. Cover and chill.)* Garnish tart with fresh mint sprigs and serve.

*\*Available at specialty foods stores and some supermarkets.*

8 SERVINGS

# Rhubarb Tart

◆ ◆ ◆

CRUST

1⅔ cups all purpose flour

¼ teaspoon salt

½ cup (1 stick) chilled unsalted butter, cut into small pieces

¼ cup sugar

2 large egg yolks

2 tablespoons (or more) ice water

3 tablespoons apricot jam

FILLING

1 cup sugar

⅓ cup water

3 3 x ½-inch strips lemon peel (yellow part only)

1 cinnamon stick, broken in half

2 pounds fresh rhubarb, trimmed, cut diagonally into ½-inch-thick pieces (about 6 cups)

◆ ◆ ◆

Though rhubarb is, in fact, a vegetable, it makes a sweet and lovely dessert. (You can prepare the dough for the crust a day ahead, and the entire tart up to six hours ahead.)

◆ ◆ ◆

FOR CRUST: Mix flour and salt in processor. Add butter and cut in, using on/off turns, until mixture resembles coarse meal. Add sugar and egg yolks and process briefly to blend. Add 2 tablespoons water and process just until moist clumps form. If dough is dry, add more water by teaspoonfuls to moisten. Gather dough into ball; flatten into disk. Wrap in plastic and refrigerate until dough is firm enough to roll, about 30 minutes.

Preheat oven to 350°F. Roll out dough disk on floured surface to 12-inch round. Transfer to 9-inch-diameter tart pan with removable bottom. Trim crust overhang to ¼ inch. Fold overhang in, creating double-thick sides. Freeze tart crust 15 minutes.

Line crust with foil. Fill with dried beans or pie weights. Bake until sides are set, about 20 minutes. Remove foil and beans. Bake until crust is golden brown, piercing with fork if bubbles form, about 15 minutes. Brush crust with jam and bake until jam is set, about 5 minutes more. Transfer pan to rack and cool.

FOR FILLING: Combine sugar and water in heavy large skillet over low heat. Stir until sugar dissolves. Add lemon peel and cinnamon stick. Increase heat and bring to boil. Add rhubarb and bring to boil. Reduce heat to medium-low. Cover pan and simmer until rhubarb is just beginning to soften, 5 minutes. Remove from heat. Let stand until rhubarb is tender, 15 minutes. Uncover and cool.

Using slotted spoon, remove rhubarb from cooking liquid and arrange in concentric circles in crust. Strain cooking liquid into heavy small saucepan. Boil liquid until reduced to ¼ cup, about 5 minutes. Cool syrup completely. Spoon syrup over rhubarb.

8 SERVINGS

# Country-Style Plum Tart

◆ ◆ ◆

CRUST

| 2 | cups all purpose flour |
| ¼ | cup sugar |
| ½ | teaspoon salt |
| 1 | cup (2 sticks) chilled unsalted butter, cut into ½-inch pieces |
| 5 | tablespoons (about) ice water |

FILLING

| 1½ | pounds red-skinned plums, sliced |
| ⅓ | cup plum jam or preserves |
| 1 | teaspoon vanilla extract |
| ¼ | teaspoon ground allspice |
| 3 | tablespoons sugar |
| 1 | egg, beaten to blend (for glaze) |

FOR CRUST: Mix flour, sugar and salt in processor. Add butter and cut in using on/off turns until mixture resembles coarse meal. Add water by tablespoonfuls; process just until moist clumps form. Gather into ball; flatten into disk. Wrap in plastic; chill 1 hour.

Preheat oven to 375°F. Roll out dough on large sheet of floured parchment paper to ¼-inch-thick round. Trim dough round to 14-inch diameter. Transfer dough on paper to large baking sheet.

FOR FILLING: Mix plums, jam, vanilla and allspice in large bowl. Mound plum mixture in center of dough, leaving 3-inch border. Sprinkle fruit with 2 tablespoons sugar. Fold dough border over fruit, pleating loosely and pinching to seal any cracks. Brush dough with beaten egg. Sprinkle dough with 1 tablespoon sugar.

Bake tart until crust is brown and filling bubbles, about 45 minutes. Transfer baking sheet to rack and cool tart slightly, about 20 minutes. Slide metal spatula under all sides of crust to free from parchment. Using large tart pan bottom as aid, transfer tart to platter. Serve warm or at room temperature.

6 TO 8 SERVINGS

◆ ◆ ◆

A buttery free-form crust joins forces with a luscious fruit filling to make the perfect summer dessert. Just add frozen yogurt or ice cream.

◆ ◆ ◆

## A SQUEEZE OF LIME

There are basically two varieties of limes: Persian, or Tahitian, limes, which are the dark green, thick-skinned limes we usually find in the supermarket; and Key limes, which are smaller and rounder, with a thin yellow-green skin. Key limes, as they are known in this country because they grow in abundance in the Florida Keys, are also called Mexican limes, and can be found in tropical regions of Mexico and the Caribbean islands. They are not distributed commercially and can, therefore, be difficult to find. Both sweeter and more tart than regular limes, they give Key lime pie its distinctive tang.

When selecting limes, look for fresh, firm fruit that has a smooth, unwrinkled skin. If you need only the juice, pour boiling water over the lime and let stand for five minutes before squeezing; this will yield more juice than you might otherwise get.

A squeeze of lime juice goes well with a variety of foods, from sliced avocado and melon to fish and different soups. The juice is a key ingredient in a number of tropical drinks and, of course, Key lime pie.

◆ ◆ ◆

# Strawberry-topped Lime Mousse Tart

◆ ◆ ◆

CRUST
¾   cup all purpose flour
⅓   cup whole almonds, toasted
⅓   cup powdered sugar
¼   teaspoon salt
6   tablespoons chilled unsalted butter, cut into ½-inch pieces
2   teaspoons (about) cold water

FILLING
¼   cup fresh lime juice
½   teaspoon unflavored gelatin
¾   cup chilled whipping cream
5   ounces good-quality white chocolate, chopped
1   teaspoon grated lime peel

2   tablespoons sugar
2   tablespoons sour cream

TOPPING
3   12-ounce baskets strawberries, hulled, sliced
⅓   cup (about) seedless strawberry jam

FOR CRUST: Blend first 4 ingredients in processor until nuts are ground but some small pieces still remain. Add butter; cut in using on/off turns until mixture resembles fine meal. Blend in enough water by teaspoonfuls until mixture begins to form clumps. Gather into ball; flatten into disk. Press dough over bottom and up sides of 9-inch tart pan with removable bottom. Freeze until firm, about 30 minutes.

Preheat oven to 375°F. Bake crust until deep golden brown, about 30 minutes. Transfer to rack and cool.

FOR FILLING: Place lime juice in small bowl; sprinkle gelatin over. Let stand 10 minutes to soften. Bring ¼ cup cream to simmer in medium saucepan. Reduce heat to low. Add white chocolate; stir until melted and smooth. Add gelatin mixture; stir to dissolve. Mix in grated lime peel. Refrigerate until cold and beginning to thicken but not set, stirring often, about 45 minutes.

Beat sugar, sour cream and remaining ½ cup cream to medium-stiff peaks in medium bowl. Fold whipped cream into white chocolate. Spoon mousse into crust. Chill until set, about 4 hours.

FOR TOPPING: Decoratively arrange berries atop mousse. Melt jam in saucepan over low heat. Brush jam over berries to glaze.

8 SERVINGS

# Lemon and Honey Tart with Walnut Crust and Honeyed Figs

◆ ◆ ◆

CRUST

1⅓ cups all purpose flour
⅓ cup walnuts
2 tablespoons sugar
¼ teaspoon salt
½ cup (1 stick) chilled unsalted butter, cut into ½-inch pieces
1 large egg yolk
1½ tablespoons cold water

FILLING

¾ cup buttermilk
⅓ cup fresh lemon juice
2 large eggs
2 tablespoons all purpose flour
½ teaspoon grated lemon peel
½ cup honey

6 fresh figs, cut crosswise into ¼-inch-thick slices
1 tablespoon honey
¼ cup walnuts, toasted, chopped

FOR CRUST: Mix first 4 ingredients in processor. Cut in butter using on/off turns until mixture resembles coarse meal. Whisk yolk and water in small bowl to blend. Add to dry ingredients and process just until moist clumps form. Gather dough into ball; flatten into disk. Wrap in plastic and chill 1 hour.

Butter and flour 9-inch tart pan with removable bottom. Roll out dough on floured surface to ⅛-inch-thick round. Transfer to pan. Trim edges; reserve trimmings. Freeze 30 minutes.

Preheat oven to 350°F. Line crust with foil; fill with dry beans. Bake until crust is set, 12 minutes. Remove foil and beans. Bake crust until golden, about 25 minutes. Repair any cracks in crust with reserved dough. Cool crust. Maintain oven temperature.

FOR FILLING: Whisk first 5 ingredients in bowl. Add ½ honey and stir until dissolved. Pour into crust. Bake until set, about 30 minutes. Cool. Chill tart until cold.

Arrange figs atop tart. Drizzle with honey; sprinkle with nuts.

6 SERVINGS

◆ ◆ ◆

If figs are unavailable, use plums (pit them and cut lengthwise into ¼-inch-thick slices). The results will be every bit as delicious.

◆ ◆ ◆

# Apple-Rhubarb Crisp

♦ ♦ ♦

Oats, brown sugar and chopped walnuts team up with cinnamon and cloves in the terrific streusel topping for this homespun treat.

♦ ♦ ♦

TOPPING

¾ cup all purpose flour
¾ cup (packed) golden brown sugar
½ cup old-fashioned oats
½ teaspoon ground cinnamon
¼ teaspoon ground cloves
6 tablespoons (¾ stick) unsalted butter, room temperature
½ cup finely chopped walnuts

FILLING

1½ pounds Golden Delicious apples, peeled, cored, cut into ½-inch pieces (about 4 cups)
¾ pound rhubarb, cut into ½-inch pieces (about 3 cups)
3 tablespoons sugar
2 teaspoons all purpose flour
½ teaspoon vanilla extract

Vanilla ice cream or frozen yogurt

FOR TOPPING: Mix first 5 ingredients in medium bowl. Rub in butter until mixture begins to clump together. Mix in nuts. *(Can be made 1 day ahead. Refrigerate.)*

FOR FILLING: Preheat oven to 400°F. Combine apples, rhubarb, sugar, flour and vanilla extract in large bowl and toss to coat. Transfer apple mixture to 8 x 8 x 2-inch glass baking dish.

Sprinkle topping evenly over fruit. Bake until fruit is tender when pierced with knife and topping is crisp, covering with foil if topping is browning too quickly, about 45 minutes. Cool 20 minutes. Serve warm with vanilla ice cream.

6 SERVINGS

# Poached Asian Pears with Star Anise and Tropical Fruit

◆ ◆ ◆

| | |
|---|---|
| 2 | cups water |
| 1 | cup dry white wine |
| ¾ | cup sugar |
| 2 | tablespoons fresh lemon juice |
| 2 | star anise* |
| 1 | 2-inch piece cinnamon stick |
| 1 | 2-inch piece fresh ginger, sliced |
| 4 | large (10 ounces each) Asian pears |
| 1 | 1¼-pound papaya, diced |
| 1 | 14- to 16-ounce mango, diced |

Bring first 7 ingredients to boil in heavy large saucepan, stirring until sugar dissolves. Cover and simmer 5 minutes.

Peel and core pears. Add to syrup. Add enough water to cover pears. Cover pan; simmer until pears are tender, about 40 minutes. Using slotted spoon, transfer pears to bowl. Increase heat; boil liquid until reduced to ¾ cup, about 25 minutes. Strain syrup; pour over pears. Chill until cold. *(Can be made 2 days ahead. Chill.)*

Stand 1 pear in center of each plate. Spoon papaya and mango around pear. Spoon syrup over and serve.

*A brown star-shaped seed pod; available at Asian markets and specialty foods stores and some supermarkets.*

4 SERVINGS

◆ ◆ ◆

A light, refreshing and very sophisticated dessert. Asian pears have a crisp texture, a round shape, and a sweet and floral aroma that's quite unlike that of the more familiar, buttery, "pear-shaped" pear.

◆ ◆ ◆

# Apricot-Blackberry Cobbler

**◆ ◆ ◆**

FRUIT

2¼ to 2½ pounds apricots (about 18), quartered, pitted

2   5- to 6-ounce baskets blackberries

1   cup sugar

¼   cup quick-cooking tapioca

2   tablespoons (¼ stick) chilled unsalted butter, diced

BISCUIT TOPPING

1½   cups all purpose flour

2   tablespoons sugar

2   teaspoons baking powder

½   teaspoon salt

6   tablespoons (¾ stick) chilled unsalted butter, diced

½   cup plus 1 tablespoon chilled whipping cream

Vanilla ice cream or frozen yogurt

FOR FRUIT: Preheat oven to 375°F. Butter 8 x 8 x 2-inch glass baking dish. Combine apricots, berries, sugar and tapioca in large bowl; toss gently to blend. Let stand 15 minutes, tossing fruit occasionally. Transfer fruit mixture to prepared dish. Dot with butter. Bake until fruit is tender and juices bubble thickly, about 50 minutes. Cool completely in dish. *(Can be made 4 hours ahead. Let stand at room temperature.)*

FOR BISCUIT TOPPING: Preheat oven to 400°F. Combine flour, sugar, baking powder and salt in medium bowl; whisk to blend. Add butter; rub in with fingertips until mixture resembles coarse meal. Gradually add ½ cup cream, mixing with fork until moist clumps form. Knead gently in bowl until dough holds together.

Roll out dough on lightly floured surface to 9 x 6-inch rectangle. Cut dough lengthwise into 8 strips, each about ¾ inch wide. Arrange 4 strips across dish, spacing evenly. Arrange 4 strips in opposite direction, forming lattice. Press ends of pastry strips firmly into fruit. Brush dough with 1 tablespoon cream.

Bake cobbler until filling is heated through and lattice is golden brown, about 30 minutes. Spoon warm cobbler into deep bowls; top with ice cream or frozen yogurt.

8 SERVINGS

**◆ ◆ ◆**

Tender, biscuit-like dough is formed into an attractive lattice pattern atop this easy treat (opposite, with a plum cobbler with hazelnut topping, page 182).

**◆ ◆ ◆**

# Individual Plum Cobblers with Hazelnut Topping

◆ ◆ ◆

◆ ◆ ◆

What's fun about this recipe is that everyone gets their own mini cobbler. (To get a look at this appealing dessert, turn to page 181.)

◆ ◆ ◆

FRUIT

2 to 2¼ pounds red-skinned plums, pitted, each plum cut into 8 wedges

⅔ cup sugar

2 tablespoons quick-cooking tapioca

½ teaspoon ground cinnamon

2 tablespoons (¼ stick) chilled unsalted butter, diced

TOPPING

¾ cup all purpose flour

2 tablespoons (packed) golden brown sugar

1 teaspoon baking powder

¼ teaspoon salt

3 tablespoons chilled unsalted butter, diced

½ cup hazelnuts, toasted, chopped

½ cup chilled whipping cream

1 tablespoon sugar

Vanilla ice cream

FOR FRUIT: Preheat oven to 375°F. Butter eight ⅔-cup soufflé dishes or custard cups. Combine plums, sugar, tapioca and cinnamon in large bowl; toss to blend. Let stand 15 minutes, tossing occasionally. Divide among prepared dishes (dishes will be full). Place on baking sheet. Dot fruit with butter. Bake until plums are tender and fruit bubbles thickly, about 45 minutes. Cool in dishes. *(Can be made 4 hours ahead. Let stand at room temperature.)*

FOR TOPPING: Preheat oven to 375°F. Whisk flour, golden brown sugar, baking powder and salt in medium bowl. Add butter; rub in with fingertips until mixture resembles coarse meal. Mix in nuts. Gradually add cream, stirring until batter holds together.

Drop large spoonful of batter atop fruit in each dish, dividing equally. Sprinkle with 1 tablespoon sugar.

Bake until topping is golden, about 25 minutes. Cool at least 15 minutes. Top with ice cream; serve warm.

8 SERVINGS

# Mixed Fruit with Honey Cream

◆ ◆ ◆

1½  cups light sour cream
3   tablespoons honey
8   cups mixed fresh fruit (such as blueberries; pitted cherries; sliced
    strawberries; sliced pitted nectarines, plums and peaches)

3   tablespoons almond slices, toasted
    Mint sprigs (optional)

Whisk sour cream and honey in medium bowl to blend. Toss
fruit together in large bowl. *(Can be made 3 hours ahead. Cover
sauce and fruit separately and chill.)*

Spoon fruit mixture into individual bowls. Whisk chilled sauce
to loosen if necessary. Spoon sauce over fruit. Garnish with toasted
almonds and mint sprigs, if desired.

6 SERVINGS

# Fruit in Spiced White Wine

◆ ◆ ◆

2   cups dry white wine
4   ⅓-inch-thick orange slices (unpeeled), quartered
¼   cup honey
1   cinnamon stick
½   vanilla bean, split lengthwise

6   apricots, pitted, sliced
1½  pounds fresh cherries, pitted or one 16-ounce bag frozen
    unsweetened pitted sweet dark cherries, thawed, well drained

Combine first 4 ingredients in heavy medium saucepan. Scrape
in seeds from vanilla bean; add bean. Bring to boil. Reduce heat to
medium-low; simmer 30 minutes to blend flavors.

Combine apricots and cherries in large bowl. Pour hot wine
mixture over. Cool to room temperature. Cover and chill. *(Can be
made 1 day ahead. Keep chilled.)* Serve fruit with liquid.

6 SERVINGS

Honey, cinnamon, vanilla and
orange slices spice up the wine marinade in this delicious low-fat dessert.
Serve the fruit with the Low-Fat
Almond-Cinnamon Biscotti (pictured
above) on page 219.

◆ ◆ ◆

# Banana-Walnut Upside-Down Cake

◆ ◆ ◆

◆ ◆ ◆

The upside-down cake—so popular in the fifties and sixties—has been making a comeback lately. This version has a banana, walnut and maple topping and tender cake.

◆ ◆ ◆

TOPPING

1 cup (packed) golden brown sugar
¼ cup (½ stick) unsalted butter
3 tablespoons pure maple syrup
¼ cup coarsely chopped toasted walnuts
4 large ripe bananas, peeled, cut diagonally into ¼-inch-thick slices

CAKE

1 cup all purpose flour
2 teaspoons baking powder
½ teaspoon ground cinnamon
¼ teaspoon salt
¾ cup sugar
6 tablespoons (¾ stick) unsalted butter, room temperature
1 large egg
½ teaspoon vanilla extract
6 tablespoons milk

Sweetened whipped cream

FOR TOPPING: Preheat oven to 325°F. Combine sugar and butter in heavy medium saucepan. Stir over low heat until butter melts and mixture is well blended. Pour into 9-inch-diameter cake pan with 2-inch-high sides. Spread to coat bottom of pan. Pour maple syrup over sugar mixture. Sprinkle nuts evenly over. Place banana slices in concentric circles on nuts, overlapping slightly and covering bottom of pan.

FOR CAKE: Stir flour, baking powder, cinnamon and salt in medium bowl to blend. Beat sugar and butter in another medium bowl until creamy. Add egg and vanilla; beat until light and fluffy. Beat in flour mixture alternately with milk in 3 additions. Spoon batter over bananas. Bake until tester inserted into center comes out clean, about 55 minutes.

Transfer cake to rack. Run knife around sides. Cool cake on rack 30 minutes. Place plate over pan; invert cake. Let stand 3 minutes, then gently lift off pan. Serve warm with whipped cream.

8 SERVINGS

# Layered Lemon Cake with Lemon Curd

◆ ◆ ◆

CAKE

6   tablespoons (¾ stick) unsalted butter, room temperature
¾   cup plus 1 tablespoon sugar
3   large eggs
1   teaspoon grated lemon peel
1¼  cups self-rising flour
2   tablespoons fresh lemon juice

LEMON CURD

2   large eggs
6   tablespoons sugar
6   tablespoons fresh lemon juice
¼   cup (½ stick) unsalted butter, cut into pieces
2   teaspoons (packed) grated lemon peel

    Powdered sugar
    Whipped cream (optional)

FOR CAKE: Preheat oven to 325°F. Butter two 8-inch-diameter cake pans with 2-inch-high sides. Line bottom of pans with parchment paper. Butter parchment.

Beat butter and sugar in medium bowl until well blended. Add eggs 1 at a time, beating well after each addition. Mix in lemon peel. Beat in flour alternately with lemon juice in 2 additions each. Divide batter between prepared pans. Bake until cakes begin to pull away from sides of pan and tester inserted into center of cakes comes out clean, about 28 minutes. Cool cakes in pans on racks 2 minutes. Turn cakes out onto racks and cool completely. Peel off parchment.

FOR LEMON CURD: Whisk eggs and sugar in top of double boiler to blend. Add lemon juice, butter and lemon peel. Set pan over simmering water (do not allow bottom of pan to touch water). Whisk until mixture thickens to pudding consistency and thermometer inserted into mixture registers 165°F, about 4 minutes. Remove from over water; cool. Press plastic onto surface; chill until cold.

Place 1 cake layer on platter. Spread lemon curd evenly over. Top with second cake layer. Place decorative stencil or doily atop cake. Sprinkle heavily with powdered sugar. Carefully remove stencil. Serve cake with whipped cream, if desired.

8 SERVINGS

This sponge cake is light and moist—perfect for dessert or an afternoon tea. (And if you're entertaining, consider that both the cake and the lemon curd can be made a day ahead. Store the cake at room temperature; chill the lemon curd.)

◆ ◆ ◆

# Espresso-Hazelnut Cheesecake

Cheesecake is as popular these days as ever; coffee shows no signs of slowing down both as a drink and a flavoring. This recipe combines the two for a spectacular finale. Decorate it with chocolate-covered espresso beans, if you like. (Begin preparing the cake one day before serving.)

CRUST

8½ ounces butter biscuit cookies
½ cup hazelnuts, toasted, husked
2 tablespoons sugar
1 teaspoon ground cinnamon
5 tablespoons unsalted butter, melted

FILLING

2 pounds cream cheese, room temperature
1¼ cups sugar
4 large eggs
1 cup sour cream
½ cup plus ⅔ cup chilled whipping cream
3 tablespoons instant espresso powder
2 tablespoons warm water
2 teaspoons vanilla extract
¾ cup hazelnuts, toasted, husked, coarsely chopped

FOR CRUST: Preheat oven to 350°F. Generously butter bottom and sides of 9-inch-diameter springform pan with 2¾-inch-high sides. Wrap outside of pan with double layer of foil. Finely grind cookies, hazelnuts, sugar and cinnamon in processor. Add butter; process until moist clumps form. Press crumb mixture onto bottom and up sides of pan. Chill while preparing filling.

FOR FILLING: Using electric mixer, beat cream cheese in large bowl until smooth. Add sugar and beat until well blended. Add eggs 1 at a time, beating just until blended and scraping down sides of bowl after each addition. Beat in sour cream and ½ cup cream. Stir

espresso powder and 2 tablespoons warm water in small bowl until powder dissolves. Add to filling and beat until blended. Beat in vanilla. Stir in chopped hazelnuts.

Pour filling into prepared pan. Place pan in large baking pan. Pour enough hot water into baking pan to come halfway up sides of springform pan. Bake cake until top is puffed and center is almost set, about 1 hour 15 minutes. Turn off oven; open door slightly. Let cake stand in oven with door ajar 1 hour. Remove pan from water; transfer to rack. Cool. Wrap in foil and chill overnight. *(Can be made 3 days ahead. Keep cheesecake refrigerated.)*

Run small knife around sides of pan to loosen cheesecake. Remove pan sides. Beat ⅔ cup cream in medium bowl until stiff peaks form. Spoon whipped cream into pastry bag fitted with large star tip; pipe around top edge of cake.

14 SERVINGS

# Grilled Pound Cake with Sour Cherry and Pecan Ice Cream

◆ ◆ ◆

¾    cup dried sour cherries (about 4 ounces)
1    cup boiling water
5    tablespoons brandy

1½    pints vanilla ice cream, softened slightly
4½    tablespoons coarsely chopped semisweet chocolate (about 2½ ounces)
⅓    cup coarsely chopped toasted pecans

1    16-ounce loaf pound cake
¼    cup (½ stick) unsalted butter, melted

Place cherries in medium bowl. Pour 1 cup boiling water over. Let stand until softened, about 10 minutes. Drain and pat dry. Mix cherries and 1 tablespoon brandy in small bowl.

Place ice cream in large bowl. Mix in cherries, semisweet chocolate and pecans. Cover and freeze until firm, about 2 hours.

Prepare barbecue (medium heat). Cut pound cake into sixteen ½-inch slices. Brush both sides of each cake slice with melted butter. Grill slices until lightly toasted, about 30 seconds per side. Place 2 slices on each of 8 dessert plates. Place 1 scoop ice cream atop cake on each plate. Drizzle 1½ teaspoons brandy over each serving.

8 SERVINGS

## INSTANT DESSERTS

Delicious desserts come together quickly and easily with the help of purchased pound cake or angel food cake. Here are some ideas for dessert-in-an-instant from Sarah Tenaglia, *Bon Appétit's* associate food editor.

◆ Use pound cake as a substitute for ladyfingers or génoise cake in desserts such as trifle.

◆ Cut pound cake or angel food cake and fresh fruit into cubes and serve with skewers for dipping in a warm chocolate fondue made of dark chocolate melted with a little cream and liqueur.

◆ Slice pound cake horizontally into three or four slices and layer with lemon curd, sliced strawberries and whipped cream, using more whipped cream to frost the cake.

◆ Mix crushed, chocolate-toffee candy into whipped cream and spread it between layers of pound cake. Ice with a fudge frosting.

◆ Toast slices of angel food cake and serve with ice cream and fruit.

◆ Top slices of pound cake or angel food cake with ice cream, hot fudge sauce and whipped cream flavored with almond extract and brown sugar. Sprinkle with toasted sliced almonds.

◆ ◆ ◆

# Lemon and Blueberry Shortcakes

◆ ◆ ◆

◆ ◆ ◆

Lemon curd, lemon-cornmeal
shortcakes, blueberry sauce and fresh
blueberries come together in this win-
ning dessert. (You can make the curd
a day ahead and refrigerate it.)

◆ ◆ ◆

CURD

7    tablespoons fresh lemon juice

6    tablespoons sugar

4    large egg yolks

BISCUITS

1    lemon

5    tablespoons sugar

1¼   cups all purpose flour

¼    cup yellow cornmeal

1½   teaspoons baking powder

½    teaspoon salt

¼    teaspoon baking soda

6    tablespoons (¾ stick) chilled unsalted butter, diced

8    tablespoons chilled whipping cream

SAUCE

3¼   cups blueberries (from about two 12-ounce baskets)

6    tablespoons water

3    tablespoons all-fruit blueberry spread

1    tablespoon sugar

⅔    cup chilled whipping cream

FOR CURD: Combine lemon juice, sugar and egg yolks in heavy medium saucepan. Whisk over medium heat until mixture thickens and just comes to boil, about 6 minutes. Transfer to bowl; cool.

FOR BISCUITS: Preheat oven to 400°F. Using vegetable peeler, remove peel from lemon in strips. Squeeze 2 tablespoons juice from lemon; reserve juice. Place peel and 3 tablespoons sugar in processor. Blend until peel is finely ground. Add flour, cornmeal, baking powder, salt and baking soda; process to blend. Add butter; process until mixture resembles coarse meal. Add 6 tablespoons cream and 2 tablespoons lemon juice; process just until moist clumps form. Gather dough into ball; flatten into disk.

Pat out dough on lightly floured surface to ¾-inch-thick round. Using floured 2½-inch-diameter cutter, cut out rounds. Gather scraps; pat out to ¾-inch-thick round. Cut out enough rounds to equal a total of 6. Place on heavy large baking sheet. Brush with 2 tablespoons cream. Sprinkle with 2 tablespoons sugar.

Bake biscuits until cooked through and golden, about 15 minutes. Transfer to plate. Cool completely.

FOR SAUCE: Combine 1½ cups blueberries, water, blueberry spread and sugar in heavy small saucepan. Stir gently over medium-high heat until mixture comes to boil and berries begin to release juices, about 2 minutes. Remove from heat. Mix in 1½ cups blueberries. Cool completely.

Beat cream in medium bowl until stiff peaks form. Fold into curd in 2 additions. Cut biscuits horizontally in half. Place bottoms on 6 plates. Spoon some sauce, then curd mixture over each. Place biscuit tops over. Garnish shortcakes with ¼ cup blueberries.

6 SERVINGS

# Old-fashioned Apple Cake

◆ ◆ ◆

1½  cups plus 2 tablespoons whole wheat flour
5  teaspoons cornstarch
2¼  teaspoons baking soda
¾  teaspoon salt
⅛  teaspoon ground cloves
½  cup (1 stick) unsalted butter, diced, room temperature
4  medium Gala or Golden Delicious apples, peeled, cored, cut into ⅓-inch pieces
¾  cup plus 1 tablespoon (packed) golden brown sugar
2  large eggs
2  tablespoons milk
2  teaspoons sugar

1  9-inch doily
 Powdered sugar

◆ ◆ ◆

This moist cake is delicious served warm with dollops of sweetened whipped cream, but it can also be offered at room temperature.

◆ ◆ ◆

Preheat oven to 375°F. Butter 9-inch-diameter springform pan with 2½-inch-high sides. Sift first 5 ingredients into large bowl. Rub in butter until mixture resembles coarse meal. Mix in apples and brown sugar. Whisk eggs and milk together; stir into apple mixture (batter will be thick). Transfer to pan. Sprinkle with sugar.

Bake cake until golden and springy to touch, about 35 minutes. Cool slightly on rack. Cut around cake to loosen; remove pan sides. *(Can be made 1 day ahead. Cool completely. Wrap tightly; store at room temperature.)* Place doily atop cake. Sprinkle powdered sugar over; carefully remove doily.

8 SERVINGS

## CHOCOLATE PRIMER

There's a chocolate for everybody—and every recipe. Whether you're snacking, melting or baking, turn to this list of what's what to know just what you need.

◆ Unsweetened: Intended for baking, not eating, this kind is made of pure chocolate liquor without sugar.

◆ Bittersweet and Semisweet: Slightly sweetened bittersweet and slightly sweeter semisweet chocolate contain cocoa butter, sugar and vanilla and are used for eating out of hand and desserts of all kinds, plus frostings, fillings and sauces.

◆ Milk Chocolate: Milk solids and sugar are added to this candy-bar chocolate, which is also used in frostings, pie fillings and puddings.

◆ Cocoa Powder: Cocoa is chocolate that is ground and sieved with most of the cocoa butter removed. There are three kinds: unsweetened, used in baking; sweetened, used in drinks and not for cooking; and Dutch-process, used in some recipes, darker and less bitter than the unsweetened kind.

◆ White Chocolate: This is not really chocolate at all, since it contains no chocolate liquor, only cocoa butter, milk solids (which give it its color), sugar and flavorings.

◆ ◆ ◆

# Hot Chocolate Cakes with Mango and Ginger

◆ ◆ ◆

¼ cup whipping cream
1 tablespoon unsalted butter
1½ teaspoons unsweetened cocoa powder
1 teaspoon grated orange peel
½ teaspoon instant espresso powder
2½ ounces bittersweet (not unsweetened) or semisweet chocolate, chopped

1 large egg
2 tablespoons sugar
2 tablespoons ground walnuts
½ teaspoon vanilla extract

1 large mango, peeled, pitted, sliced or 2 oranges, peeled, sectioned, seeded
2 tablespoons minced crystallized ginger
Whipped cream (optional)

Preheat oven to 350°F. Butter four ½-cup muffin cups. Sprinkle with sugar to coat. Combine cream, butter, cocoa, orange peel and espresso powder in heavy small saucepan. Bring to simmer, whisking until blended. Remove from heat. Add chocolate; stir until melted. Cool to lukewarm, about 10 minutes.

Using electric mixer, beat egg and sugar in medium bowl until pale yellow and slowly dissolving ribbon forms when beaters are lifted, about 4 minutes. Fold in walnuts and vanilla. Gently fold in chocolate mixture. Divide batter among prepared muffin cups.

Bake cakes until puffed and tester inserted into center comes out clean, about 18 minutes. Cool in pan on rack 10 minutes (cake centers may sink). Turn cakes out onto rack. *(Can be made 1 day ahead. Cool completely. Cover and store at room temperature. Rewarm uncovered in 350°F oven about 10 minutes.)*

Arrange warm cakes bottom side up on plates. Surround with mango or orange. Sprinkle with crystallized ginger. Top cakes with whipped cream, if desired, and serve.

MAKES 4

# Orange-Clove Pound Cake
# with Strawberries

◆ ◆ ◆

CAKE

2   cups cake flour

2   teaspoons baking powder

½   teaspoon salt

¾   cup (1½ sticks) unsalted butter, room temperature

1¼  cups sugar

1½  teaspoons grated orange peel

¼   teaspoon ground cloves

½   teaspoon vanilla extract

2   large eggs

2   large egg whites

½   cup milk (do not use low-fat or nonfat)

GLAZE

½   cup powdered sugar

1   tablespoon orange juice

2   1-pint baskets strawberries, hulled, sliced

¼   cup sugar
    Sweetened whipped cream

FOR CAKE: Preheat oven to 350°F. Butter 10-inch-diameter angel food cake pan. Stir cake flour, baking powder and salt in medium bowl to blend. Beat butter, sugar, orange peel and cloves in medium bowl until light and creamy. Mix in vanilla extract. Add eggs 1 at a time, beating well after each addition. Add egg whites and beat until well blended, about 2 minutes. Beat in dry ingredients alternately with milk in 3 additions.

Spoon batter into pan (batter will come halfway up). Smooth top. Bake until tester inserted near center of cake comes out clean, about 45 minutes. Cool cake in pan on rack. Turn out onto platter. *(Can be made 1 day ahead. Cover; let stand at room temperature.)*

FOR GLAZE: Mix powdered sugar and orange juice in small bowl. Drizzle glaze over cake. Let stand until glaze sets, about 30 minutes.

Mix strawberries and ¼ cup sugar in medium bowl. Let stand at room temperature until juices form, about 20 minutes. Cut cake into slices and place on plates. Spoon strawberry mixture and sweetened whipped cream alongside cake and serve.

10 TO 12 SERVINGS

# Walnut-Spice Layer Cake with Caramel Cream Cheese Frosting

◆ ◆ ◆

CARAMEL

1½  cups sugar
½   cup water
1   cup whipping cream

SYRUP

½   cup water
⅓   cup sugar
¼   cup dark rum

CAKE

¾   cup sifted all purpose flour
3   tablespoons cornstarch
4   teaspoons pumpkin pie spice
1   cup walnuts

5   large eggs, room temperature
⅔   cup sugar
3½  tablespoons unsalted butter, melted

FROSTING

5   3-ounce packages cream cheese, room temperature
6   tablespoons (¾ stick) unsalted butter, room temperature

1   cup coarsely chopped walnuts
25  to 30 walnut halves

FOR CARAMEL: Stir sugar and water in heavy large saucepan over medium-low heat until sugar dissolves. Increase heat and boil without stirring until deep amber color, brushing down sides of pan with wet pastry brush and swirling pan occasionally, about 9 minutes. Remove from heat. Add cream. Stir until caramel is smooth. Return to medium heat. Stir until caramel returns to boil and color deepens slightly, about 1 minute. Pour into bowl. Chill until cold.

FOR SYRUP: Stir water and sugar in small saucepan over medium-low heat until sugar dissolves and syrup comes to boil. Remove from heat; add dark rum.

FOR CAKE: Preheat oven to 350°F. Butter and flour 9-inch-diameter cake pan with 2-inch-high sides; line bottom with parchment. Sift first 3 ingredients into bowl. Finely grind walnuts and 2 tablespoons dry ingredients in processor.

Combine eggs and sugar in large bowl. Set bowl over saucepan

To prevent the syrup from becoming grainy, use a pastry brush dipped into water to brush down any sugar crystals sticking to the pan sides.

For best caramel flavor, boil the syrup without stirring, swirling pan occasionally for even browning, until the syrup is a deep amber color.

of gently simmering water (do not allow bottom of bowl to touch water). Whisk until mixture resembles softly whipped cream, about 4 minutes. Remove bowl from over water. Using electric mixer, beat mixture until cool and heavy ribbon forms when beaters are lifted, about 5 minutes. Sift flour mixture over egg mixture in 3 additions; fold in each addition. Sprinkle walnut mixture and melted butter over and fold in. (Do not overfold or batter will deflate.) Transfer batter to prepared pan. Bake cake until tester inserted into center comes out clean, about 25 minutes. Cool in pan 5 minutes. Cut around cake. Turn out onto rack; cool completely.

FOR FROSTING: Using electric mixer, beat room-temperature cream cheese and unsalted butter in large bowl until blended. Beat in 1⅓ cups cold caramel sauce in 4 additions.

Cut cake in half. Place bottom half, cut side up, on plate. Drizzle with 5 tablespoons syrup. Spread 1½ cups frosting over. Place top half, cut side down, on top. Drizzle with 5 tablespoons syrup. Spread 1½ cups frosting over top and sides of cake. Drizzle 3 tablespoons caramel sauce onto top. Using tip of knife, swirl decoratively. Press chopped nuts onto sides of cake. Place nut halves around top edge. *(Can be made 1 day ahead. Chill.)*

10 TO 12 SERVINGS

Once the syrup turns deep amber, immediately remove the pan from the heat. Gradually add cream to syrup (mixture will bubble vigorously).

To finish, return the sauce to the heat. Stir the caramel with a wooden spoon until any undisolved bits are melted and the sauce is smooth.

# Chocolate Strawberry Shortcake

◆ ◆ ◆

SAUCE

⅔   cup whipping cream
2   tablespoons (packed) golden brown sugar
6   ounces bittersweet (not unsweetened) or
    semisweet chocolate, chopped
1   tablespoon brandy
1   teaspoon vanilla extract

BISCUIT

2   cups all purpose flour
5   tablespoons sugar
1½  teaspoons baking powder
½   teaspoon baking soda
½   teaspoon salt
½   cup (1 stick) chilled unsalted butter, cut into small pieces
3   ounces bittersweet (not unsweetened) or
    semisweet chocolate, chopped
⅔   cup plus 2 tablespoons buttermilk

FILLING

2   pounds strawberries, hulled
5   tablespoons sugar
1⅓  cups chilled whipping cream
½   teaspoon vanilla extract

FOR SAUCE: Combine cream and sugar in heavy small saucepan. Stir over medium-high heat until mixture comes to boil. Remove from heat. Add chocolate and stir until chocolate melts and sauce is smooth. Mix in brandy and vanilla. *(Can be prepared 2 days ahead. Cover and refrigerate.)*

FOR BISCUIT: Preheat oven to 375°F. Butter 9-inch-diameter cake pan with 1½-inch-high sides; dust with flour. Combine 2 cups flour, 3 tablespoons sugar, baking powder, baking soda and salt in large bowl; whisk to blend. Add butter and rub in with fingertips until mixture resembles coarse meal. Add chopped chocolate. Gradually add ⅔ cup buttermilk, stirring with fork until dough forms.

Transfer dough to cake pan; press gently to level top. Brush dough with 2 tablespoons buttermilk, then sprinkle with 2 tablespoons sugar. Bake until cooked through and golden on top, about 25 minutes. Cool in pan on rack (biscuit will be 1 to 1½ inches high).

FOR FILLING: Reserve 8 berries for garnish. Slice remaining

◆ ◆ ◆

Making one large shortcake is impressive and lots of fun—especially when chocolate is added to the basic combination of ingredients.

◆ ◆ ◆

berries into large bowl. Add 4 tablespoons sugar and toss to coat; let stand until berries begin to release juices, about 30 minutes. Combine whipping cream, vanilla and 1 tablespoon sugar in medium bowl. Whip to soft peaks. Cover and chill cream.

Rewarm sauce over low heat, stirring often. Cut around pan sides to loosen biscuit. Turn biscuit out onto work surface. Using long serrated knife, carefully cut biscuit in half horizontally. Using large spatula as aid, place biscuit bottom on platter. Spoon sliced berries with their juices over. Drizzle with some chocolate sauce. Spoon all but ½ cup whipped cream over; cover with biscuit top. Drop reserved whipped cream in dollops onto biscuit. Garnish with reserved whole strawberries. Serve, passing chocolate sauce.

8 SERVINGS

# Individual Chocolate Mousse Cakes

◆ ◆ ◆

14  ounces bittersweet (not unsweetened) or semisweet choclate, chopped
1¼  cups chilled whipping bream
1  teaspoon ground cinnamon
¼  cup Grand Marnier or other orange liqueur
6  large eggs
½  cup (packed) brown sugar
   Sweetened whipped cream

Preheat oven to 350°F. Butter and flour twelve ¾-cup custard cups. Stir chocolate in bowl set over simmering water until smooth. Remove from over water. Cool to lukewarm, about 10 minutes.

Using electric mixer, beat cream and cinnamon in medium bowl until soft peaks form. Add liqueur; beat until stiff peaks form. Beat eggs and sugar in large bowl until very light, 5 minutes. Gradually beat chocolate into egg mixture, then fold in cream.

Divide batter among prepared cups. Set cups in large roasting pan. Add enough hot water to pan to come halfway up sides of cups. Bake until tops of cakes look dry and tester inserted into center comes out with moist crumbs attached, about 18 minutes. Transfer cups to racks; cool cakes completely.

Cut around cakes to loosen; turn out onto plates. Serve cakes with sweetened whipped cream.

12 SERVINGS

# SWEETER THAN CREAM

What's dessert without a good dollop of whipped cream? It can top pies and pastries, soufflés and fruit desserts, and frost a cake, too. In many such recipes, it's sweetened with sugar and sometimes it's flavored. Here are some tips for sweetening this favorite topping.

Whip chilled heavy cream just until very soft peaks form, then add either sugar (powdered or granulated) for sweetened whipped cream or a flavoring (see the suggestions below). Continue whipping until soft peaks form, then use immediately or chill. For whipped cream that's firm enough to pipe through a decorating bag, whip until stiff peaks form.

Try any of these flavorings.

◆ Molasses or maple syrup
◆ Rum or rum extract
◆ Brown sugar or vanilla extract for a butterscotch flavor
◆ Lemon or orange zest or lemon or orange extract
◆ Almond extract or amaretto liqueur
◆ Ground ginger or finely minced crystallized ginger
◆ Instant espresso powder
◆ Peppermint extract or crème de menthe liqueur

◆ ◆ ◆

## ZABAGLIONE: A CLASSIC ITALIAN

Zabaglione, like that other traditional Italian dessert, tiramisù, is enjoying renewed popularity in American kitchens. Both are rich and creamy, but zabaglione has another key thing going for it: It's very easy to make. Add to that its versatility—zabaglione can be served either on its own or as a custard sauce for fresh fruit or spooned over a slice of cake—and it is simple to see why this light and foamy sweet is so popular.

Zabaglione, or *zabione* as it's called in Italy, is a richly flavored custard sauce of egg yolks, sugar and, traditionally, Marsala wine. Some restaurants still perform its preparation tableside, using a big copper bowl to whisk the sauce to a perfect froth and serving it immediately. For home cooks, it can be easier to fold in a stabilizing agent, such as whipped cream or gelatin, which allows you to make the sauce ahead.

Its versatility extends to flavoring possibilties as well. Try any of these:

◆ Coffee-flavored liqueur and espresso powder

◆ Finely grated citrus peel with juice or citrus-flavored liqueur

◆ Rum, Madeira, Sherry or Champagne in place of the Marsala

◆ ◆ ◆

# ◆ MOUSSES & PUDDINGS ◆

# Champagne Zabaglione with Fresh Fruit Compote

◆ ◆ ◆

ZABAGLIONE
1   cup dry Champagne or other sparkling wine
¾   cup powdered sugar
5   large egg yolks
2   tablespoons light corn syrup

6   tablespoons chilled whipping cream

FRUIT COMPOTE
2   large oranges

½   small pineapple, peeled, cored
1   basket strawberries, hulled, quartered
2   kiwis, peeled, sliced into rounds
1   pear, peeled, cored, diced

6   tablespoons chilled dry Champagne
6   whole strawberries

FOR ZABAGLIONE: Whisk Champagne, sugar, yolks and corn syrup in large metal bowl to blend. Set bowl over saucepan of simmering water (do not allow bottom of bowl to touch water). Whisk constantly until mixture has tripled in volume and candy thermometer registers 160°F, about 10 minutes. Remove from over water. Using electric mixer, beat zabaglione until completely cool, about 5 minutes.

Beat cream to soft peaks in medium bowl. Fold into cooled zabaglione. Chill until ready to use. *(Can be made 1 day ahead. Cover and keep chilled. Stir lightly to loosen texture before serving.)*

FOR FRUIT COMPOTE: Using small sharp knife, cut off peel and white pith from oranges. Working over bowl, cut between membranes to release orange segments. Set aside.

Using tip of vegetable peeler, cut out eyes from pineapple; discard eyes. Dice pineapple. Combine pineapple, quartered strawberries, kiwis and pear in large bowl. Mix in oranges.

Spoon fruit into 6 stemmed glasses. Pour 1 tablespoon Champagne over fruit in each goblet. Top fruit with zabaglione. Garnish each serving with whole strawberry and serve immediately.

*6 SERVINGS*

# Summer Pudding

◆ ◆ ◆

6    ½-inch-thick slices French bread (each about 6 x 4 inches)

1½   cups halved hulled strawberries (about 6 ounces)
1½   cups frozen unsweetened raspberries, unthawed
1½   cups frozen unsweetened blueberries, unthawed
1½   cups frozen unsweetened blackberries, unthawed
½    cup sugar
¼    cup cranberry juice cocktail

     Lightly sweetened whipped cream

Preheat oven to 400°F. Place bread slices on baking sheet. Bake bread until slightly dry and firm, about 8 minutes. Trim crusts and discard. Arrange enough bread slices over bottom and up sides of 6- to 6½-cup bowl or pudding mold to line completely; trim overhang from bread slices and reserve.

Combine strawberries, raspberries, blueberries, blackberries, sugar and cranberry juice cocktail in heavy large saucepan. Stir over low heat just until frozen berries thaw and sugar dissolves, about 10 minutes. Remove from heat. Ladle warm fruit and juices into

◆ ◆ ◆

This pretty dessert of bread and assorted sweetened berries gets its name from the time of year when the berries are in season. But many people want to eat this delicious pudding even when fresh berries aren't available. Fortunately, frozen ones work just as well. (Begin preparing this recipe a day before serving so that it can set up overnight.)

◆ ◆ ◆

bread-lined bowl. Cover fruit with reserved bread trimmings. Place small plate atop pudding; weigh down plate with cans or weights. Refrigerate pudding overnight.

Remove weights and plate. Invert pudding onto platter. Cut into wedges and serve with sweetened whipped cream.

6 SERVINGS

# Sweet Cherry Clafouti

◆ ◆ ◆

| | |
|---|---|
| 4 | large eggs |
| ½ | cup sugar |
| | Pinch of salt |
| ⅓ | cup all purpose flour |
| 1 | cup whole milk |
| ¼ | cup (½ stick) unsalted butter, melted |
| 1 | teaspoon vanilla extract |
| 1 | teaspoon grated lemon peel |
| 1 | 1-pound bag frozen pitted dark sweet cherries, thawed, drained |
| | Powdered sugar |
| | Ice cream |

Preheat oven to 325°F. Generously butter 8 x 8 x 2-inch glass baking dish. Whisk eggs, ½ cup sugar and salt in medium bowl to blend. Whisk in flour. Add milk, butter, vanilla and lemon peel and whisk until smooth. Arrange cherries in bottom of prepared baking dish. Spoon batter evenly over.

Bake until clafouti is set in center and golden on top, about 50 minutes. Cool completely. Sift powdered sugar over top of clafouti. Serve with scoops of ice cream.

6 SERVINGS

## ALL ABOUT CLAFOUTI

Served warm with a dusting of powdered sugar, ice cream or whipped cream, *clafouti* is a baked fruit dessert that has been showing up on menus in many of the country's hottest restaurants lately. Its humble origins, though, belie its newfound status. In the Limousin region of France, where it got its start, this puffy, custard-like pudding is commonly made with cherries— often by children, as simple as it is.

The basic recipe calls for baking sweetened fruit in a thin, crepe-like batter. There are many variations on this theme, however, and you'll find desserts that vary from refined to rustic and they're all called clafouti. Enrich the custard batter with cream or sour cream, pour it around poached pear halves in a pastry shell and bake to create an elegant dessert that can be served either hot or chilled. Or, reduce the amount of sugar in the batter, bake it with a handful of berries and serve with sour cream for a warming breakfast dish.

Clafouti adapts well to a variety of fruits; let the seasons be your guide. In spring, try berries or apricots; in the summer, peaches or nectarines; and in the the fall, pears or plums.

◆ ◆ ◆

# Lemon Custard Phyllo Cups

❖ ❖ ❖

CUSTARD

½  cup sugar

2  tablespoons cornstarch

   Pinch of salt

1  cup cold water

¼  cup fresh lemon juice

1  large egg

½  teaspoon grated lemon peel

1  teaspoon unsalted butter

1  drop yellow food coloring

PHYLLO CUPS

   Nonstick vegetable oil spray

4  sheets fresh phyllo or frozen, thawed

1  tablespoon unsalted butter, melted

1  teaspoon sugar

½  teaspoon powdered sugar

   Mint sprigs

❖ ❖ ❖

Just a few layers of phyllo make a pretty cup for the rich-tasting but light lemon custard. The leftover phyllo cups and filling can be stored separately and assembled the next day for an afternoon treat.

❖ ❖ ❖

FOR CUSTARD: Whisk sugar, cornstarch and salt in heavy medium saucepan to blend. Gradually whisk in 1 cup cold water and lemon juice. Whisk until sugar and cornstarch dissolve. Whisk in egg and lemon peel. Add butter. Whisk over medium heat until mixture boils and thickens, about 5 minutes. Remove from heat. Stir in food coloring. Transfer custard to bowl. Press plastic onto surface of custard and cool to room temperature.

FOR PHYLLO CUPS: Preheat oven to 375°F. Lightly spray eight ⅓-cup muffin cups with vegetable oil spray. Stack 4 phyllo sheets on work surface. Cut phyllo stack into six 4-inch squares, forming total of 24 squares. Press 1 phyllo square into each cup (cover remaining phyllo with plastic wrap and damp towel). Using pastry brush, dab phyllo in a few places with melted butter. Press another phyllo square atop first phyllo square, with corners at different angles. Dab with butter. Top with a third phyllo square, with corners at different angles. Sprinkle phyllo cups with sugar.

Bake until phyllo is golden brown, about 6 minutes. Transfer pan to rack and cool cups completely in pan. Remove cups from muffin tin. *(Custard and phyllo cups can be prepared 1 day ahead. Refrigerate custard. Store phyllo cups in airtight containers.)*

Spoon some of custard into each of 4 cups (save remaining custard and cups for another use.) Sift powdered sugar over edges of phyllo. Garnish with mint sprigs. Arrange on plates.

4 SERVINGS

# Panna Cotta with Crushed Raspberry Sauce

◆ ◆ ◆

1   12-ounce package frozen unsweetened raspberries, thawed, drained
3   tablespoons plus ¼ cup sugar

    Nonstick vegetable oil spray
1   tablespoon plus ⅓ cup milk (do not use low-fat or nonfat)
1¼  teaspoons unflavored gelatin

1¾  cups whipping cream
½   vanilla bean, split lengthwise
2   tablespoons Frangelico (hazelnut liqueur; optional)

Place raspberries in small bowl. Crush lightly with back of spoon. Stir in 3 tablespoons sugar. Set sauce aside.

Spray four ¾-cup custard cups with vegetable oil spray. Pour 1 tablespoon milk into a small bowl. Sprinkle gelatin over and let stand until softened, about 10 minutes.

Combine cream, ¼ cup sugar and ⅓ cup milk in heavy medium saucepan. Scrape in seeds from vanilla bean; add bean. Bring to boil over medium heat, stirring often. Remove from heat. Add gelatin mixture and stir until melted. Strain mixture into large glass measuring cup. Stir in Frangelico, if desired. Divide among prepared cups. Chill until cold, about 2 hours. Cover and chill overnight.

Run small sharp knife around sides of cups to loosen custards. Invert custards onto plates. Serve with sauce.

4 SERVINGS

*Panna cotta* means "cooked cream" in Italian, and, indeed, that is just about all these elegant little desserts consist of. A touch of hazelnut liqueur and a sauce of crushed berries add flavor interest.

# Caramel, White Chocolate and Rum Bread Pudding

◆ ◆ ◆

5    cups 1 x 1x½-inch pieces trimmed whole wheat bread

⅔    cup sugar
⅓    cup light corn syrup
⅓    cup water
¼    cup apple cider
3    tablespoons unsalted butter

½    cup raisins
1½   teaspoons ground cinnamon
1½   teaspoons ground coriander
1    teaspoon ground ginger
2    large eggs, beaten to blend
¼    cup dark rum
5    ounces good-quality white chocolate, coarsely chopped

Preheat oven to 325°F. Arrange bread on large baking sheet; bake until dry, about 10 minutes. Transfer bread to large bowl. Increase temperature to 350°F.

Stir sugar, syrup and water in heavy medium saucepan over low heat until sugar dissolves. Increase heat and boil without stirring until amber color, brushing down sides of pan with wet pastry brush and swirling pan occasionally, about 12 minutes. Remove from heat. Add cider and butter. Return to low heat; stir until sauce comes to simmer. Cover pan and simmer until caramel bits dissolve, stirring occasionally, about 5 minutes. Set pan over ice; stir until caramel cools to lukewarm, about 5 minutes.

Mix raisins, spices, eggs, then rum into caramel. Add to bread. Mix in white chocolate. Let stand 10 minutes, stirring occasionally.

Butter eight ½-cup custard cups. Divide pudding among cups. Place in large baking pan. Pour hot water into pan to come halfway up sides of cups. Bake puddings until set in center, about 30 minutes. Cool 10 minutes before serving.

MAKES 8

◆ ◆ ◆

A cider-flavored caramel sauce, raisins, aromatic spices, rum and chunks of white chocolate all take this pudding beyond the ordinary.

◆ ◆ ◆

# Dried Apricot Soufflés

◆ ◆ ◆

9   ounces dried apricots (about 1½ cups)
2   cups boiling water

2   teaspoons unsalted butter, melted
3   teaspoons plus 2½ tablespoons sugar
5   teaspoons amaretto liqueur
2   teaspoons fresh lemon juice

5   large egg whites
    Pinch of salt
    Pinch of cream of tartar

Place apricots in large bowl. Pour boiling water over. Cover; soak apricots in water 2 hours.

Preheat oven to 400°F. Brush six 1¼-cup soufflé dishes with butter. Sprinkle bottom and sides of each dish with ½ teaspoon sugar. Drain apricots, reserving 3 tablespoons soaking liquid. Transfer apricots and reserved soaking liquid to processor. Puree until smooth. Blend in 1½ tablespoons sugar, amaretto and lemon juice. Transfer to bowl. *(Can be made 2 days ahead. Cover and chill.)*

Using electric mixer, beat egg whites, salt and cream of tartar to soft peaks in another large bowl. Gradually add 1 tablespoon sugar and beat until stiff but not dry. Stir ¼ of egg whites into apricot mixture to lighten. Gently fold remaining beaten egg whites into apricot mixture in 2 additions.

Divide batter among prepared dishes. Place dishes on baking sheet and bake soufflés until puffed and golden on top, about 20 minutes. Serve immediately.

MAKES 6

These individual soufflés make an excellent dessert at brunch (see the menu on page 117). And as delicious as they are, they are also surprisingly low in fat and calories.

◆ ◆ ◆

# Chocolate Soufflé-filled Crepes

◆ ◆ ◆

SAUCE

2     cups half and half
½     vanilla bean, split lengthwise
2     large eggs
½     cup sugar

CREPES

½     cup whole milk
1     large egg
2½   tablespoons sugar
1     tablespoon unsalted butter, melted
½     teaspoon vanilla extract
2     tablespoons unsweetened cocoa powder
2     tablespoons all purpose flour
    Pinch of salt

    Nonstick vegetable oil spray
    Additional melted butter

SOUFFLE FILLING

4½   ounces semisweet chocolate, chopped
2     tablespoons half and half
1     tablespoon dark rum
2     large egg yolks
¼     cup sugar

3     large egg whites
    Pinch of salt

FOR SAUCE: Pour half and half into heavy medium saucepan. Scrape in seeds from vanilla bean; add bean. Bring to simmer. Remove from heat. Whisk eggs and sugar in bowl to blend. Gradually whisk in hot half and half mixture. Return mixture to same saucepan; stir over low heat until sauce thickens and coats spoon, about 4 minutes (do not boil). Strain sauce. Chill.

FOR CREPES: Blend first 5 ingredients in blender. Add cocoa, flour and salt and blend until smooth. Chill 1 to 3 hours.

Spray 9-inch-diameter nonstick skillet with 6-inch-diameter bottom with vegetable oil spray. Brush with melted butter. Heat over low heat 1 minute. Whisk batter; pour 2 tablespoons into skillet. Swirl batter to coat bottom of skillet. Cook until crepe edges are very dry, about 2 minutes (do not undercook; crepe is fragile). Using spatula, loosen edges and turn crepe over; cook until set, about 1 minute. Place crepe on paper towel. Top with another paper towel. Repeat with remaining crepe batter, brushing skillet with butter before cooking each crepe. Cool crepes. *(Sauce and crepes can be made 1 day ahead. Cover separately; chill.)*

FOR FILLING: Preheat oven to 400°F. Line baking sheet with parchment paper. Stir chocolate in large metal bowl set over saucepan of simmering water until melted and smooth. Cool chocolate 5 minutes. Whisk in half and half and rum. Using electric mixer, beat yolks and sugar in medium bowl until thick and pale yellow ribbon forms when beaters are lifted, about 3 minutes. Whisk yolk mixture into chocolate mixture.

Using clean dry beaters, beat whites and salt in another large bowl until stiff but not dry. Fold ⅓ of whites into chocolate mixture. Fold in remaining whites.

Place crepes on prepared baking sheet. Place ⅓ cup soufflé mixture on 1 half of each crepe; fold second half of crepe over filling (do not press). Bake until soufflés are set, about 6 minutes. Using large spatula, carefully transfer crepes to plates. Serve with sauce.

6 SERVINGS

# Cardamom Crème Brûlée

◆ ◆ ◆

| | |
|---|---|
| 8 | large egg yolks |
| ¾ | cup plus 6 teaspoons sugar |
| 1½ | teaspoons ground cardamom |
| 3 | cups whipping cream |

Preheat oven to 350°F. Place six ¾-cup ramekins or custard cups in large roasting pan. Whisk yolks and ¾ cup sugar in large bowl to blend. Stir in cardamom. Bring cream to boil in medium saucepan. Gradually whisk into yolks. Pour custard into ramekins.

Pour hot water into roasting pan to come halfway up sides of ramekins. Bake custards until set in center, about 40 minutes. Cool; refrigerate custards overnight.

Preheat broiler. Arrange ramekins on baking sheet. Sprinkle 1 teaspoon sugar over each. Broil until sugar browns, rotating baking sheet for even broiling and watching closely, about 2 minutes. Chill custards at least 1 and up to 6 hours before serving.

6 SERVINGS

◆ ◆ ◆

Cardamom adds a hint of exotic flavor to these creamy custards. (Make them ahead of time—up to six hours— to give them time to chill.)

◆ ◆ ◆

# White Russian Sorbet

♦ ♦ ♦

1¾  cups water
½  cup sugar
3½  teaspoons instant espresso powder
1  tablespoon dark corn syrup
½  cup whipping cream
¼  cup vodka
¼  cup Kahlúa or other coffee liqueur

Coffee beans

Stir water and sugar in heavy medium saucepan over medium heat until sugar dissolves. Increase heat and bring to boil. Remove from heat. Add espresso powder and stir to dissolve. Pour into medium bowl. Mix in corn syrup, then whipping cream, ¼ cup vodka and Kahlúa. Refrigerate mixture until cold, about 2 hours.

Transfer sorbet mixture* to ice cream maker; process according to manufacturer's instructions. Transfer sorbet to container; cover and freeze until firm, about 2 hours. *(Can be made 2 days ahead.)*

Freeze 4 coffee cups for 30 minutes. Scoop sorbet into frozen cups. Garnish with coffee beans and serve immediately.

*\*To make this into a granita, mix an additional ½ cup water into sorbet mixture. Freeze until semifirm, whisking occasionally, about 3 hours. Cover and freeze until solid, at least 6 hours or overnight. Using fork, scrape surface of granita to form crystals. Scoop crystals into frozen cups and serve immediately.*

**4** SERVINGS

♦ ♦ ♦

Taking a cue from the classic drink, this dessert has a rich and creamy coffee flavor. It looks pretty spooned into glass coffee cups or mugs and topped with a few coffee (real or chocolate) beans. (Pictured opposite, with the Blue Tidal Wave Sorbet. page 208, and the Kir Royale Sorbet, page 209. All three were prepared using the "granita" technique.)

♦ ♦ ♦

# Frozen Fruit Fantasy

◆ ◆ ◆

3    cups finely ground gingersnap cookies (about 13½ ounces)
½    cup (packed) golden brown sugar
2    teaspoons ground ginger
¾    cup (1½ sticks) unsalted butter, melted

2    pints mango sorbet, slightly softened
1    pint lime sorbet, slightly softened

½    small pineapple, peeled, cored, chopped
1    small papaya, peeled, seeded, chopped
1    small mango, peeled, pitted, chopped
2    ½-pint baskets blackberries
     Shredded sweetened coconut, toasted

Combine gingersnap cookie crumbs, brown sugar and ginger in large bowl. Stir in melted butter. Press over bottom and up sides of 9-inch-diameter springform pan with 2½-inch-high sides. Freeze crust until firm, about 20 minutes.

Spread mango sorbet in crust; freeze until firm, about 20 minutes. Spread lime sorbet over mango. Freeze until firm, about 30 minutes. *(Can be made 1 day ahead. Cover and keep frozen.)*

Mix fruit in medium bowl. Remove pan sides from dessert. Place dessert on platter. Spoon fruit atop lime sorbet. Sprinkle with shredded coconut and then serve.

8 SERVINGS

# Blue Tidal Wave Sorbet

◆ ◆ ◆

1½   cups water
¼    cup sugar
½    cup plus 1 tablespoon frozen lemonade concentrate
5    tablespoons vodka
3    tablespoons blue curaçao

Stir water and sugar in heavy saucepan over medium heat until sugar dissolves. Increase heat; bring to boil. Remove from heat. Add concentrate; stir until dissolved. Pour into bowl. Mix in vodka and blue curaçao. Chill until cold, about 2 hours.

◆ ◆ ◆

This lemon-based frozen treat is accented with blue curaçao for a striking color. For fun, serve the sorbet in scallop shells, which are sold at cookware stores nationwide.

◆ ◆ ◆

Transfer sorbet mixture* to ice cream maker; process according to manufacturer's instructions. Transfer to container; cover and freeze until firm, about 2 hours. *(Can be made 2 days ahead.)*

Freeze 4 stemmed coupes or scallop shells for 1 hour. Scoop sorbet into frozen coupes and serve immediately.

*\*To make this into a granita, place the bowl of sorbet mixture directly in freezer. Freeze until semifirm, whisking occasionally, about 3 hours. Cover; freeze until solid, at least 6 hours or overnight. Using fork, scrape surface to form crystals. Scoop into coupes.*

4 SERVINGS

# Kir Royale Sorbet

◆ ◆ ◆

1¼  cups water

⅔  cup sugar

5  tablespoons crème de cassis (black currant liqueur)

1⅓  cups chilled dry Champagne

Champagne grapes or other grapes (optional)

Stir water and sugar in heavy medium saucepan over medium heat until sugar dissolves. Increase heat and bring mixture to boil. Pour mixture into medium bowl. Mix in 5 tablespoons crème de cassis. Refrigerate mixture 2 hours.

Stir Champagne into sorbet mixture. Process sorbet mixture* in ice cream maker according to the manufacturer's instructions. Transfer sorbet to container; cover and freeze until firm, about 2 hours. *(Can be prepared 2 days ahead; keep frozen.)*

Freeze 4 Martini glasses or Champagne coupes for 1 hour. Scoop sorbet into frozen glasses. Garnish each with small cluster of grapes, if desired, and serve.

*\*To make this into a granita, mix an additional 1 cup water into sorbet mixture. Freeze until semifirm, whisking occasionally, about 3 hours. Cover and freeze until solid, at least 6 hours or overnight. Using fork, scrape surface of granita to form crystals. Scoop crystals into frozen glasses; serve immediately.*

4 SERVINGS

◆ ◆ ◆

Kir royale, the French apertif of Champagne with a splash of crème de cassis becomes a sophisticated sorbet in this recipe. If you have them, Champagne coupes or Martini glasses make elegant servers.

◆ ◆ ◆

# Vanilla Ice Cream and Ginger Molasses Cookie Sandwiches

◆ ◆ ◆

COOKIES

| | |
|---|---|
| 2 | cups all purpose flour |
| 2 | teaspoons baking powder |
| 2½ | teaspoons ground ginger |
| 1 | teaspoon ground cinnamon |
| 1 | teaspoon ground cloves |
| 1 | teaspoon salt |
| ½ | cup (1 stick) unsalted butter, room temperature |
| ¼ | cup vegetable shortening, room temperature |
| 1 | cup (packed) brown sugar |
| 1 | egg |
| ¼ | cup unsulfured (light) molasses |
| 1 | tablespoon grated orange peel |
| | Sugar |

SANDWICHES

| | |
|---|---|
| 1 | pint vanilla ice cream, softened slightly |
| ½ | cup chopped stem ginger in syrup |
| | Fresh strawberries, hulled, sliced |

Ice cream sandwiches—but better. The cookies are also superb on their own. (You can make the sandwiches a day ahead. Wrap them tightly in plastic and keep frozen.)

FOR COOKIES: Sift first six ingredients into medium bowl. Combine butter, shortening and brown sugar in large bowl. Using electric mixer, beat butter mixture until fluffy. Add egg, molasses and peel; beat until blended. Add dry ingredients; mix just until incorporated. Cover; chill 1 hour.

Preheat oven to 350°F. Butter 2 baking sheets. Place sugar in small bowl. Using wet hands, form dough into 12 equal pieces; shape pieces into balls. Roll in sugar to coat. Transfer to prepared sheets, spacing 2½ inches apart. Bake until cookies are pale golden and cracked on top but still soft, about 15 minutes. Cool on sheets 1 minute. Transfer to racks; cool completely.

FOR SANDWICHES: Place ice cream in medium bowl. Stir in ginger. Freeze until almost firm, about 30 minutes.

Place 6 cookies on work surface, flat side up. Top each with ⅓ cup ice cream. Spread to ¼ inch from edge of cookies. Top each with second cookie. Press to adhere. Freeze until firm, at least 2 hours. Garnish with berries and serve.

MAKES 6 SANDWICHES

# Pistachio Ice Cream

◆ ◆ ◆

½ cup shelled unsalted pistachios
6 tablespoons sugar
3 large egg yolks
1 cup whole milk
¾ cup whipping cream

Combine nuts and 4 tablespoons sugar in processor. Grind until mixture forms moist clumps, occasionally scraping down sides of bowl, about 3 minutes. Whisk yolks with 2 tablespoons sugar in medium bowl until very thick. Combine milk and cream in heavy medium saucepan. Bring to boil. Gradually whisk hot milk mixture into yolk mixture. Mix in nut paste. Return custard to same saucepan; stir over medium-low heat until mixture thickens and leaves path on back of spoon when finger is drawn across, about 4 minutes (do not boil). Transfer to bowl. Cover custard and refrigerate until cold, at least 3 hours.

Transfer custard to ice cream maker; process according to manufacturer's instructions. Place in container; cover and freeze. *(Can be prepared up to 3 days ahead.)*

6 SERVINGS

◆ ◆ ◆

This delicious ice cream is excellent with the Sweet Cherry Clafouti on page 199. It would also make a fitting ending to an Asian-themed meal.

◆ ◆ ◆

# Peanut Brittle Ice Cream Sundaes with Chocolate Sauce

◆ ◆ ◆

PEANUT BRITTLE
¾  cup sugar
⅔  cup light corn syrup
2  tablespoons water
½  teaspoon baking soda
1½ cups salted cocktail peanuts

ICE CREAM
1  cup milk (do not use low-fat or nonfat)
1  cup sugar
1  vanilla bean, split lengthwise
4  large egg yolks
3  cups chilled whipping cream

Chocolate Sauce (see recipe opposite)
Whipped cream

◆ ◆ ◆

An ice-cream parlor special comes home in this outstanding treat. The brittle has to be cooked to a very high temperature, so be sure to have a bowl of ice water nearby to cool down your fingers in case of any spills.

FOR PEANUT BRITTLE: Lightly butter large baking sheet. Combine sugar, corn syrup and water in heavy medium saucepan. Stir over medium-low heat until sugar dissolves. Attach clip-on candy thermometer to side of pan. Increase heat to medium. Using wooden spoon, stir constantly but slowly until temperature reaches 300°F, occassionally brushing down sides of pan with wet pastry brush, about 20 minutes. Remove from heat; immediately add baking soda and stir in peanuts. Working quickly, pour out onto baking sheet. Cool completely. Coarsely chop peanut brittle. *(Can be made 3 days ahead. Store in airtight container.)*

FOR ICE CREAM: Combine milk and sugar in heavy medium saucepan. Scrape in seeds from vanilla bean; add bean. Stir over medium heat until sugar dissolves. Bring to boil. Remove from heat. Whisk yolks in medium bowl to blend. Gradually whisk in hot milk mixture. Return mixture to saucepan. Stir over medium-low heat until custard thickens and leaves path on back of spoon when finger is drawn across, about 2 minutes (do not boil). Strain into bowl. Whisk in cream. Refrigerate until chilled.

Process custard in ice cream maker according to manufacturer's instructions. Transfer to large container. Mix in 2 cups chopped peanut brittle. Cover and freeze. Reserve remaining brittle for garnish. *(Can be made 3 days ahead. Keep frozen.)*

Top ice cream with sauce, whipped cream and brittle.

8 SERVINGS

## Chocolate Sauce

⅔  cup water

2  tablespoons light corn syrup

8  ounces semisweet chocolate, chopped

2  ounces bittersweet (not unsweetened) chocolate, chopped

Bring water and corn syrup to simmer in heavy medium saucepan. Reduce heat to low. Add both chocolates and stir until smooth. *(Can be made 1 day ahead. Cover and refrigerate sauce. Rewarm over low heat.)* Serve sauce warm.

MAKES ABOUT 1½ CUPS

## Tropical Fruit Granita

3  cups tropical fruit juice blend (such as
   pineapple-orange-passion fruit)

4½  tablespoons sugar

1½  tablespoons dark rum

1  tablespoon fresh lime juice

¾  teaspoon vanilla extract

Stir juice and sugar in large bowl until sugar dissolves. Add rum, lime juice and vanilla. Pour mixture into shallow baking dish. Freeze until mixture is entirely crystallized, stirring frequently and scraping crystals from around edges, about 5 hours. *(Can be prepared 2 days ahead. Cover and keep frozen.)*

Using tines of fork, scrape frozen juice mixture to form small flakes. Spoon granita into goblets and serve.

6 SERVINGS

A light dessert that absolutely no one need feel guilty about (only 119 calories and no fat per serving). It's easy, too, since you don't need an ice cream maker to prepare it.

◆ ◆ ◆

# ◆ COOKIES ◆

# Irish Coffee Meringues

◆ ◆ ◆

MERINGUES

7 tablespoons sugar

3 tablespoons (packed) dark brown sugar

1 teaspoon instant espresso powder or instant coffee powder

2 large egg whites

FILLING

1¼ cups chilled whipping cream

2 tablespoons sugar

2 tablespoons Irish whiskey

2 teaspoons instant espresso powder or instant coffee powder

Chocolate-covered coffee beans (optional)

FOR MERINGUES: Preheat oven to 250°F. Line 2 heavy baking sheets with parchment paper. Stir 3 tablespoons sugar, 1 tablespoon brown sugar and 1 teaspoon instant espresso powder in small bowl to blend well. Using handheld electric mixer, beat 2 egg whites in medium bowl until medium-stiff peaks form. Add remaining 4 tablespoons sugar and 2 tablespoons dark brown sugar to egg whites by tablespoonfuls and beat until stiff peaks form. Fold coffee-sugar mixture into meringue.

Drop meringue by rounded tablespoonfuls onto prepared baking sheets, spacing evenly. Using knife, gently spread meringues to 2½- to 3-inch rounds. Bake until meringues are dry and can easily be lifted from parchment, about 45 minutes. Transfer meringues to racks and cool completely. *(Can be prepared 2 days ahead. Store in airtight containers at room temperature.)*

FOR FILLING: Beat 1 cup whipping cream in medium bowl to medium-firm peaks. Add sugar, Irish whiskey and instant espresso powder and beat until firm peaks form.

Place 1 meringue on plate, flat side down. Spoon 1 generous tablespoon of espresso cream filling over. Top with another meringue, flat side down, and press gently until filling spreads to edge. Repeat with remaining meringues and filling. *(Can be prepared 1 hour ahead. Cover with plastic wrap and refrigerate.)*

Beat remaining ¼ cup whipping cream in small bowl until firm peaks form. Spoon small dollop of cream atop each meringue. Garnish each with chocolate-covered coffee beans, if desired.

6 SERVINGS

# Coconut Cup Cookies

◆ ◆ ◆

Nonstick vegetable oil spray
1    cup sweetened shredded coconut (about 4 ounces)
¾    cup sugar
1    egg
1    teaspoon vanilla extract
¼    cup (½ stick) butter, melted, cooled

2    refrigerated pie crusts (one 15-ounce package), room temperature
¼    cup (about) apricot jam or orange marmalade

Preheat oven to 375°F. Spray 12-cup muffin pan with oil spray. Mix coconut, sugar, egg and vanilla in medium bowl. Stir in butter.

Unfold 1 crust on work surface. Using 3-inch-diameter cutter, cut out 12 rounds from crust, patching crust scraps as needed to form 12 rounds. Press rounds gently into prepared muffin cups; bake until light brown, about 10 minutes. Drop about ½ teaspoon jam, then 1 scant tablespoon coconut filling into each warm pastry. Bake until filling is brown, about 15 minutes. Cut around cookies to loosen. Using spatula, transfer cookies to rack and cool. Repeat with remaining crust, jam and filling to make 12 more cookies.

MAKES 24

Shaped in muffin cups, these cookies have a crisp pie-pastry bottom and a chewy jam-accented coconut filling.

◆ ◆ ◆

# Mexican Brownies

The traditional Mexican flavor combination of cinnamon and chocolate adds interest to these brownies, which are enhanced by a brown sugar and almond topping.

◆ ◆ ◆

BROWNIES

4 ounces unsweetened chocolate, chopped
½ cup (1 stick) unsalted butter
1¼ cups (packed) golden brown sugar
1 tablespoon ground cinnamon
¼ teaspoon salt
3 large eggs
1 teaspoon vanilla extract
¾ cup all purpose flour
1 cup milk chocolate chips (about 6 ounces)

BROWN SUGAR TOPPING

1 cup (packed) golden brown sugar
¼ cup whipping cream
1 tablespoon unsalted butter
¾ teaspoon vanilla extract
½ cup sliced almonds

FOR BROWNIES: Preheat oven to 325°F. Line 8-inch square baking pan with foil, extending foil over sides. Stir unsweetened chocolate and butter in heavy large saucepan over low heat until melted and smooth. Cool 5 minutes. Whisk in sugar, cinnamon and salt. Whisk in eggs, 1 at a time, then vanilla. Continue to whisk until batter is smooth, about 2 minutes. Add flour and whisk just until blended. Stir in chocolate chips. Pour batter into prepared pan, smoothing surface. Bake until tester inserted into center comes out with a few moist crumbs attached, about 35 minutes. Cool brownie completely in pan on rack.

FOR TOPPING: Whisk sugar, cream and butter in heavy small saucepan over low heat until mixture is smooth and comes to boil. Remove from heat; mix in vanilla. Cool 10 minutes. Whisk until thick enough to spread. Spread over brownie. Sprinkle with almonds. Let stand until topping sets, about 1 hour. *(Can be made 1 day ahead. Cover brownie and keep chilled.)*

Using foil as aid, lift brownie from pan. Cut brownie into 16 squares. Serve cold or at room temperature.

MAKES 16

# Peanut Butter and Chocolate Chunk Brownies

◆ ◆ ◆

6 tablespoons (¾ stick) unsalted butter, room temperature

½ cup nutty old-fashioned-style or freshly ground peanut butter

1¼ cups (packed) golden brown sugar

2 large eggs

2 teaspoons vanilla extract

¾ cup all purpose flour

1 teaspoon baking powder

¼ teaspoon salt

4 ounces bittersweet (not unsweetened) or semisweet chocolate, coarsely chopped

Preheat oven to 350°F. Generously butter and flour 8-inch square baking pan. Using electric mixer, beat butter in large bowl until smooth. If oil has separated from peanut butter, stir to blend. Add peanut butter to butter; beat until well blended, scraping down sides of bowl occasionally. Beat in brown sugar. Add eggs 1 at a time, beating well after each addition. Beat in vanilla. Sift flour, baking powder and salt into medium bowl. Add to peanut butter mixture; beat until blended. Stir in chocolate.

Transfer batter to pan. Using spatula, smooth top. Bake until toothpick inserted 2 inches from edge of pan comes out with moist crumbs attached, about 33 minutes. Transfer pan to rack and cool. *(Can be made 3 days ahead. Cover; store at room temperature.)* Cut brownies into squares and serve.

MAKES ABOUT 25

◆ ◆ ◆

What sets these brownies apart from the rest is peanut butter, used as a flavoring, and chunks of bittersweet chocolate. Anyone who likes the classic candy that combines those two flavors will love these.

◆ ◆ ◆

# Almond Shortbread Cookies

◆ ◆ ◆

6 tablespoons (¾ stick) chilled unsalted butter, cut into 8 pieces
¼ cup (packed) golden brown sugar
¾ teaspoon vanilla extract
  Pinch of salt
¾ cup all purpose flour
1 tablespoon cornstarch
¼ cup sliced almonds (about 1 ounce)

Preheat oven to 375°F. Place 9-inch-diameter metal pie pan in freezer to chill. Combine butter, brown sugar, vanilla and salt in processor. Blend until smooth, about 20 seconds. Add flour and cornstarch. Using on/off turns, process until dough clumps together. Press dough evenly onto bottom of chilled pie pan. Sprinkle almonds over; press almonds lightly into dough to adhere. Freeze until chilled, about 5 minutes.

Bake shortbread until edges are golden brown, about 22 minutes. Transfer pan to rack. Cut warm shortbread into 8 wedges; cool completely in pan. *(Cookies can be prepared 1 day ahead. Cover; store at room temperature.)*

MAKES 8

# Cottage Cheese Rugelach with Walnuts

◆ ◆ ◆

*Rugelach* are classic cookies in the Jewish culinary repertoire. The surprise ingredient in this version—cottage cheese—makes for tender, rich cookies. Walnuts add flavor, too.

◆ ◆ ◆

⅔ cup small-curd cottage cheese
⅔ cup plus 3 tablespoons stick margarine, room temperature
1⅓ cups all purpose flour

½ cup (packed) golden brown sugar
½ cup chopped walnuts (about 2 ounces)
½ teaspoon ground cinnamon
½ teaspoon vanilla extract

1 egg
2 tablespoons milk

Mix cheese and ⅔ cup margarine in medium bowl. Stir in flour. Knead in bowl until dough is smooth, about 1 minute. Divide dough into 2 balls. Flatten into disks. Wrap each in plastic; freeze until firm enough to roll, about 10 minutes.

Meanwhile, combine brown sugar, walnuts, cinnamon, vanilla and 3 tablespoons margarine in processor. Blend until almost smooth paste forms. set aside.

Preheat oven to 350°F. Roll out 1 dough disk on lightly floured surface to 10-inch round. Spread half of brown sugar mixture evenly over. Cut round into 16 wedges. Starting at wide ends, roll up wedges. Bend ends in, forming crescents. Place on ungreased heavy baking sheet. Repeat rolling, filling and shaping crescents with remaining dough disk.

Beat egg and milk to blend in small bowl. Brush glaze over crescents. Bake until cooked through and light brown, about 25 minutes. Transfer cookies to racks and cool. *(Can be made 2 days ahead. Store airtight at room temperature.)*

MAKES 32

# Low-Fat Almond-Cinnamon Biscotti

◆ ◆ ◆

| | |
|---|---|
| 3 | large eggs |
| 1 | cup sugar |
| 1 | teaspoon vanilla extract |
| ¾ | teaspoon almond extract |
| 3 | cups all purpose flour |
| ½ | cup chopped toasted almonds |
| 1 | teaspoon ground cinnamon |
| ¾ | teaspoon baking soda |
| ¼ | teaspoon salt |

Preheat oven to 350°F. Grease 18 x 12 x 1-inch baking sheet. Combine first 4 ingredients in bowl of heavy-duty electric mixer fitted with paddle attachment. Beat until well blended. Mix flour, almonds, cinnamon, baking soda and salt in bowl. Gradually add to egg mixture, beating until blended (dough will be soft).

Turn dough out onto floured surface and gather together. Roll dough between palms and work surface into 16-inch-long log. Transfer to prepared sheet. Flatten log to 1-inch thickness. Bake until light brown and cracked on top, about 30 minutes. Transfer sheet to rack; cool log 10 minutes. Reduce oven temperature to 325°F.

Transfer warm log to work surface. Using serrated knife, cut log on sharp diagonal into ¼- to ⅓-inch-thick slices. Arrange on baking sheets. Bake 10 minutes per side. Transfer to racks and cool (biscotti will harden while cooling).

MAKES ABOUT 36

◆ ◆ ◆

There's no butter or oil in these crisp cookies (and so, only two grams of fat each). For the best texture, be sure to slice them thinly.

◆ ◆ ◆

# ⋄Index⋄

Page numbers in *italics* indicate color photographs.

*Strawberry-topped Lime Mousse Tart (page 176)*

# Acknowledgments

◆ ◆ ◆

The following people contributed the recipes included in this book: Bruce Aidells; Darina Allen; Allures, Nemacolin Woodlands Resort, Farmington, Pennsylvania; Mary Barber; Melanie Barnard; Beach Plum Inn & Restaurant, Menemsha, Martha's Vineyard, Massachusetts; Davina Besford; Lena Cederham Birnbaum; Bix, San Francisco, California; Carole Bloom; Marilyn Bright; Caffe Trinity, San Francisco, California; Georgina Campbell; Susan Campoy; Mary Cech; Château de Madières, Madières, Ganges, France; China House Bistro, San Francisco, California; Sara Corpening; Jameson Cox; Lane Crowther; Charles Dale; Robin Davis; Janet Hazen De Jesus; The Dining Room, The Ritz-Carlton, Chicago, Illinois; Brooke Dojny; Terry Doyle; Durbin and Trux Emerson; Linda and John Finn; Jim Fobel; Susanna Foo; Leslie and Kirk Francis; Gerri Gilliland; Sophie Grigson; The Heartline Cafe, Sedona, Arizona; Elizabeth Heizig; Hotel Hana-Maui, Hana, Maui, Hawaii; Ruth Jacobson; Raji Jallepalli; Karen Kaplan; Mollie Katzen; Jeanne Thiel Kelley; Kristine Kidd; Ellen Lebow; Joanne Levy; Longueville House and Presidents' Restaurant, Mallow, County Cork, Ireland; Maguy Maccario-Doyle; Lisa Mann; Michael McLaughlin; Michael's, Santa Monica, California; Rick Moonen; Jinx and Jefferson Morgan; Selma Brown Morrow; Kitty Morse; Dawn Murray; James G. Nichols, Jr.; Nancy Oakes; The Olde Bryan Inn, Saratoga Springs, New York; The Palace Restaurant, The Cincinnatian Hotel, Cincinnati, Ohio; Rochelle Palermo; Pancho Villa Taqueria, San Francisco, California; The Porthole Restaurant, Lynn, Massachusetts; Post Hotel, Lake Louise, Alberta, Canada; Stephan Pyles; The Restaurant, Meadowood, St. Helena, California; Ristorante Chianti, Geneva, Illinois; Riversong Lodge, Anchorage, Alaska; Betty Rosbottom; St. Francis Fountain and Candy Store, San Francisco, California; Richard Sax; Martha Rose Shulman; Marie Simmons; Joachim Splichal; Steak & Sticks, Sedona, Arizona; Maureen Tatlow; Sarah Tenaglia; Marjorie Thompson; Mary Jo Thoresen; Tinakilly Country House & Restaurant, Rathnew, County Wicklow, Ireland; John Toler; Lucia Watson; Joanne Weir; Charles Wiley; Pierre Wolfe; Zenzero, Santa Monica, California.

The following people contributed the photographs included in this book: Jack Andersen; David Bishop; Angie Norwood Browne; Shelby Burt; Wyatt Counts; Julie Dennis; Colleen Duffley; Alison Duke; Susan Goldman; Charles Imstepf; Jeff Katz; Deborah Klesenski; Lannen/Kelly; Brian Leatart; Rita Maas; Andrew Martin; Gary Moss; Judd Pilossof; Stephanie Rausser; Jeff Sarpa; Charles Schiller; Ellen Silverman; Dave Slivinski; Rick Szczechowski; Mark Thomas; Rai Uhlemann; Elizabeth Zeschin.

Front jacket photo: Mark Thomas, Photographer; Dora Johenson, Food Stylist; Nancy Micklin, Prop Stylist.